# SHAW 6

continuing

# *The Shaw Review*

**Stanley Weintraub,** *General Editor*

# The Annual of Bernard Shaw Studies
## Volume Six

*Edited by*
## Stanley Weintraub

The Pennsylvania State University Press
University Park and London

ISBN 0-271-00426-6

Note to contributors and subscribers. *SHAW*'s perspective is Bernard Shaw and his milieu—its personalities, works, relevance to his age and ours. As "his life, work, and friends"—the subtitle to a biography of G.B.S.—indicates, it is impossible to study the life, thought and work of a major literary figure in a vacuum. Issues and men, economics, politics, religion, theatre and literature and journalism—the entirety of the two half-centuries the life of G.B.S. spanned—was his assumed province. *SHAW*, published annually, welcomes articles that either explicitly or implicitly add to or alter our understanding of Shaw and his milieu. Address all communications concerning manuscript contributions (in 2 copies) to S234 Burrowes Building South, University Park, Pa. Unsolicited manuscripts are welcomed but will be returned only if return postage is provided. In matters of style *SHAW* recommends the *MLA Style Sheet*.

# CONTENTS

# CONTENTS

REVIEWS

# Alan G. Brunger

# POINTE BERNARD SHAW— IDENTIFICATION AND NAMING

In June, 1983, the name Pointe Bernard Shaw was officially bestowed on an elongated southward-projecting peninsula on the southern end of the largest of the Iles Radisson in the southwestern area of Ungava Bay, northern Quebec. The eastern shore of the peninsula possesses a rocky surface whose form—when viewed from the air 5,000 feet above—bears a close resemblance to the angular, high-browed profile of George Bernard Shaw as seen from his left hand side (Fig. 1). This effect is created by the chance arrangement of coast-line and adjacent cliffs and hills whose shadows accentuate the areas of Shaw's left eye, his nose and hirsute mouth and chin.

The person who first identified Shaw's features on this tiny peninsula in the vastness of the Canadian North is unknown. The word to describe the feature is topo-anthropomorph—a man-like place. I first became aware of its existence in October, 1973, during a field-trip with my class of Geography students from Trent University. We were in Ottawa inspecting the facilities of the Canadian Centre for Remote Sensing in which all aerial photographs and satellite images are processed and stored. Many examples of photographs were shown us, and I was informed by one of the gentlemen in the processing department about the presence of the Shavian peninsula. He did not say if he had discovered it or indicate the name of the original discoverer. I obtained a black-and-white copy from him although I did not, unfortunately, ascertain his identity.

I retained the photograph for several years and found it useful as a class-room illustration of a novel kind. The point arrived, during an office move, at which I was in the process of getting rid of material. I resisted discarding the photograph and wondered what use it could have. The thought occurred to me that the Shaw Festival company might find it interesting. Consequently, I wrote them enclosing the aerial photograph in the fall of 1978. I heard nothing more of the

Fig. 1. Aerial view of Pointe Bernard Shaw, Iles Radisson, Ungava Bay, Quebec, Canada. Photo by Surveys & Mappings Branch, Energy, Mines & Resources, Ottawa; rephotographed by David Cooper, courtesy of Shaw Festival Theatre, Niagara-on-the-Lake, Ontario, Canada.

photo until I was 'phoned at 1 A.M. in England on July 5 1983 by an eager newsman from the Toronto *Star* seeking details on the Canadian Press wire-story that had just been received on Pointe Bernard Shaw.

The process of officially naming the peninsula was begun (in 1981) by Christopher Banks, the Shaw Festival General Manager. In that year, the photo which I had sent to the Festival in 1978 had been excavated from the drawer in which it had been placed. A long time passed while Festival authorities sought the proper government department to which they had to apply for the official name. The appropriateness of the name needed justification before the two committees concerned with toponymy: the federal Canadian Permanent Committee on Geographical Names and the equivalent committee in the Province of Quebec—La Commission de toponymie du Quebec—within whose boundary the Pointe lies.

Final approval occurred in June, 1983, although the Shaw Festival delayed announcement of newly named Pointe Bernard Shaw until July in order for it to coincide with the opening day of one of Shaw's spoofs of the British Empire entitled *The Simpleton of the Unexpected Isles*.

# Sean Morrow

# THE MISSIONARY IN
# *THE BLACK GIRL*

Bernard Shaw started to write his fable on religion, *The Adventures of the Black Girl in Her Search for God,* in Knysna, South Africa, early in 1932. Shaw's South African trip provided the occasion for the writing of the story, but its inspiration dates to 1927. In 1927–28 Bernard Shaw had a three-cornered correspondence with Mabel Shaw, an English missionary teacher who worked at Mbereshi, Northern Rhodesia, from 1915 to 1940, and with J. E. Whiting, of the Leeds-based Arthington Trust, which disbursed money to Mabel Shaw's Girls' Boarding School. Mabel Shaw, who was not related to Bernard Shaw, was the model for the missionary in the first pages of the *Black Girl.*

Shaw pictures the missionary who launches the black girl in her search for God as "a small white woman, not yet thirty." She is a masochist who, jilting a succession of clergyman suitors and taking "an extraordinary joy" in the suicide on her account of one of them, goes off to "plant the cross in darkest Africa." At her remote station, in response to the interrogation of the black girl, she develops a religion which, while professedly Christian, is "really a product of the missionary's own direct inspiration." Armed with a Bible from the missionary, and taking literally the injunction to "Seek and ye shall find me," the black girl sets out to look for God.[1]

The woman who inspired Bernard Shaw to create his missionary was an important figure in mission education in Northern Rhodesia in the 1920s and 1930s. Mabel Shaw's Girls' Boarding School, in spite of its position in a remote area of the country, was the foremost educational institution for African girls in Northern Rhodesia, and its Principal had an international reputation. She wrote a number of widely-read books, and on retiring from the London Missionary Society in 1940 she became an advisor on the education of girls in East Africa and India to the Church Missionary Society, an Anglican organization.[2] Her school at Mbereshi was designed to serve as a defence for its girls, educated above all for Christian marriage, against what Mabel Shaw saw as the superstition and degradation of village "paganism" and against the viciousness and materialism of what she considered to be the neo-paganism of urban life, increasingly prominent with the growth of large-scale copper mining in Northern Rhodesia from the mid-1920s.

Mabel Shaw was born in 1888 in Bilston, Wolverhampton, in the industrial English midlands, and was brought up in an intellectually limited and unhappy lower-middle-class home. She taught briefly as an unqualified primary teacher, and was accepted as a missionary candidate by the London Missionary Society in 1912, studying at the Missionary College of the Church of Scotland in Edinburgh until 1915, when she was posted to Northern Rhodesia.[3] At Edinburgh she had a love affair with a young parson whom she jilted in favour of her missionary career. He joined the British forces at the outbreak of the First World War, and was killed in France.[4] It is this segment of her life that Shaw embellishes in the *Black Girl* by having his missionary fall in love "with earnest clergymen" and become engaged "to six of them in succession," one of the jilted parsons committing suicide. His death, in Shaw's version, "gave her an extraordinary joy. It seemed to take her from a fool's paradise of false happiness into a real region in which intense suffering became transcendent rapture."[5]

Mabel Shaw's religious and literary sensibility was of a kind with which it is difficult for those not sharing her preoccupations to relate, and she can appear over-intense, cloying and glib. *My Sanctuary,* a poem written in 1922, is an example of this mawkish religiosity suffused with an almost sadistic sexuality.

> A House of prayer
> All softly grey and shadows hushed.
> And lily lamps agleam within, without;
> And music pregnant sweet
> From daffodil trumpets blown, and caught and held
> In the heart of a thousand springing flowers
> Within—a deep sweet haunting peace,
> One little lamp agleam
> Love's flame before love's altar burning—
> My Sanctuary.
>
> A beating heart—
> All filled with love's divine delight.
> Love's glory flame in all its deep recesses.
> A tender tremulous yearning to enfold within itself

Its dear beloved, and hide it from the storm;
Hands, strong, tender, true, outstretched to gather in and hold;
Evenings that hold all Love's radiance, light of earth and heaven,
A voice in which throbs and thrills Love's triumph song
A breast—the resting place of one loved weary head
　　　My Sanctuary.

A Cross crowned hill—
All stark and desolate and bare.
Yet up its slopes Love's pilgrims throng
Dear Cross: the very heart of God
Love's hiding place—the wide world's
　　　Sanctuary.[6]

In her school Mabel Shaw operated a system of extreme isolation and discipline. Girls were enclosed in a walled, convent-like environment for a single term of ten months each year, from as young as five years old until they left school to get married in their late teens.[7] Within these walls, punishments such as washing out with soap the mouth of a four-year-old child who swore, and, in the case of a girl who called a fellow-pupil a dog, chaining the malefactor to the dog's kennel and encouraging the schoolgirls to bark at her as they went by, were utilized.[8] Corporal punishment often took the form of getting girls to stand with arms outstretched crucifix-fashion, while Mabel Shaw gave strokes with a stick on each hand alternately, often until a girl's "pride" was broken and she apologized and begged forgiveness. Enuresis was punished severely. One past-pupil remembers a sixteen-year-old girl suffering from this condition having a chamber-pot tied around her neck and her fellow-pupils being encouraged to push her here and there. A girl who called another a swine had her tongue scrubbed until she screamed.[9] So complete was Mabel Shaw's dominance of the school that few hints of rebellion are apparent, perhaps because so all-enveloping and isolated an environment gave very little opportunity for girls to grasp the possibility of alternative models of school life.

The school, however, stood for more than rigorous discipline, and past pupils are in general positive in their attitudes to their school days. Mabel Shaw was a feminist, though an ambivalent one. With what she called her "kind of sex pride" she rejected all efforts by male missionaries to control her work,[10] yet at the same time she attempted to grasp and use in a Christian neo-traditionalism the rich store of customary ceremonial associated with the puberty, marriage and giving birth of the African women of her area of Northern Rhodesia. Her aim was

> To conserve all that is true and good in the old life and build upon it
> . . . so as to present the Christian faith to the community and the indi-
> vidual that they see it not as the white man's religion, something likely
> to be as useful to them as his money is, but as the fulfillment of that
> towards which their fathers grasped.[11]

Her aim was to prepare Christian wives and mothers in an all-female
environment, and the school was organized with this end in view. She
presided over and sometimes organized the marriage-negotiations of
her pupils; "No girl," she wrote in 1929, "leaves the school unmarried."[12]

Mabel Shaw was unwilling to bow to pressures from any source,
and her stubbornly Christian view of education led her to take stands
that could conflict with colonial officialdom. Education for Mabel
Shaw was primarily a moral rather than an academic process. In
1935, for instance, she noted that Standard IV girls were eagerly
studying for their government certificate. "We are determined," she
said, "to correct this, and bring their thoughts back to a worthier concept of education."[13] This concept meant teaching the children to be

> colonists of heaven. . . . To make it concrete, every book we read, every
> exercise given and done, every story and game must be an exercise in
> the seeing of the Lord of all good life, in learning from Him how the
> kingdom of the world may be so cleansed and renewed and recreated
> that it becomes the one Eternal Kingdom of Our Lord. That is our
> faith, "educational" faith, our definition of education.[14]

Mabel Shaw became known to Bernard Shaw through Whiting. Whiting was an admirer of Mabel Shaw's missionary work and of her writing, and with an amazing misjudgment of Bernard Shaw's literary
tastes, he sent some of her letters to him for his critical scrutiny. On
5 July 1927 Bernard Shaw told Whiting that "Miss Shaw's letters
ought to be printed," but he also attacked her for emphasizing what
he considered the vicious symbol of the cross rather than the figure
of Christ as teacher.[15] Whiting showed this letter to Mabel Shaw, and
she wrote to Whiting passionately denying Bernard Shaw's interpretation of the cross, saying that "to know our Lord as a Teacher one
must know Him in His Life and Death . . . you cannot divorce His
Life and Death from His teaching, and unless we understand His
death, can we ever fully understand His teaching." When in England
she had seen *Saint Joan:* "The man who wrote that can never have

been an agnostic. There are bits in St. Joan I turn to when I need to be near the heart of God."[16]

Further exchanges of letters took place between Whiting and Bernard Shaw, and Whiting sent more of Mabel Shaw's letters to Bernard Shaw on 25 November. He read these on 11 January 1928.[17] On 30 January, Bernard Shaw wrote as Whiting had requested him to do to Mabel Shaw. This letter has been reprinted elsewhere, and only a brief summary need be given.[18]

Bernard Shaw acknowledged Mabel Shaw's competence as a writer, but argued that matter as well as manner is vital if literary facility is to lead to literature. Mabel Shaw, he implied, had a mission, like St. Paul, Voltaire (who appeared in the *Black Girl*), Bunyan and Bernard Shaw himself; "I assure you," he said, "the question of becoming a professional writer is a pretty deep one when the intention behind it extends to becoming a prophet as well. I am in that line myself, and I KNOW."

Bernard Shaw criticized Mabel Shaw's motivation and approach: "Jesus, who was strongly anti-missionary, as his warning about the tares and the wheat shews, would probably tell you to mind your own business and suffer little children to find their own way to God, even if it were a black way!" He explained Mabel Shaw's missionary zeal in psychological terms, with the Cross, "the horrible emblem of Roman cruelty and Roman terrorism," interweaving with Mabel Shaw's masochism. She had driven a young parson to his death through her rejection of him, but revelled in this and made "a propaganda of voluptuous agony. . . . But I, who loathe torture, and object most strongly to being tortured, my lusts being altogether normal, should take you and shake you were it not that you are out of my reach and that you would rather enjoy being shaken if it hurt you enough."

This letter, devastating though it was, was not the end of the episode. Whiting was anxious to know the upshot of his introduction of Mabel Shaw's work to Bernard Shaw, and he pressed both parties for details of the correspondence, to the point where Bernard Shaw on 15 May 1928 urged Whiting not to request from Mabel Shaw a copy of his letter of 30 January, as "It was not the sort of letter that one can ask to see." He also asked Whiting for a photograph of Mabel Shaw, which was sent.[19]

Though Bernard Shaw refused to do so, Mabel Shaw herself, with considerable intellectual honesty, though possibly also with the masochism that Bernard Shaw recognized in her, sent a copy of the letter to Whiting. Mabel Shaw also wrote a covering letter to Whiting. The

comments of the missionary who was to figure later in the *Black Girl*
are sufficiently penetrating to reproduce in full:

> At last I enclose G.B.S.'s letter . . . [*sic*] In this letter there is much I can
> never agree with, as you will see; but under everything there is Kind-
> liness and there is Truth, and that is something that makes for security.
> God is Truth to me, supremely; and G.B.S. knows God, and not a little,
> it seems to me. He has God unclouded by mists of theology, unimpris-
> oned within organized Christianity. He is fearless because God for him
> is truth. I should like to be set free as G.B.S. is. I am still imprisoned
> in many ways. I imagine G.B.S. in a Mission like ours. —What a shat-
> tering there'd be! Even I with my little strivings after absolute Truth
> am a storm centre; he is a positive volcano, in eruption. I am glad I
> have let his letter lie deep within my thought for months. At first I rose
> up hotly against much in it. Now I see only a man who is not afraid to
> stand before the blaze of Truth.
>
> But he hasn't seen the whole Truth; not the glorious, burning, un-
> veiled face of God. If he had, he would see the Cross, and see it not as
> a disgusting symbol of cruelty, but as the symbol of all-glorious life.
>
> What he says about St. Paul puzzles me. Always St. Paul puzzles me.
> And yet I love him. But I turn more and more to Our Lord and less
> and less to St. Paul. The Church has more of St. Paul in it than of Our
> Lord, don't you think? But how St. Paul loves! If only I have one spark
> of the fire that burned within him! St. Paul gives me that right "fear";
> and so does G.B.S. in a different way. I sometimes think of them to-
> gether. They are both so ruthless in their going forward. I've told him
> he seems curiously like the St. Paul he disapproves of to me. I wish
> he'd write about the God he knows so well.[20]

In May 1930, when Mabel Shaw was on home leave, Bernard Shaw
invited her to lunch.[21] Mabel Shaw next appeared in the opening
pages of the *Black Girl*, thus entering the Shavian oeuvre five years
after the author's first contact with her. A figure reminiscent of Bernard Shaw also appears in the *Black Girl*. However, Bernard Shaw did
not give this figure the austere Pauline aspect that Mabel Shaw identified in her namesake.


# Notes


LMS = London Missionary Society
NAZ = National Archives of Zambia

The Shaw-Morton papers are in the keeping of Dr. Margaret Morton, of Leicester. The L.M.S. Archive is housed in the School of Oriental and African Studies, London University. The Arthington Archive is in Sheepscar Branch Library, Leeds Public Libraries. I would like to thank these and the other institutions mentioned in the notes for their help. I would particularly like to thank Mr. Dan H. Laurence, who alerted me to the existence of Bernard Shaw's letter of 30 January 1928 to Mabel Shaw, and to the correspondence between the Shaws and J. E. Whiting now preserved in the Houghton Library, Harvard University.

1. George Bernard Shaw, *The Adventures of the Black Girl in Her Search for God* (London, 1932), pp. 1–2.

2. Mabel Shaw, *Children of the Chief* (London, 1921); *Dawn in Africa* (London, 1927); *God's Candlelights* (London, 1932); *Treasure of Darkness* (London, 1936).

3. LMS/Candidates' Papers, 1900–1940/34, Mabel Shaw, 16 January 1912; J. Sibree, *A Register of Missionaries, Deputations etc. from 1796 to 1923* (London, 1923), p. 164; Interview J. J. Tawney/Mabel Shaw, Haslemere, 20 October 1972 (Oxford Colonial Records Project), 1–2.

4. Shaw-Morton Papers, "The Life and Work of Miss Mabel Shaw, O.B.E. at Mbereshi Mission," N.D. (but probably 1973), no author.

5. Shaw, *The Black Girl*, pp. 1–2.

6. Shaw-Morton Papers, notebook containing poems, mostly 1914–1924, where dated.

7. LMS/Central Africa/6, Winifred Bishop's Report for 1930, Report of the Livingstone Memorial G.B.S., 1930.

8. Shaw, *God's Candlelights*, 122, 167.

9. Interviews, unattributable.

10. LMS/Central Africa Correspondence/23/Shaw's file, Shaw to Chirgwin, 2 April 1930, Highgate.

11. Shaw, *God's Candlelights*, 13.

12. NAZ/C1/8/9/4/3, African Education, L.M.S., Mbereshi Girls' School, Shaw to Latham, 3 December 1929, R.M. *Arundel Castle*.

13. LMS/Central Africa Reports/4, Shaw's Report on Mbereshi Girls' Boarding School, 1935.

14. NAZ/NR 2/240, L.M.S., Mbereshi Girls' School and Jeanes 1938–54, Shaw to Tyndale-Biscoe, 8 April 1938, Mbereshi.

15. Shaw mss., Houghton Library, Harvard University, G. B. Shaw/J. E. Whiting, 5 July 1927, Ayot St. Lawrence.

16. Ibid., Mabel Shaw/J. E. Whiting, N.D.

17. Ibid., G. B. Shaw/J. E. Whiting, 11 January 1928, Ayot St. Lawrence.

18. G. B. Shaw/Mabel Shaw, 30 January 1928, Ayot St. Lawrence, in Stanley Weintraub, ed., *The Portable Bernard Shaw*, (London, 1977), pp. 632–35.

19. Shaw mss., Houghton Library, Harvard University, G. B. Shaw/J. E. Whiting, 28

April 1928, London; J. E. Whiting/G. B. Shaw, 3 May 1928; G. B. Shaw/J. E. Whiting, 15 May 1928, Ayot St. Lawrence; J. E. Whiting/G. B. Shaw, 17 May 1928, Leeds.

20. Arthington Archive, C/1/53, copy of Mabel Shaw/J. E. Whiting, 17 February 1929, Mbereshi.

21. Weintraub, ed., *Portable Bernard Shaw*, p. 632.

# Fred D. Crawford

# SWIFT AND SHAW AGAINST THE WAR

When Bernard Shaw published *What I Really Wrote about the War* in 1931, he declared in his draft jacket copy that his *Common Sense About the War* had "no parallel in literature since Swift's classic pamphlet on The Conduct of the Allies."[1] The identification with Swift which Shaw invites is true in more ways than he may have consciously intended, for Shaw's activity during the years of World War I curiously mirrored aspects of Jonathan Swift's during the years of the War of the Spanish Succession.

When each took up his pen in defense of peace, he did so in the belief that the literary work should not exist in an aesthetic vacuum but must exert its power to direct the course of political change. In 1711, the year of Swift's *The Conduct of the Allies and of the Late Ministry in beginning and carrying on the present war,* Swift had already demonstrated his literary power in *A Tale of a Tub* (never acknowledged by him publicly), *The Bickerstaff Papers,* several numbers of the *Examiner,* and his *Discourse on the Contests and Dissentions of Athens and Rome,* as well as pamphlets defending the sacramental test. His masterpiece, *Gulliver's Travels,* would later grow from the stormy 1710–1714 period in which he became intimately involved with the great men of the Tory Ministry, Harley and St. John.

By 1914, the year of *Common Sense about the War,* Shaw had some thirty years' experience of polemical writing behind him, including Fabian and other political pamphlets, letters, prefaces, speeches, and criticism. He had also published a score of plays, but, except for the 1904 *John Bull's Other Island,* Shaw's political masterpieces and extravaganzas did not appear until after the 1914–1918 war. Swift in his mid-forties and Shaw in his late fifties set out to put the world right.

Each regarded himself as a cool observer viewing the irrational activity and unruly passion of the world at large. Each, in his own view, stood above the interests of party or faction. Such a stance was easier to maintain for Shaw than for Swift, since Swift was writing for the Tory Ministry while Shaw was writing independently. Swift, however, managed to maintain the illusion of his own independence by identifying himself as a man of the cloth and as a friend rather than hired subordinate of Harley and St. John, acting solely for the best interests of church and state.

In two instances Swift's actions supported his sense of moral integrity. When he realized that the Whig Junto, despite earlier promises, had no intention of supporting the sacramental test but could still extend preferment to him, Swift put the church above his private interests and published his *Letter Concerning the Test,* which he knew would antagonize the Junto. "In the first partisan pamphlet that he ever brought out, the job-hungry vicar had broken through the restraints of prudent self-interest in what amounted to a public declaration of war against the Whigs."[2] In February 1711 (new style), Robert Harley, who knew of Swift's financial difficulties, provoked Swift when Harley "pressed upon him a bankbill for fifty pounds. Swift . . . reacted with a furious sense of outrage and . . . sent the bill back by way of Erasmus Lewis, to whom he also wrote 'a very complaining letter' that was shown to Harley."[3]

The strength of Swift's reaction resulted partly from his unwillingness to put a financial value on his services and partly from his desire to keep his relationship with Harley on a personal rather than working level. To accept a gift of money would have compromised both his personal dignity and his stance of supporting the Ministry because it was right, not because it paid. The conflict of motives, however, was one of Swift's major difficulties. He did desire preferment for his services but was reluctant to admit it and thus placed himself in an awkward position. As Swift's biographer Irvin Ehrenpreis commented, "Once a man has identified virtue with failure, he is condemned to moral discomfort unless promotion is thrust upon him."[4] The conflict between Swift's moral discomfort and desire for independence on the one hand, and his acute desire for recognition and promotion on the other, was to plague him not only in his dealings with his "great men," but also throughout his career in the church.

Shaw, like Swift, placed his ideals above self-interest when writing about the war. If his lack of direct involvement with statesmen made this somewhat easier for him than for Swift, his already formidable reputation handicapped him. Swift tended to exaggerate the personal risk he ran as a political writer although his anonymity protected him to a degree, but Shaw signed his work and his risk was real. His "outrages" were identifiable immediately as his own. Without the protection of a ministry or the approval of the war-delirious British public, he was vulnerable to charges of treason and to physical abuse of the kind that Swift had feared from the Mohawks. Despite the risk he ran, Shaw steadfastly refused to profit from his war writings. During the early months of the war, as he was writing *Common Sense about the War,* he abandoned all remunerative literary work, and except for several letters to the editor, several short newspaper pieces hardly more than letters to the editor with the signature under the title rather than under the text, and an interview with Mary Boyle O'Reilly for a New York paper, he toiled on his manifesto, and "asked no fee from the *New Statesman* when it was published, although ever since the war began he could have named his price for pieces on the war."[5]

Because of his identifiability, Shaw was the object of bitter personal attacks, ranging from the vituperations of H. G. Wells and the mudslinging of lesser superpatriots, to political caricatures portraying Shaw adorned with the Iron Cross. Describing the polemical responses to his *Proposal for Correcting, Improving, and Ascertaining the English Tongue,* Swift complained, "I believe if I writt an Essay upon a Straw some Fool would answer it."[6] Shaw might have made this complaint with more justice. As Robert Lynd put it, "the war was spoken of and written about as a war between the Allies on the one hand, and, on the other, Germany, Austria, Turkey, and Bernard Shaw."[7] Shaw himself later joked about painting a sign on his roof to warn off zeppelins from their "ally"—"HIER WOHNT DER DICHTER SHAW / BITTE / FAHREN SIE WEITER"[8]—for most of his critics felt his affinity with the Germans was greater than with the English, and Germany actually quoted Shaw's articles to support Germany's cause. The Duchess of Marlborough once remarked of Swift that he would be a fine writer in the opposition. Shaw was never anywhere else.

Despite some experience, neither Swift nor Shaw fully understood the workings of the machinery that governs man. Swift had functioned within the framework of the ecclesiastical hierarchy, and Shaw had served on the executive committee of the Fabians since the 1880s and as a vestryman on the St. Pancras Borough Council from 1897 to 1904. Such experience was too narrow to provide an understanding of international or even national politics. Swift and Shaw both viewed history as a drama of personalities of individual men and tended to simplify the processes of English politics.

In his dealings with St. John and Harley, Swift, slow to realize that these men were struggling against each other for control of the gov-

ernment, never understood the intensity of their struggle. Swift,
courted by both men, assumed that they were acting in harmony until
March 1711, when circumstances compelled him to revise his estimate. The government discovered that the Marquis de Guiscard, an
employee of Harley, had begun to spy for the French. While being
examined by government leaders, Guiscard asked St. John for a private interview. St. John refused. Guiscard then stabbed Harley. Since
St. John had signed the order against Guiscard, it is likely that St.
John was Guiscard's preferred victim, but Harley had the wound and
Harley thus received credit for being the chief enemy of France.
Guiscard's death, a result of the pummeling he received during his
"apprehension" directly after the stabbing, prevented any wide-
spread denial that Harley was his original target.

Swift put himself into an awkward position by writing in the *Examiner* (15 March 1711) that

> The Murderer confessed in *Newgate,* that his chief Design was against
> Mr. Secretary *St. John,* who happened to change seats with Mr. *Harley,*
> for more Convenience of examining the Criminal: And being asked
> what provoked him to stab the Chancellor [of the Exchequer]? He said,
> that not being able to come at the Secretary, as he intended, it was some
> Satisfaction to murder the Person whom he thought Mr. *St. John* loved
> best.

Swift's "error" of mentioning St. John as the primary target was
speedily pointed out to him. In *The Journal to Stella* (16 April 1711),
Swift wrote that he felt his allegiance was divided and "sent hints to
the author of the *Atlantis* [Mrs. Manley]," dropping the whole business
rather than taking sides. In this instance and in his later attempts to
reconcile his "friends," Swift revealed how little he understood the
ruthless ambition and bitter rivalry behind Harley and St. John's efforts to control England.

For Swift, the opposing forces of the world were religion, good
government, and civilization on the one hand, and heathens, anar-
chists, and barbarians on the other. He divided political groups into
opposing, although unequal, groups: Queen, clergy, Ministry, and
people on one side, and a minority consisting of Marlborough,
Whigs, and Junto on the other. Thus in his writing he purported to
write for the reasonable majority against a minority group of politicians and profiteers. Shaw did essentially the same. Like Swift, he
oversimplified the political process to the point of proposing seriously
that to stop a war, France, England, and Germany need only agree
that if Germany committed an aggressive act, France and England

would unite against Germany, and if France began a war, Germany and England would unite against France. For Shaw this was the only diplomacy required, although determining the identity of the "aggressor" in armed conflict is usually among the prerogatives of the victor. Unlike Swift, Shaw directed his message to a minority, but one composed of those members of the intelligentsia immune to war delirium, capable of rational thought, and committed to the higher causes of humanity and peace.

Shaw's division between the reasonable forces for good and the warmongering politicians and profiteers was as rigid as Swift's. Shaw's generalizations and views were far removed from the actual workings of politics and diplomacy, for, like Swift, he believed that reason and common sense were sufficient to direct and even predict political events. Ehrenpreis speaks of such belief in terms of both sacrifice and gain for a pamphleteer:

> If this is the great axiom of Swift's political philosophy, it cannot be said to reveal a deep understanding of how institutions evolve. By identifying the right course of action only as the obvious, established course, Swift gives us no clue for recognizing it ahead of time; and people differ bitterly as to what is either obvious or customary. By stigmatizing the wrong course as eccentric or irrational, he supplies us not with a logical analysis but with a means of ridicule. Furthermore, to limit oneself to the advocacy of self-evident truths, the common consent of mankind, is to isolate oneself—as Swift regularly did—from the most profound intellectual transactions of one's time; and these are the forces ultimately responsible for self-evident truths.
>
> Nevertheless, what would mean loss for the philosopher is gain for the polemicist. Any pamphleteer who holds privately to the view that the science of government is a simple matter of "nothing but common sense" will find himself powerfully driven and powerfully equipped to destroy the logic of his political antagonists.[9]

Like Swift, Shaw constantly appealed to common sense and placed his opposition into a position of irrationality.

When Swift wrote *Conduct* and Shaw wrote *Common Sense,* they shared the assurance given by previous literary successes, a belief in their independence and detachment, a sense of acting without self-interest, an oversimplified view of the political process, and a sense of confidence in the effectiveness of their ability to direct thought with their pens. Both men justifiably rated themselves highly as writers, but many effects of their political writing resulted from factors independent of their rhetorical skills. The effects of timeliness, inside information, and an infusion of moral idealism outweigh those of mere rhetorical or literary power. Swift and Shaw both wrote their pamphlets when the issues were explosive and both had a great deal of moral idealism, but the advantage of inside information clearly was Swift's.

Swift's *Conduct* appeared in November 1711 after the war had lasted for so many years and taxes had become so burdensome that almost any appeal for peace would have been effective. A series of political events made the pamphlet even more timely. While Harley was recuperating from his wound, St. John discovered that Harley had begun secret negotiations for a peace. With surprising quickness St. John secured agreement on preliminary articles which included the cession of Gibraltar, the Assiento, Newfoundland, and other commercial interests to England, denying Spain to the Hapsburgs and the barrier to the Dutch. After the secret articles were signed in September 1711, public articles appeared which vaguely protected the Allies and conformed to the Grand Alliance.

Two weeks later St. John distributed, in confidence, copies of earlier peace negotiations, made by the Whig Ministry in 1708, to representatives of the Allied courts. In these negotiations the Whigs, ostensibly suing for peace, had made demands so excessive that France could never have accepted them. The Whig *Daily Courant* published these confidential articles on 13 October 1711. The inflammatory situation resulting from the publication of state secrets, which indicated that the war had been deliberately prolonged was ideal for the appearance of a pamphlet arguing for peace and fixing blame on those who were profiting from the war. Publication of Swift's pamphlet in November was even more timely because Parliament was to meet to consider St. John's preliminary articles. Swift's pamphlet not only argued for peace when the majority was war-weary, but also appeared in coordination with a scheduled program of legislation for the Ministry's peace articles.

Shaw's audience was not nearly as receptive as Swift's, for Shaw's courage was to argue against the war before the majority was war-weary. When *Common Sense* appeared in November 1914 the war had hardly begun, but enough time had elapsed for the British public to whip itself into a war frenzy. Neither taxes nor oppressive death lists had made themselves felt, and the populace supported a war waged against despised German militarism. There was no peace faction as such, nor much opposition since the war made the Conservatives reluctant to attack the Liberal Government. Many writers had responded wholeheartedly to the government's invitation to support the war through propaganda, and, since conscription had not begun, conscientious objection had not become a burning public issue or produced other voices of moral outrage.

The only preparation the public had for Shaw's pamphlet was his established reputation for paradoxical utterance. Shaw spent two valuable months writing, revising, and researching, and he "thought afterward that he had held back his fire too long for optimum effect."[10] Had Shaw's *Common Sense* appeared within a week of the war's beginning, his article might have been more judiciously received and accurately reported. Certainly his timing suffered further from his scattering of letters-to-the-editor and his interview with Mary Boyle O'Reilly, which revealed his main ideas and stole the thunder of the *New Statesman* version. *Common Sense* could not have appeared at a worse moment in terms of its reception—there was no popular support for his position, no peace legislation in progress, and no desire even to question or examine the motives for entering the war. Unlike Swift, Shaw was timely in the sense of being ahead of his time instead of writing what the majority had already begun to think.

The advantage of inside information was Swift's without question. St. John and Harley supplied him with copies of the alliance and additional secret information to give him ample ammunition. Swift's command of secret information was so extensive that both Whigs and Tories referred to the pamphlet during the ensuing parliamentary debates. Swift worked closely with Harley and St. John in the process of composition and was able to supply minute and personal details which gave his pamphlet an air of complete authority. This added power to his misleading translation of the Eighth Article of the Grand Alliance. His access to the personages and secrets of state was an advantage which completely overwhelmed opponents and which has no journalistic parallel in literary history. Shaw had none of these advantages. He had no access to Asquith or Grey, no secret documents to reveal, and no sense of being privy to matters of state. At Torquay, where he isolated himself to write *Common Sense,* he lacked materials for research and, in any case, had only information which was at everyone's disposal.

Swift's infusion of moral idealism and outrage resulted from his identification with the ministers' case for peace. His attachment to them and his consequent rigid division between the forces for good and the war-prolonging Whig profiteers added a sense of personal involvement to his work. His course was clear before him—to undermine identifiable opponents who were impeding negotiations to stop an unprofitable and undesirable war. He could castigate his oppo-

nents on the grounds of pure greed. Shaw's position was not so clearly
one of moral outrage stemming from personal loyalties, and his attacks, in most cases, were indirect and levelled at incompetence or
irrationality rather than at specific vices. He could not identify his
stance with anyone else's cause. In addition, his own position was ambiguous, for even as he condemned the war, its causes, and its probable effects, he maintained that the war had to be won and that it had
to result in the downfall of the Junkers in both Germany and England. The impact of Shaw's outrage suffered because it was not directed against one side, but against all sides. Even when a pamphleteer perpetuates the illusion of objectivity or detachment, he usually
profits from a partisan stance. Swift was a partisan of a defined group
with a rigid policy and program. Shaw was arguing from an extremely lonely position.

Both Swift and Shaw adopted an ostensibly non-partisan stance in
their pamphlets, preferring to set themselves up as objective historians impartially reviewing the actions related to the war. Each began
by establishing a framework for examination. Swift began with a preface that stated,

> . . . no reasonable Person, whether Whig or Tory (since it is necessary to use
> those foolish Terms) can be of Opinion for continuing the War, upon the Foot it
> now is, unless he be a Gainer by it, or hopes it may occasion some new Turn of
> Affairs at Home, to the Advantage of his Party; or lastly, unless he be very
> ignorant of the Kingdom's Condition, and by what Means we have been reduced
> to it.

Swift summarily dismissed the prospects of victories gained, towns
taken, and articles hoped for, and listed his complaints: the heavy
burden of taxes, the advancement of private interest at public expense, the neglect of beneficial campaigns in the war, and the delu-
sion by a "Mock Treaty" so excessive that it deliberately prevented
peace. He then offered a rough outline of his pamphlet by listing the
questions he intended to answer: where lies the difficulty of securing
peace, what is our present condition, how long can we continue, what
are the consequences, and can a peace "without that impractical Point
which some People do much insist on" be worse than continuing
the war.

After reading this preface, Swift's audience, despite any protesta-
tions of impartiality on his part, could recognize the Tory position.
The heavy burden was a common Tory complaint since taxes on land
supported the war. The reference to private interest pointed to the
Godolphin-Marlborough faction and was already familiar to readers

of the *Examiner*, especially those who had seen the famous letter to Crassus. The neglect of the proper means to wage the war reflected the Tory preference for fighting with fleets, since a continental army was more expensive (the Whigs, whose moneyed interest was untaxed and who were therefore less concerned with the cost, preferred that the fleet remain free to guard the merchant marine). The Mock Treaty referred to the recently revealed Whig negotiations of 1708. The "impractical Point" was the slogan "No Peace Without Spain" raised by those who favored the war and opposed the Tory ministers. Swift's preface clearly supported negotiations for peace along Tory lines.

The identifiability of Swift's position as Tory partisan required him to place his arguments and facts not into a party framework, but into a larger context governed by established principles of higher law. Instead of beginning with contemporary issues, Swift proceeded to examine the principles of war in general by considering "The Motives that may engage a wise Prince or State in a War," the condition a country must be in to undertake a war, and the reasons for accepting overtures of peace. From there Swift moved to consider further implications arising from a war waged by confederates, arguing mainly that the allies' burdens should be proportionate to their respective shares in the quarrel, and that, should a "generous" ally assume more than its fair share of the burden, it should receive a larger share of the gain.

With these general statements on war Swift had not brought in England or her Allies explicitly, but, when he began to examine the history of English wars since the Norman Conquest, he revealed his partisan position and introduced his grievances against the war under the guise of impartial examination. In the wars he considered, Swift stressed the relative advantages which had accrued from previous struggles. Public debts were either avoided entirely or paid off quickly. In wars against Spain and Holland, "managing it by their Fleets, [the English] encreased very much the Riches of the Kingdom, instead of exhausting them." In foreign wars, England was prudent enough to fight only for herself. In each instance, England emerged without substantial loss because she was prudent in the motives and methods of her warfare.

When Swift spoke of the war between Louis XIV and the Grand Alliance (1689–1697), he introduced what he considered the true causes of England's difficulties:

> About this time the Custom first began among us of borrowing Millions upon Funds of Interest. . . . The Person said to have been Author

of so detestable a Project, is still living, and lives to see some of its fatal Consequences, whereof his Grand-Children will not see an End. And this pernicious Counsel closed very well with the Posture of Affairs at that time: For, a Set of Upstarts, who had little or no part in the *Revolution,* but valued themselves by their Noise and pretended Zeal when the Work was over, were got into Credit at Court, by the Merit of becoming Undertakers and Projectors of Loans and Funds: These, finding that the Gentlemen of Estates were not willing to come into their Measures, fell upon those new Scheams of raising Mony, in order to create a Mony'd-Interest that might in time vie with the Landed, and of which they hoped to be at the Head.

When assaulting the moneyed interest Swift was attacking a Whig faction, but he went farther:

> . . . during that whole War, the Sea was almost entirely neglected, and the greatest Part of *Six* Millions Annually employed to enlarge the Frontier of the *Dutch.* For the King was a General, but not an Admiral; and although King of *England,* was a Native of *Holland.*

Swift used this war to show how England's allies had exploited her in the past, for the Treaty of Ryswick gave enormous advantages to the Empire and to Holland but nothing more than a staggering war debt to England.

At this point Swift began to discuss the present war, ostensibly in objective terms, applying the principles he had mentioned at the outset to determine whether England's motives, circumstances, and proposed advantages justified her entry into the war. After determining that England was still in debt, that she had little to gain, and that the aims of the war helped only the Allies, Swift concluded his introductory section:

> . . . without offering at any other Remedy, without taking time to consider the Consequences, or to reflect on our own Condition, we hastily engaged in a War which hath cost us sixty Millions; and after repeated, as well as unexpected Success in Arms, hath put us and our Posterity in a worse Condition, not only than any of our Allies, but even our conquered Enemies themselves.

Swift had already indicated his antipathy to the Whig-Godolphin-Marlborough faction in the course of his historical exposition, but now, after he had written one-fourth his pamphlet, he defined his stance in no uncertain terms:

> ... I presume it will appear, by plain Matters of Fact, that no Nation was ever so long or so scandalously abused by the Folly, the Temerity, the Corruption, the Ambition of its domestic Enemies; or treated with so much Insolence, Injustice and Ingratitude by its foreign Friends.

Swift then proposed to prove three points: that England should have entered the war as an auxiliary rather than as a principal, that England neglected those parts of the war where she could do most damage to the enemy and bring most gain to herself, and that England allowed her Allies to break agreements, leaving England with most of the burden.

Swift's introduction is both lengthy and elaborate, but he needed to establish his position on three foundations. First, he required the illusion that he spoke not only for the Ministry as such but also for the national interest on purely objective grounds. He was able to do this in his introduction by attacking the moneyed interest and hinting at private advantages gained by the proponents of the war, but he did not mention the Tory faction or even refer to the Tory Ministers. Second, he needed to convince his readership that the peace supporters were more numerous than the supporters of a prolonged war, and that the corrupt few at home and abroad had duped this majority into the war. To gain support for the Tory peace negotiations, he needed to place the controversy in terms of the nation against a small faction rather than of one party against another. Only an "objective" appeal to prudence or reason could accomplish this. Third, he needed to establish his authority and superior facility by demonstrating both his familiarity with facts and his ability to ascertain the causes of those events which many did not understand. Only by doing this could he prepare his audience to accept the serious charges that he was about to make and to regard the Allies' demands as greedy while English gains were justifiable matters of national interest.

Shaw also adopted the stance of the objective historian in his introduction, but Shaw's historical position was more intellectual and social than political. While Swift had dismissed the "foolish Terms" of Whig and Tory in his preface, Shaw claimed a different type of detachment. Where Swift refused to call himself part of a party explicitly, Shaw repudiated the entire nation:

> ... my inborn dramatic faculty and professional habit as a playwright prevent me from taking a one-sided view even when the most probable result of taking a many-sided one is prompt lynching. Besides, until Home Rule emerges from its present suspended animation, I shall retain my Irish capacity for criticizing England with something of the

detachment of a foreigner, and perhaps with a certain slightly mali-
cious taste for taking the conceit out of her.[11]

Shaw claimed that although he was not without prejudice, his "prejudices in this matter are not those which blind the British patriot, and
therefore I am fairly sure to see some things that have not yet struck
him." Like Swift, Shaw saw the English as "deliberately duped" into
the war, not by a moneyed interest but by Junkers and militarists in
both England and Germany. As Shaw presented the situation, the
masses fought to advance no interest of their own, but to help "the
Junkers and Militarists of England and Germany jumping at the
chance they have longed for in vain for many years of smashing one
another and establishing their own oligarchy as the dominant military
power in the world." He addressed the dreadful waste of military op-
erations and then announced that, by way of introduction to his analysis of the war, he would "break it gently by expatiating for a while
on the subject of Junkerism and militarism generally, and on the history of the literary propaganda of war between England and Potsdam
which has been going on openly for the last forty years on both sides."
Swift had traced examples of foreign policy in an attempt to establish
the recent undermining of a nation's interests. Shaw traced the evolution of a pro-war attitude.

Shaw began by using the definition of *Junker* from Muret-Sanders's
*Encyclopädisches Wörterbuch* to demonstrate that the word meaning
"young nobleman, younker, lording, country squire, country gentleman, squierarch" was more applicable in England than in Germany.
After establishing that the governing classes in England were either
Junker or moneyed, he traced anti-German feeling in England from
the Franco-Prussian War of 1870 to 1914, which had evolved from
defensive to offensive as Germany's fleet began to rival England's. He
dismissed the belief that "smashing this or that particular Power" was
likely to relax pressure in England since another power would rise to
take its place, and, as Swift had feared that England's beaten opponents would fare better than England after the war, Shaw showed
Austria's numerous defeats that had not prevented her from being
one of the "Great Powers." Shaw then referred to another historical
example:

> . . . the effect on England's position of the repeated defeats of our
> troops by the French under Luxembourg in the Balance of Power War
> at the end of the seventeenth century differed surprisingly little, if at
> all, from the effect of our subsequent victories under Marlborough.

As Swift had argued that the war was doing England little or no good but excessive harm, Shaw argued that the war was pointless:

> The only rule of thumb that can be hazarded on the strength of actual practice is that wars to maintain or upset the Balance of Power between States, called by inaccurate people Balance of Power wars, and by accurate people Jealousy of Power wars, never establish the desired peaceful and secure equilibrium.

Having dismissed the war aim as impractical and militarism as a bogus science, Shaw proceeded to treat the "peculiar psychology of English statesmanship," which consisted mainly of intellectual laziness, resulting in discord between a statesman's conscious professions and illusions on one hand, and his actions on the other. Shaw presented English statesmanship as muddleheaded blundering from one crisis to the next, and he placed responsibility for the war on Grey's errors during secret negotiations. By making commitments to France and Belgium, and then publicly disavowing them, Grey convinced the Germans that England would not fight, thereby guaranteeing that Germany would proceed, thus drawing England into the conflict on the basis of her previous agreements.

Shaw presented this analysis using two techniques. To lend the proper historical perspective to his discussion, he proceeded "to tell the story of the diplomatic negotiations as they will appear to the Congress which, I am assuming, will settle the terms on which Europe is to live more or less happily ever after." Second, he documented his case by quoting from the White Paper, Miscellaneous, Numbers 6, 17, and 123, claiming that in his history "All this is recorded in the language of diplomacy in the White Paper on or between the lines." Once he had done this, his case momentarily took the same course as Swift's. Swift had argued that England should have entered the war as an auxiliary rather than as a principal, but that against her own self-interest she bound herself to play a major part for limited gains. Shaw, offering the government the proper position to take, posed a situation in which England had been hopelessly outwitted. In both cases the action resulted from a minority's desire for immediate gain. Swift concentrated on the lust for wealth and power of the moneyed interests, particularly of Godolphin, Marlborough, and the Junto. Shaw cited Sir Edward Grey, the English militarists, and a moneyed interest.

Shaw, considering the problem of imposing restraints on diplomacy, wrote,

A far graver doubt is raised by the susceptibility of the masses to war
fever, and the appalling danger of a daily deluge of cheap newspapers
written by nameless men and women whose scandalously low payment
is a guarantee of their ignorance and their servility to the financial
department, controlled by a moneyed class which not only curries favor with the military caste for social reasons, but has large interests in
war as a method of raising the price of money, the only commodity the
moneyed class has to sell.

Swift had spoken of private interest in similar terms:

Thus it plainly appears, that there was a Conspiracy on all sides to go
on with those Measures, which must perpetuate the War; and a Conspiracy founded upon the Interest and Ambition of each party; . . . It
is to be supposed, that what I am to say upon this Part of the Subject,
will have little Influence on those, whose particular Ends or Designs of
any sort, lead them to wish the Continuance of the War. I mean the
General and our Allies abroad; the Knot of late Favourites at home;
the Body of such, as Traffick in Stocks; and lastly, that Set of Factious
Politicians, who were so violently bent, at least, upon *Clipping* our Constitution in Church and State.

Shaw also deplored the inability of constitutional procedures to pre-
vent war, referring to Grey's committing England to war before letting Parliament know about it and mentioning the possibility of an
American president's being able to prosecute a war without the approval of Congress. For both Swift and Shaw, pro-war factions can
drive a nation to war contrary to its own desire or interest, although
Swift assigned the role of beginning war to factions while Shaw
blamed similar factions for failing to stop war.

Entangling alliances themselves were evils for both Swift and Shaw.
For Swift, England's neglect of profitable aspects of the war was due
to the interests of the Allies and to England's supposed obligations to
them. Swift represented the Allies as deliberately furthering their
own ends and opposing any campaign that would be advantageous to
the English:

. . . it could hardly enter into any Imagination, that while we are Confederates in a War, with those who are to have the whole Profit, and
who leave a double share of the Burthen upon us, we dare not think
of any Design, though against the Common Enemy, where there is the
least prospect of doing Good to our own Country, for fear of giving
Umbrage and Offence to our Allies; while we are ruining our selves to
Conquer Provinces and Kingdoms for them. . . . While the Design of

Mr. *Hill's* Expedition remained a Secret, it was suspected in *Holland* and *Germany* to be intended against *Peru;* whereupon the *Dutch* made every where their Publick Complaints, and the Ministers at *Vienna* talked of it as *an Insolence in the Queen to attempt such an Undertaking;* which, however it has failed, partly by the Accidents of a Storm, and partly by the Stubbornness or Treachery of some in that Colony, for whose Relief, and at whose Entreaty it was in some measure designed, is no Objection at all to an Enterprize so well concerted, and with such fair Probability of Success.

Swift's version of Hill's expedition to Quebec is at odds with fact. Through the incompetence of the British and their unfamiliarity with the St. Lawrence River, the fleet went on the rocks. In October, with winter approaching and inadequate provisions for the winter, the leaders voted unanimously to return to England. The venture, designed by St. John while Harley was recuperating from his wound, resulted in the loss of eight transports and eight hundred men. Harley, who had opposed the venture from the start, was unable to reveal what he subsequently learned—that of the 28,036 pounds, five shillings authorized for the venture, only 7,000 pounds went to provision the fleet. Sir Arthur Moore and St. John pocketed the rest, thereby guaranteeing failure.

With the sympathy of the public won by Guiscard's assassination attempt and the Tory peace articles about to be presented in Parliament, Harley could ill afford to split his party by revealing St. John's ill-timed cupidity. St. John's political purposes in fostering the undertaking were to acquire some military prestige for himself and to ingratiate himself, at Harley's expense, with Abigail Hill (Mrs. Masham), who believed her brother was as capable in the field as Marlborough. General Hill later assumed command of the British forces occupying Dunkirk and botched the assignment as spectacularly as he had bungled the Quebec expedition, but for St. John this was of secondary importance. He had the ear of Abigail, and therefore of Queen Anne, throughout the rest of his struggle with Harley. That was all St. John had really wanted. Swift's objections to the Allies, however, were sound.

Shaw also felt such alliances were detrimental to England's cause, but he emphasized England's initial involvement rather than the ultimate conduct of the war.

We must get rid of the monstrous situation that produced the present war. France made an alliance with Russia as a defence against Germany. Germany made an alliance with Austria as a defence against

Russia. England joined the Franco-Russian alliance as a defence
against Germany and Austria. The result was that Germany became
involved in a quarrel between Austria and Russia. Having no quarrel
with France, and only a second-hand quarrel with Russia, she was,
nevertheless, forced to attack France in order to disable her before she
could strike Germany from behind when Germany was fighting with
France's ally, Russia. And this attack on France forced England to come
to the rescue of England's ally, France. Not one of the three nations (as
distinguished from their tiny Junker-Militarist cliques) wanted to fight;
for England had nothing to gain and Germany had everything to lose;
whilst France had given up hope of her Alsace-Lorraine *revanche*, and
would certainly not have hazarded a war for it. Yet because Russia, who
has a great deal to gain by victory and nothing except military prestige
to lose by defeat, had a quarrel with Austria over Servia, she has been
able to set all three western friends and neighbors shedding "rivers of
blood" from one another's throats: an outrageous absurdity.

For Swift, England fought the war for her Allies' profit. For Shaw,
England, Austria, Germany, and France were fighting Russia's war.

Both Swift and Shaw posed, as the gloomiest of possibilities, an
extension of the war beyond its original aims. Swift's target was the
"No Peace Without Spain" slogan of the war adherents. He devoted
a large portion of his pamphlet to it, ultimately dropping the bomb-
shell of the Eighth Article of the Grand Alliance from which, in his
translation, he showed that dispossessing the Duke of Anjou was not
an original war aim. He then showed that since Austria would gain
Spain without much effort, and since the Dutch would still have their
barrier as a consolation, the Allies had reason to adopt this new aim.
England had not. Shaw foresaw a similar situation:

> For see what the first effect of the nonsense about Belgium has been!
> It carried with it the inevitable conclusion that when the last German
> was cleared off Belgian soil, peace-loving England, her reluctant work
> in this shocking war done, would calmly retire from the conflict, and
> leave her Allies to finish the deal with Potsdam. Accordingly . . . the
> Allies very properly insisted on our signing a solemn treaty between
> the parties that they must all stand together to the very end.

What this amounted to for Shaw was a "blank cheque":

> Just consider what the blank cheque means. France's draft on it may
> stop at the cost of recovering Alsace and Lorraine. We shall have to be
> content with a few scraps of German colony and the heavy-weight
> championship. But Russia? When will she say "Hold! Enough!"? Sup-

pose she wants not only Poland, but Baltic Prussia? Suppose she wants Constantinople as her port of access to the unfrozen seas, in addition to the dismemberment of Austria? Suppose she has the brilliant idea of annexing all Prussia, for which there is really something to be said by ethnographical map-makers, Militarist madmen, and Pan-Slavist megalomaniacs? . . . The only limit there is to the obligation is the certainty that the cheque will be dishonored the moment the draft on it becomes too heavy. And that may furnish a virtuous pretext for another war between the Allies themselves.

The possibility that Shaw foresaw is similar to the actuality Swift had explicated. Although Swift opposed the Allies on materialistic grounds and Shaw on more ideological ones, Swift castigating the Allies for greed and Shaw opposing the Russian Tsar as an enemy of liberty, neither desired to further Allied ends at the cost of England's well-being.

Both Swift and Shaw supported the continuance of the war "within reason," Swift posing limited war aims and Shaw suggesting new aims for the war. Swift concluded that the Tory Ministers

> think it infinitely better, to accept such Terms as will secure our Trade, find a sufficient Barrier for the *States,* give *Reasonable Satisfaction* to the Emperor, and restore the Tranquility of *Europe,* though without adding *Spain* to the Empire: Rather than go on in a languishing way, upon the vain Expectation of some improbable Turn, for the Recovery of that Monarchy out of the *Bourbon* Family; and at last be forced to a worse Peace, by some of the Allies falling off, upon our utter Inability to continue the War.

His plea was for the most advantageous peace rather than a stance against war. Shaw also limited the war's aims, but his objectives were different. England had to win the war without the help of Tsarist Russia, be generous in settlement, abolish war, remove the illusion of moral superiority by either England or Germany, recognize English militarism as the enemy of democracy, admit that outrages had been committed by both sides, and convince the world that democracy is invincible. As Swift had opposed aims that were excessive beyond all probability, Shaw dismissed such impractical aims as disarmament and excessive reparations. In their attempts to place the wars into proper perspective, Swift and Shaw both demanded a close scrutiny of war aims, actual motives for conflict, and reasons for continuing.

Nevertheless Swift and Shaw both revealed biases unrelated to the

war. Swift upheld the Tory Ministry and attacked Godolphin, Marlborough, and the Allies *ad hominem*. Shaw, too, upheld the Labour
Party and attacked various officials by name, notably Sir Edward
Grey. Swift alluded to relatively minor issues such as Hill's expedition
to Quebec and Queen Anne's domestic difficulties with Sarah
Churchill. Shaw treated the issues of soldiers' pensions, the oath of
allegiance, Ireland's role fighting for England, and post-war jobs for
soldiers. Swift did not miss a chance to uphold the present Ministry,
citing Harley's honest use of public funds and the Ministry's selfless
sacrifice in negotiating for peace. Shaw emphasized a socialist stance
and even argued that some good might arise from the war in terms
of political and economic reforms. In their pamphlets, neither neglected to grind his own axe.

Both Swift and Shaw took a great deal of pride in their political
writing. In *Journal to Stella* (18 December 1711), Swift wrote, "all
agree, that never any thing of that kind was of so great consequence,
or made so many converts." *Conduct* was quoted in the parliamentary
debates "and in the Commons, heavy majorities passed resolutions
which were almost quotations from it."[12] Swift justifiably took credit
for the success of the Tory articles of peace, yet he was amazingly
short-sighted in terms of the ultimate result. Those who opposed the
war seemed to oppose the Successor, and the Tory triumph turned to
defeat when George assumed the throne. The effectiveness of *Conduct* buried the Tory party for thirty years. Also, it revealed Swift's
ignorance of events in his own party. Even as he continued to mini-
mize the danger of the Pretender, Harley and St. John were negotiating with him, inviting him to renounce his religion to accept the
British throne. Swift seemed not to realize how much he had been
misled by his great men, or what the actual stakes were. By not understanding the duplicity of his political leaders, his own ambivalent
stance of partisan above party, and the animosity and vindictiveness
of his political onslaughts, Swift demonstrated he was completely out
of his depth. He functioned, despite his belief to the contrary, merely
as a tool in the hands of the Ministers who, as Steele wrote later,
laughed at Swift behind his back.

Shaw, too, revealed his basic misunderstanding of the situation, for
while his grasp of the political forces at work was basically sound, the
effect of his pamphlet could only be to provoke outrage. In a letter to
Clifford Sharp (24 October 1914), Shaw indicated that he expected
resistance, but he clearly underestimated the opposition he would encounter:

Finally, as to annoying a lot of people, of course it will. It will make everyone who reads it howl like a dog at a ballad concert at certain passages. But then in other passages it says something they want to have said so badly that they will have to submit. Besides, I mean it to be read in Germany. It will finally impose itself, for though of course it is not "just" (am I God Almighty?) it is, on the whole, as nearly so as human nature can bear.[13]

If Swift erred in exalting his political leaders' motives, Shaw over-estimated the objectivity of his audience. His widely (and mislead-ingly) quoted suggestion that the soldiers should shoot their officers and go home, his suggestion that England was as culpable as Ger-many, and his flippant attitude culminating in the suggestion that the way to crush Germany would be to kill 75% of her women affected his audience more than his comments on the plight of the soldiers, his statements that Germany was more militaristic than England and that England could justify the war, and his insistence that settle-ment with Germany must be made in the name of the democratic powers.

Swift could not resist an opportunity to attack every opponent in his "objective" pamphlet. Shaw could not resist telling his audience exactly what it did not want to hear. By being less partisan, Swift might have secured the peace without destroying his party. By being less abrasive, Shaw might have been able to direct public opinion and would not have been required to justify his *Common Sense* for the rest of the war. *Conduct* put Swift's party in a hopeless situation. Shaw's *Common Sense* put Shaw in a defensive position, so much so that his later war writings, which defended the same stance he had taken in his most notorious pamphlet, were taken as contradictions. Ehren-preis wrote of Swift, "It's a token of the potency of human self-deception that a satirist like Swift, who expressly described himself as a libeller, could picture himself as so innocent, and feel baffled be-cause his victims paid more attention to their gaping wounds than to his exalted motives."[14] The same power of self-deception was behind Shaw's belief that his *Common Sense* could, at that time, provoke a re-sponse other than outrage and that his audience could see through his stance to his higher motive.

In their immediate effects, one can call Swift's *Conduct* a rhetorical success and Shaw's *Common Sense* a rhetorical failure, yet Shaw re-mained proud of it because in the long run the truth of his statements prevailed. In his 1931 collection of his wartime writings, Shaw ended,

> One last word. In calling this book What I Really Wrote about the War,
> I have exposed myself to the obvious repartee "Does it matter?"
>     My reply is that it does.

Such an attitude is a closer literary parallel between Swift and Shaw
than the two major pamphlets themselves, for both men believed
strongly that their positions deserved the attention of humanity, and
they felt that their political writing entitled them to some measure of
esteem.

# Notes

1. Stanley Weintraub, *Journey to Heartbreak* (New York: Weybright and Talley, 1971), p. 328.
2. Irvin Ehrenpreis, *Swift: The Man, his Works, and the Age* (London: Methuen & Co., Ltd., 1967), II, 275.
3. Ibid., p. 461.
4. Ibid., p. 618.
5. Weintraub, p. 56.
6. *Journal to Stella*, 31 May 1712. Quotations of Swift are from *The Prose Works of Jonathan Swift*, ed. Herbert Davis (Oxford: Basil Blackwell, 1939–1968).
7. *Sixteen Self Sketches* (London, 1949), p. 118.
8. Weintraub, p. 176.
9. Ehrenpreis, pp. 50–51.
10. Weintraub, p. 48.
11. Quotations of Shaw are from *The Ayot St. Lawrence Edition of the Collected Works of Bernard Shaw*, Volume 21: *What I Really Wrote About the War* (New York: William H. Wise & Company, 1931).
12. Ehrenpreis, p. 500.
13. Dan H. Laurence, ed., *The Collected Letters of Bernard Shaw*, III (New York: Viking, 1985), 260.
14. Ehrenpreis, p. 736.

# Desmond J. McRory

# SHAW, EINSTEIN AND PHYSICS

At the Savoy Hotel in 1930 Bernard Shaw delivered this toast: "Health and length of days to the greatest of our contemporaries, Einstein." How is it that a man who was widely regarded as anti-science came to give the most prominent scientist of the past three hundred years such praise? The answer to that question reveals a good deal about Shaw's general philosophy and his attitude toward science.

On 6 November 1919 an event had occurred that extended Albert Einstein's fame from scientific circles to the world at large. On that day the British Royal Society and the Royal Astronomical Society heard the results of an expedition to Africa and South America they had commissioned to test Einstein's assertion that light had mass and consequently would be affected by a gravitational field. The validity of his General Theory of Relativity depended on the expedition's photographically recording light from a star being bent by the sun's gravity during a solar eclipse. Einstein predicted the deflection to be approximately 1.75 seconds of arc; the expedition reported the deflection to be 1.64 seconds of arc. Einstein was right.

The news of the verification of his theory made Einstein an international celebrity overnight, a status which had obligations that were to grow and bedevil him for the remainder of his life. England's reaction to the proof was particularly enthusiastic. Three things accounted for this enthusiasm: A small group of British scientists, led by Sir Arthur Eddington, had sponsored Einstein's ideas in learned societies as early as 1914; the verification of the General Theory by a British expedition had stimulated national pride; and English astronomers verifying the work of a German scientist suggested a new era of cooperation for a war-weary generation.[1] The *Times* of London on 7 November made clear to the British people the significance of Einstein's ideas, reporting that the "greatest experts" confidently believed "enough has been done to overthrow the certainty of ages, and to require a new philosophy of the universe, a philosophy that will sweep away nearly all that has hitherto been accepted as the axiomatic basis of physical thought." On 15 November the *Times* underscored the revolutionary importance of Einstein's theories in an article entitled "The Revolution in Science."[2] Some months later the *Times Educational Supplement* devoted three full-page articles to interpretations of relativity by three prominent scientists, and in 1920 the House of Commons authorized an Einstein Society.

When the news of the proof of General Relativity broke, Shaw must have felt the surge of interest and excitement that went through London in late 1919 and early 1920—interest and excitement which was not limited to intellectual circles. Even the London Palladium, hoping to cash in on Einstein's popularity, tried, without success, to book him for a three-week "performance."[3] Although no direct account exists of Shaw's reaction to the epoch-making verification, the toast that Shaw delivered to Einstein ten years later contained a capsulization of the history of physics very much like the one that appeared in "The Revolution in Science." Archibald Henderson said of this part of the toast that "undoubtedly" Shaw composed it carefully, "briefed by some scientific authority," but Shaw may have remembered the short histories of physics given in the newspapers a decade earlier, or perhaps he was drawing on information supplied in one of a number of accounts of relativity that Henderson himself mentioned having given him. Even the amusing, but fictional, story told in the toast about the workman who sensed relativity during a fall from a building dated from this time.

Worldwide acclaim grew so great that Einstein undertook a series of tours during the first half of the nineteen-twenties. These tours were loathsome to him because "He always hated excessive recognition, well aware that in spite of what he had done, he was in some way like the men on Everest who metaphorically stood upon the shoulders of their predecessors. He was never in any doubt about his own worth; he had no reason to be. But he hated the hubbub created around him by those ignorant of the very language of science which he spoke."[4]

Nevertheless, Einstein felt obliged to use his fame in America to benefit the Zionist cause and to help the forces at work in England and France to rebuild Europe on a more enlightened basis. It was in this spirit that he traveled to England in 1921. During this visit Shaw and he met at a private dinner party on 10 June given by Richard Burdon Haldane, former Secretary for War and Lord Chancellor. Although no verbatim account exists of what passed in conversation between the two men, we know that Einstein very much enjoyed meeting Shaw, whose wit delighted him.[5] A Shavian reference to Einstein occurs soon after, in a letter to St. John Ervine, 21 September 1921, in which Shaw refers to the difference between the child and the adult as akin to that "between Reggie de Veulle (or whatever his silly name is) and Einstein."[6]

Two years after the face-to-face meeting between Shaw and Einstein, a close association was established between them through Shaw's biographer Archibald Henderson. Henderson was a skilled mathematician who had earned a doctorate from the University of Chicago in the early years of the century and became professor of mathematics at the University of North Carolina. In late December of 1923 Henderson traveled to Germany as Kenan Traveling Research Professor in Mathematics to work with Einstein on relativity and atomic theory at the Institute of Physics at the University of Berlin.[7] The two met frequently both professionally at the Institute and at the physicist's home at 5 Haberlandstrasse.[8] Archibald Henderson's new friendship with Einstein and continuing relationship with Shaw acted as a powerful influence in raising mathematics and physics in Shaw's esteem.

Shaw's attitude toward science is more diverse and complex than critics have realized. He is commonly remembered for his attacks on the cruelty of vivisection, the danger of vaccination, the incompetence of the medical profession, and the claims of physics, mathematics, and astronomy. Yet by 1920 Shaw's attitude toward science seemed to change. He began to soften his stand against the biological sciences and to admire much about the physical sciences. This shift in Shaw's attitude is evident in his work after the First World War. A variety of things caused him to alter his strident tone against science. In the biological sciences, Shaw did not so much change his mind as simply stop making his mind known. In the physical sciences, Shaw made his newfound esteem for mathematics and physics explicitly known through his plays. A significant reason for this new respect was Shaw's personal relationship with the physicist Albert Einstein and the mathematician Archibald Henderson, biographer of Shaw and elucidator of Einstein.

Shaw remained suspicious of the biological sciences to the end of his life. (He made a biochemist the villain of the "First Fable" of *Farfetched Fables* written in 1950.) Yet this hostility toward the biological sciences lessened after 1920, or at least he spoke less frequently about them after that time. One reason was that Shaw's attention was taken by other cultural, philosophical, and political matters. And too, Shaw must have felt that he would have been arguing an issue that had become less relevant. The benefits derived from vaccination and improvements in other fields of medicine had made the biological sciences a widely recognized boon to mankind.

Though biology had been the major target of Shaw's denunciation of science, he felt that the physical sciences had also been corrupted by the credulity afforded science as the result of Darwin's assault on Christian doctrine. Physicists and astrophysicists among the physical scientists were particularly excoriated because they took advantage of the people's need for cosmological belief.

As a boy, Shaw had read the works of the English physicist John Tyndall and the German physicist Herman Von Helmholtz, who contributed arguments on the side of mechanism in the vitalist-mechanist debate. This debate greatly influenced not just Shaw's attitude toward science but his entire worldview, as expressed in his philosophy of Creative Evolution. It also accounted for the out-of-date character of many of his attacks on science. He continued to debate a nineteenth-century issue into the middle of the twentieth century. In fact Shaw once called himself a "doddering relic" of the nineteenth century.[9] In the *Simpleton of the Unexpected Isles,* written in 1934, Shaw asserted that science would never be able to explain human life in chemical terms alone (6:747). In 1949, when few scientists doubted that a complete understanding of man's makeup would be possible in electrochemical terms, Shaw had composed *Farfetched Fables.* In the futuristic "Fifth Fable," Rose and the Hermaphrodite discuss the inability of science to explain man as the sum of his chemical constituents:

> ROSE. We all want the Just Man Made Perfect; but when our chemists ask us for an exact prescription of the necessary protoplasm, hormones, vitamins, enzymes and the rest, we never agree on the last milligram of each ingredient; and it is that milligram that determines whether the resulting product will be a poet or a mathematician.
> HERMAPHRODITE. I'm against all that. It revolts me. I tell you again and again we shall never make decent human beings out of chemical salts. [7:452]

Although Shaw considered the foolish credulity afforded the physical sciences to spring from the same misplaced religious devotion that characterized the biological sciences, he believed that the physical scientists erred in ways peculiar to themselves. One aspect of Shavian scepticism concerned the numeration used by geologists, physicists, and astronomers (to a lesser degree Shaw also attacked the microbiologists on this point). For example, in Shaw's estimation Archbishop Ussher, who calculated the origin of the universe to have occurred in

4004 B.C., was succeeded in spirit by nineteenth-century scientists who erred in the other direction: they had a "craze for big figures" and "talked very glibly about geological periods, and flung millions of eons about in the most lordly manner" (5:278). Physicists in the late nineteenth century spoke of the number of electrons in an atom in the same way that medieval theologians spoke of the number of angels on the head of a pin. Astrophysicists calculated the distance between stars to be billions of miles, and helped to give rise to people who would not have believed anything unless it contained "billions of millions in space." Shaw for his part "refused to conceive this conception of an enormous number of billions of miles."[10] He concluded in the preface to *Saint Joan* that clairvoyants, hand readers, slate writers, Christian Scientists, and electronic vibration diviners belong in the same category with astronomers who "tell us that the sun is nearly a hundred million miles away and that the Betelgeuse is ten times as big as the whole universe" and physicists who "balance Betelgeuse by describing the incredible smallness of the atom," and a "host of other marvelmongers whose credulity would have dissolved the Middle Ages in a roar of sceptical merriment" (6:68).

*Back to Methuselah,* completed in 1920, was the first play in which Shaw recognized the type of thinking used in mathematics and physics as characteristic of an advanced human intellect. Pygmalion even speaks of the children of the future possessing an innate perception of Einsteinian "space-time." Certainly we can safely infer that Henderson's influence was at work here. Indeed, Henderson said that he explained to Shaw the "meaning of many terms used by Einstein": invariant and covariant, vector and tensor, quadractic differential form, frame of reference, and the like. The mathematical concept of tensor fascinated Shaw, and Henderson said that tensors "occupied his attention during the remainder of his life." Shaw once wrote drolly to Henderson, "I can't imagine why you take such interest in the Shavian drama when you could be devoting all your time to the study of Tensors."[11] Henderson not only explained the individual mathematical components operating in Einstein's theories, but he also set forth a comprehensive explanation in *Relativity: A Romance of Science.*[12] In 1923 he sent Shaw a copy of the newly published book. Shaw said it was the "most lucid exposition of the subject he had seen." The clarity of the book so impressed Shaw that he asked Henderson to send copies to H. G. Wells, G. K. Chesterton, Hilaire Belloc, Max Beerbohm, and others.[13] Henderson also provided Shaw with other books on the philosophy of relativity as well as numerous technical papers on the subject.[14] Henderson, in effect, tutored Shaw in the latest advances in physics and their mathematical foundations, giving Shaw a privileged, intimate view of the revolution in the physical sciences that enhanced his opinion of them.

Henderson facilitated the deepening of the relationship between Shaw and Einstein during the mid-twenties by carrying correspondence between the two great men. Their acquaintance grew into a long-distance friendship. This was not surprising since they had much in common: both were internationally famous European intellectuals; both were socialists; Einstein was a pacifist during the First World War and Shaw a critic of the British position; both professed scientific humanism as a personal philosophy and substitute for conventional religion; and both were outsiders—Shaw, an Irishman in England; Einstein, a Jew in Germany.[15]

The closeness of feeling was apparent in the letters exchanged between the men. On a postcard that bore his photograph, dated 2 December 1924, Shaw wrote to Einstein, "I venture to send you this little portrait of myself because I have had for some years a much bigger one of you in my house. Your letter gives me the greatest pleasure, not only as a compliment to me, but because only a very exact and penetrating mind could have said the right thing so precisely. You are the only sort of man in whose existence I see much hope for this deplorable world."[16]

Einstein's name appeared for the first time in Shaw's writings in the 1924 preface to *Saint Joan*. In it Shaw used Einstein as a representative of human genius. All told, Shaw mentioned Einstein twenty times in his plays and prefaces (excluding the six times it appeared in his 1922 adaptation of Siegfried Trebitsch's *Jitta's Attonement*) and nine times in *The Intelligent Woman's Guide to Socialism, Capitalism, Sovietism, and Fascism* and *Everybody's Political What's What?* In his two political tracts Shaw primarily contrasted Einstein's professorial income with more lucrative but less socially beneficial occupations (such as prize-fighting) in order to highlight the inequalities in the distribution of wealth in capitalist societies. In his plays and prefaces, however, Shaw used Einstein for two different purposes: as an exemplar of human genius, the supreme mathematician and physicist of the age; and as a subject of Nazi persecution, the victim of the corrupt moral and intellectual character of the Nazi regime.

Further face-to-face meetings between Shaw and Einstein occurred in London in October of 1930. Throughout the nineteen-twenties Einstein had lent his support to specific Jewish causes and to the international Zionist movement. And it was as the guest of honor that Einstein attended the dinner at the Savoy Hotel on 28 October, presided over by Lionel Rothschild and sponsored by the Joint British

Committee of Ort and Oze, organizations which sought to promote the economic and physical well-being of Eastern European Jewry. During this visit, Einstein and Shaw also met at a luncheon. Einstein had previously "skillfully evaded" an invitation to meet other "prominent men,"[17] and this luncheon was a demonstration of Einstein's special affection for Shaw. Shaw's secretary, Blanche Patch, described this meeting in her book, *Thirty Years With G.B.S.*, and recounted a brief exchange between them. Shaw with characteristic bold humor told Einstein that "he had made a mess of science." To which the physicist replied jokingly, "What does it matter? This is not your business!"[18]

No person ever received higher praise from Shaw than did Einstein in Shaw's toast at the Ort-Oze dinner.[19] In his most significant expression of the respect and admiration that he felt for Einstein, Shaw put forth two ideas that lay at the heart of his speech and that help to explain his high regard for Einstein, ideas derived from his theory of Creative Evolution: one, Einstein was a genius and a great man among great men; two, the true artist was a scientist and the true scientist was an artist.

Men of genius, "great men," were of special importance in the scheme of Creative Evolution. All nature was its agent, but man as a reasoning being represented the highest expression yet of its struggle for realization. Among men the Life Force created individuals with varying mental capacities and talents, just as each sex exhibited different general characteristics. As Shaw explained in the preface to *Farfetched Fables*, "providence" made certain that mankind had the right mix of individuals:

> Providence, which I call the Life Force, when not defeated by the imperfection of its mortal instruments, always takes care that the necessary functionaries are born specialized for their job. When no specialization beyond that of common mental ability is needed, millions of "hands" (correctly so called industrially) are born. But as they are helpless without skilled craftsmen and mechanics, without directors and deciders, without legislators and thinkers, these also are provided in required numbers. Chaucer and Shakespear, Dante and Michael Angelo, Goethe and Ibsen, Newton and Einstein, Adam Smith and Karl Marx arrive only once at intervals of hundreds of years, whilst carpenters and tailors, stockbrokers and parsons, industrialists and traders are all forthcoming in thousands as fast as they are needed. [7:385–86]

As implied in this passage, Shaw had a high regard for geniuses because of their scarcity. On two occasions Shaw set the percentage of

people especially useful to society at only five percent of the population, and out of that five percent only a handful were great men. In
*Village Wooing* the character A speaks of the percentage in a dialogue
with the character Z:

> About five percent of the human race consists of positive masterful
> acquisitive people like you, obsessed with some passion which they
> must gratify at all hazards. The rest let them have their own way be-
> cause they have neither the strength nor the courage to resist, or be-
> cause the things the masterful ones want seem trifling beside the starry
> heavens and the destiny of Man. [6:566]

In a passage quoted previously from *Farfetched Fables,* Thistle,
speaking of the men of the twentieth century, also sets the percentage
at five:

> They wasted millions of hours every day because they could not or
> would not do the simplest things; when their five percent of geniuses
> made wonderful machines for them . . . they accepted them as gifts
> from some imaginary paradise called heaven. [7:450]

Not only were great men to be valued because they were scarce
ingredients in the evolutionary mix, but also because they were the
highest expression of the Life Force's movement to realize itself; and
therefore they were examples of what every person might become in
terms of increased intellectual and moral power. Shaw wrote in the
preface to *Geneva,* "The apparent freaks of nature called Great Men
mark not human attainment but human possibility and hope" (7:41).
Indeed, in the future as depicted in *Back to Methuselah,* the hope that
one day every person might possess the faculties of Einstein was realized in the children who were born with a "simple direct sense of
space-time."

Shaw recognized a characteristic of genius in Einstein's thinking
that he prided himself in possessing:

> I am myself by profession what is called an original thinker, my busi-
> ness being to question and test all the established creeds and codes to
> see how far they are still valid and how worn out or superseded, and
> even to draft new creeds and codes. [*IWG,* p. 336]

This overturning of conventions and widely held beliefs was precisely
the aspect of Einstein's work that Shaw praised near the conclusion of
his toast:

I rejoice in the fact that he has destroyed all the circles, all the old axioms, all the old cut-and-dried conceptions, even of time and space, which were so discouraging because they seemed all so solid that you never could get any further. I want to get further always. I want more and more problems, and our visitor has raised endless and wonderful problems and has begun solving them. [p. 87]

In his toast Shaw made a clear distinction between great men. There was Napoleon's type and there was Einstein's type. Just as the Life Force raised animals above plants, men above animals, and great men above ordinary men, the Life Force raised Einstein above great men. He acted as an epoch-making agent of Creative Evolution, but he did not make the advancement by shedding men's blood, by wasting the energy of the Life Force. Einstein was, in fact, an example of the highest level of development yet achieved in the process of Creative Evolution, one of its heroes:

If you take the typical great man of our historic epoch and suppose that I had arrived here tonight to propose the toast to Napoleon—well, undoubtedly I could say many very flattering things about Napoleon, but the one thing which I should not be able to say about him would be perhaps the most important thing and that was that it would perhaps have been better for the human race if he had never been born. Tonight, at least, we have no suppressions to make, no hypocrisy to be guilty of.

I have said that great men are a mixed lot, but there are orders of great men. There are great men who are great among small men, but there are great men who are great among great men, and that is the sort of great man you have among you here tonight. Napoleon and other great men of his type, they were makers of empires, but there is an order of men who get beyond that. They are not makers of empires, but they are makers of universes. Their hands are unstained by the blood of any human being on earth. They are very rare. I go back 2,500 years, and I can count on the fingers of my two hands: Pythagoras, Ptolemy, Aristotle, Copernicus, Kepler, Galileo, Newton, Einstein, and I still have two fingers left vacant. [p. 82]

Near his conclusion, Shaw made these remarks about Einstein and his theories, setting forth the second of the two ideas that help to explain Shaw's special feeling for the man:

But this man is not challenging the fact of science, he is challenging the axioms of science, and what is more, not only is he challenging the axioms of science, but the axioms of science have surrendered to his challenge. And then came in my special and particular point of view. These are not the results of equations marked out on paper; these are the intuitions of an artist, and I as an artist claim kinship with that great authority. I claim to be a man of science, and in the same sense that he is a man of science. I remind myself that Leonardo da Vinci, an artist, born twenty-one years before Copernicus, wrote down in his notebook—not as the result of elaborate calculation, but as perfectly simple and plain and obvious matter of fact—he wrote, "The earth is a moon of the sun." And later on the English artist, William Hogarth, a contemporary of Newton—their lives overlapped by thirty years— and when Newton said, "The line of nature is a straight line," William Hogarth said, "The line of nature is a curve." He anticipated our guest. But he was not mathematician enough to work out the entire problem and so—I flatter myself that I too am an artist—I think my speech will be understood by our guest here tonight. [pp. 86–87]

That scientific theories were often dogmatic was what Shaw was objecting to when he said that "religion is always right and science always wrong." It was a theme often repeated.[20] In "The Conflict Between Science and Common Sense," published in the *Humane Review* in 1900, Shaw delivered a denunciation of science, whose focus was the changing theories of the composition of the atmosphere and the shape of the earth:

Ten years ago, I no more doubted that I was breathing nothing but nitrogen and oxygen with a trace of carbon, than I doubt that the sun will rise tomorrow morning. The "trace of carbon" was conclusive: it cut off retreat by replying that there was not even a trace of anything else. But I reckoned without the reluctance of the "man of science" to say "I dont know." The fact that the old formula was an imposture would never have been discovered had not someone discovered argon in the atmosphere, and insisted on the others finding room for it, and confessing (or pretending) that they had known all along that the old formula was incomplete. How many physicists have been able since that disgraceful day to look the public in the face, is more than I can understand. Now that the gaff is blown, the show given away, the scientists have become reckless. They own that the earth formerly described by them, in their precisionist jargon, as "an oblate spheroid" (I believe it as I believe the first chapter of Genesis), is an object probably resembling a twopenny loaf in its general outline, and has no pretension to symmetry. Then why did they say it did? Can no man, when once he is given the entire confidence of the world, refrain from abusing it? . . . I have found out the man of science: and in the future my attitude towards him will be one of more or less polite incredulity. Impostor for impostor, I prefer the mystic to the scientist—the man who at least has the decency to call his nonsense a mystery, to him who pretends that it is ascertained, weighed, measured, analyzed fact.[21]

In *The Adventures of the Black Girl in Her Search for God,* the Black Girl encounters a jumble of rival scientific theories. Written in 1932, this passage from Shaw's short novel was a brief outbreak of his old prejudice against physical science. In it, the characters, after an argument over Natural Selection, discuss whether the sun was getting hotter or colder:

> "What is the use of all this?" groaned a depressed gentleman. "The only thing that we know for certain is that the sun is losing its heat, and that we shall presently die of cold. What does anything matter in the face of that fact?"
>
> "Cheer up, Mr Croker" said a lively young gentleman. "As chief physicist to this expedition I am in a position to inform you authoritatively that unless you reject cosmic radiation and tidal retardation you have just as much reason to believe that the sun is getting hotter and hotter and will eventually cremate us all alive."[22]

At this point in the story Shaw had a character voice his position in what he considered to be the most important of all scientific debates, the one between the mechanists and the vitalists. In answer to Mr. Croker's comment that we must perish whether from the extreme heat or extreme cold, a gentleman replies:

> Pooh! . . . our bodies, which are the only part of us to which your temperatures are fatal, will perish in a few years, mostly in well ventilated bedrooms kept at a comfortable temperature. But what of the something that makes the difference between the live body and the dead one? Is there a rag of proof, a ray of probability even, that it is in any way dependent on temperature? It is certainly not flesh nor blood nor bone, though it has the curious property of building bodily organs for itself in those forms. It is incorporal: if you try to figure it at all you must figure it as an electromagnetic wave, as rate of vibration, as a vortex in the ether if there be an ether; that is to say something that, if it exists at all—and who can question its existence?—can exist on the coldest of the dead stars or in the hottest crater of the sun.[23]

Beneath the alleged danger, cruelty, and greed of the biological sciences and the pretentiousness of the physical sciences, Shaw saw in scientific thinking basic epistemological errors that limited science as a field of intellectual inquiry. He objected to science when it pretended to answer what he termed the *why* of existence. Science could provide an equation to describe how a planet moved in an elliptical path under the gravitational influence of the sun, but it could not answer the question of why there was gravity or an ellipse or a planet or a sun. As Shaw explained in *Everybody's Political What's What?*,

> American psychologists who have studied the minds of children tell me that a child's first questions, five in number, are What? Where? When? How? Why? Secular science can answer the first three, and partly answer or hope to answer the fourth; but the fifth, the Why? is absolute checkmate to the scientist. [p. 64]

Again, further on in the discussion,

> The child's final question, which is always Why, is unanswerable, and should perhaps be always answered by a frank "Nobody knows," though stupid scientists put themselves out of court too often by mistaking hows for whys. [p. 71]

Shaw objected to science behaving as if it were religion, issuing dogma in the form of scientific theory. The business of religion was to answer the whys of existence, but science since the advent of creed-shattering Darwinism had taken over the role.

For Shaw even the scientific method was unreliable. In 1920 he described the problem in his "Foundation Oration" in the course of a general denunciation of science:

> One of the things that you must understand is that you can prove anything. (Laughter.) There is nothing so absurd that you cannot prove. But there is another thing. If you will only take trouble enough to prove things you will make this discovery, that proving a thing will not establish it, either with you or anybody else, for the reason, that when you have proved a thing up to the hilt by every law of logic, by every operation of the human mind, by every operation of the laws of evidence and conditions of proof you can possibly imagine, you will not have established a thing. You will have established a certain alternative. You will have to say to yourself, "Either this thing is true, or what I have achieved is a *reductio ad absurdum*. That is to say, the conclusion is so entirely unacceptable to me, that I prefer to say that my logical process has either been wrong or else, if you prove to me my process was right, and that I omitted nothing, I shall have to set to work to overthrow the whole scheme of logic and all the laws of evidence, and to scrap them rather than accept this thing that I have proved."[24]

When we consider Shaw's attitude as represented in this quote, we can see why he preferred the mystic to the scientist, and why he said in a letter to G. K. Chesterton in 1908, "Nothing is more natural than that you should reconstruct me as the last of the Rationalists . . . ; and nothing could be more erroneous. It would be nearer the truth to call me . . . the first of the mystics."[25]

Considering that Shaw held traditional Christian religions in low regard, representing as they did for him an obsolescent stage in the evolution of culture, that he would want to be known as a mystic (he would repeat that regularly) revealed an important element of his thinking, one that greatly influenced his estimation of scientific knowledge. He believed that religions at their best could inspire men by expressing truths about life in a poetic way and that this poetic expression promoted holiness—holiness meaning a sense of awe at the *why* of life, a sense of the brotherhood of man, a sense of an intelligence in the design of nature that inspired moral obligation, and a sense of the kinship of living things. Science, on the other hand, when it established truth (Shaw never argued that scientific knowledge was not truth of a kind), did so in a way that did not inspire holiness. In the preface to *On the Rocks* (1933) Shaw spoke of the contrast:

> . . . if instead of telling me that Jesus was taken up into the clouds and the disciples saw him no more, which still makes me feel quite holy, you tell me that he went up like a balloon into the stratosphere, I do not feel holy; I laugh obstreperously. The exalting vision has suddenly become a ribald joke. [6:610]

In *Back to Methuselah* The Elderly Gentleman explains the difference between knowledge that promotes goodness and knowledge that promotes evil:

> I assure you, madam, the merest mediocrities can discover the most surprising facts about the physical universe as soon as they are civilized enough to have time to study these things, and to invent instruments and apparatus for research. But what is the consequence? Their discoveries discredit the simple stories of our religion. . . . When the priests themselves ceased to believe in the Deity and began to believe in astronomy, they changed their name and their dress, and called themselves doctors and men of science. They set up a new religion in which there was no Deity, but only wonders and miracles, with scientific instruments and apparatus as the wonder workers. Instead of worshipping the greatness and wisdom of the Deity, men gaped foolishly at the million billion of miles of space and worshipped the astronomer as infallible and omniscient. They built temples for his telescopes. Then they looked into their own bodies with microscopes, and found

there, not the soul that they had formerly believed in, but millions of micro-organisms, so they gaped at these as foolishly as at the millions of miles, and built microscope temples in which horrible sacrifices were offered. They even gave their own bodies to be sacrificed by the micro-scope man, who was worshipped like the astronomer, as infallible and omniscient. Thus our discoveries, instead of increasing our wisdom, only destroyed the little childish wisdom we had. All I grant you is that they increased our knowledge. [5:513–14]

It is clear that knowledge for Shaw could be of varying quality and that the quality depended on the effect that knowledge had on man's moral character. Religion and science both described and explained reality, both arrived at knowledge; but scientific knowledge was often detrimental to man's moral sense, and therefore was often of lesser value. In *Back to Methuselah* a group of characters discusses the difference between the explanations of the Bible and the explanations of science. Through Conrad and Franklyn, Shaw again made his position clear:

> LUBIN. . . . Surely Science knows nothing of Genesis; or of Adam and Eve.
> CONRAD. Then it isnt Science: thats all. Science has to account for everything; and everything includes the Bible.
> FRANKLYN. The Book of Genesis is a part of nature like any other part of nature. The fact that the tale of the Garden of Eden has survived and held the imaginations of men spellbound for centuries, whilst hundreds of much more plausible and amusing stories have gone out of fashion like last year's popular song, is a scientific fact; and Science is bound to explain it. You tell me that Science knows nothing of it then Science is more ignorant than the children at any village school.
> CONRAD. Of course if you think it more scientific to say that what we are discussing is not Adam and Eve and Eden, but the phylogeny of the blastoderm—
> SAVVY. You neednt swear, Nunk.
> CONRAD. Shut up, *you:* I am not swearing. [*To Lubin*] If you want the professional humbug of rewriting the Bible in the words of four syllables, and pretending it's something new, I can humbug you to your heart's content. I can call Genesis Phylogenesis. Let the Creator say, if you like, "I will establish an antipathetic symbiosis between thee and the female, and between thy blastoderm and her blastoderm." Nobody will understand you; and Savvy will think you are swearing. The meaning is the same.
> HASLAM. Priceless. The one version is poetry: the other is science.

FRANKLYN. The one is classroom jargon: the other is inspired human language. [5:425–26]

Shaw's attitude toward science, as evident in this play written as the First World War was closing, was showing signs of change. Still, his Creative Evolution remained an idealist philosophy that viewed the apprehensible world as the manifestation of a great motivating will or idea. This will or Life Force sought to realize itself by using the living beings of the world as its agents, a Shavian adaptation of the Lamarckian view that change in living creatures was brought about by their desire to improve their chances of survival. In this respect, Shaw remained unreformed, describing the process in the preface to *Back to Methuselah* much as he had dramatized it twenty years before in *Don Juan in Hell:*

> Let us fix the Lamarckian evolutionary process well in our minds. You are alive; and you want to be more alive. You want, consequently, additional organs, or additional uses of your existing organs: that is, additional habits. You get them because you want them badly enough to keep trying for them until they come. Nobody knows how: nobody knows why: all we know is that the thing actually takes place. We relapse miserably from effort to effort until the old organ is modified or the new one created, when suddenly the impossible becomes possible and the habit is formed. The moment we form it we want to get rid of the consciousness of it so as to economize our consciousness for fresh conquests of life; as all consciousness means preoccupation and obstruction. [5:273–74]

The question of what men were evolving toward and which men were farthest along arises in any consideration of Shaw's Creative Evolution. It also has a direct bearing on Shaw's changed attitude toward mathematics and physics and specifically his admiration for Einstein.

Shaw was to express man's quest toward greater self-consciousness and self-understanding as a desire to become god. As Koholeth tells the black girl in *The Adventures of the Black Girl in Her Search for God* (1932) when she says that she must know god, "You mean that you must *be* God."[26] In the preface to *The Doctor's Dilemma*, Shaw said, "Everybody, by the deepest law of the Life Force, desires to be godlike" (3:263). Again, in *Back to Methuselah*, Franklyn says,

> The pursuit of omnipotence and omniscience. Greater power and greater knowledge: these are what we are all pursuing even at the risk

of our lives and the sacrifice of our pleasures. Evolution is that pursuit and nothing else. It is the path to godhead. A man differs from a microbe only in being further on the path. [5:423]

In the Shavian philosophy there was an intrinsic inferiority of matter relative to things of a spiritual nature. This became more apparent when Shaw in his futuristic dramas such as *Back to Methuselah* and *Farfetched Fables* characterized the advanced states of human intelligence. These plays owe much to Platonism and suggest a good deal about Shaw's attitude toward Einstein.

When he projected the evolution of the Life Force in the distant future, a dichotomy between matter and spirit, body and mind, was a prominent theme. The human intellect continued on the evolutionary path that set it apart from other creatures. It moved toward pure thought. As the She-Ancient in *Back to Methuselah* says, "The day will come when there will be no people, only thought" (5:620). And in *Village Wooing* a character speaks of a future in which the "world of senses will vanish" (6:568). Lilith at the conclusion of *Back to Methuselah*, Shaw's play about the entire history of human development from Adam and Eve to a science fiction-like future, speaks of men's and women's evolution toward pure thought:

> . . . they press on to the goal of redemption from the flesh, to the vortex freed from matter, to the whirlpool in pure intelligence that, when the world began, was a whirlpool in pure force. And though all that they have done seems but the first hour of the infinite work of creation, yet I will not supercede them until they have forded this last stream that lies between flesh and spirit, and disentangled their life from the matter that has always mocked it. . . . I brought life into the whirlpool of force, and compelled my enemy, Matter, to obey a living soul. But in enslaving Life's enemy I made him Life's master; for that is the end of all slavery; and now I shall see the slave set free and the enemy reconciled, the whirlpool become all life and no matter. [5:630]

This pressing on to the "redemption from flesh, to the vortex freed from matter" was expressed in a number of other plays. Rose in the *Farfetched Fables* states it plainly: "I would like to be a mind without a body" (7:453).

In *Farfetched Fables* Shaw also used a variation of the theme of man's evolution toward pure thought. In "The Sixth and Last Fable," set far in the future, the Teacher, a character representing Shavian ideas, and her students discuss the origin of ideas. The Teacher agrees with the "Theory of the Disembodied Races" as explained by a student.

According to the theory, a race of men some time in the past (our future) branched off from the human race and achieved complete disembodiment. As Youth 1 explains:

> I was brought up to consider that we are the vanguard of civilization, the last step in creative evolution. But according to the theory we are only a survival of the sort of mankind that existed in the twentieth century, no better than black beetles compared to the supermen who evolved into the disembodied. [7:460]

The Teacher goes on to explain that "the Disembodied Races still exist as Thought Vortexes, and are penetrating our thick skulls in their continual pursuit of knowledge and power, since they need our hands and brains as tools in that pursuit." The influence of the Disembodied Races is the origin of ideas. It is the Life Force willing men to greater knowledge and power.

That Shaw began to write futuristic plays after the First World War perhaps indicated his despair over the failure of his contemporaries and his desire to deal with a time distant enough to be hopeful. Whatever the reason, this change in Shaw's general outlook paralleled a change in his attitude toward mathematics and the rest of physical sciences.

As a schoolboy, Shaw himself was a duffer at mathematics. As he came into contact with theories and theorists of socialism, he quickly learned the importance of mathematics to his social and political thinking. To his radical contemporaries, socialism was a *scientific* analysis of history and economics. Marx and Engels had marshalled statistics, and the Fabians with their emphasis on the statistical analysis of social issues confronted Shaw with the practical benefits of a mathematical perspective. Only later would he turn to higher mathematics as a metaphor for advanced intellectual development in the scheme of Creative Evolution. Higher mathematics would come to represent for Shaw the closest that contemporary man could reach toward pure thought, the direction of the Life Force. On his way to becoming what Arthur Nethercot would call a "mathematical mystic,"[27] Shaw in *Back to Methuselah* would use mathematical speculation to characterize advanced intelligence. In the play Martellus desires to spend his time in mathematical thought. The longing for this thought is the Life Force urging him to higher development:

> There is a prehistoric saying that has come down to us from a famous woman teacher. She said: "Leave women; study mathematics." It is the only remaining fragment of a lost scripture called The Confessions of

St. Augustine, the English Opium Eater. That primitive savage must have been a great woman to say a thing that still lives after three hundred centuries. I too will leave women and study mathematics, which I have neglected too long. Farewell, children, my old playmates, I almost wish I could feel sentimental about parting from you; but the cold truth is that you bore me. Do not be angry with me: your turn will come. [5:625]

Earlier in the play The Maiden expresses a similar urge to think about mathematics as she explains in her conversation with The Youth:

THE MAIDEN. What does it matter what I did when I was a baby? Nothing existed for me then except that I tasted and touched and saw, and I wanted all that for myself, just as I wanted the moon to play with. Now the world is opening out for me. More than the world: the universe. Even little things are turning out to be great things, and becoming intensely interesting. Have you ever thought about the properties of numbers?
THE YOUTH [sitting up, markedly disenchanted] Numbers!!! I cannot imagine anything drier or more repulsive.
THE MAIDEN. They are fascinating, just fascinating. I want to get away from our eternal dancing and music, and just sit down by myself and think about numbers. [5:569]

As Shaw grew older his estimation of mathematics as an activity of man greatly increased, and in Buoyant Billions Shaw at ninety revealed the height to which his admiration rose in this conversation between Sir Ferdinand, Mrs Thirdborn, and Dick Secondborn, a character for which Archibald Henderson was apparently the model:

SIR FERDINAND. I do not think, Mr Buoyant, that you can treat this question as altogether a mathematical one. You must take account of feelings, passions, emotions, intuitions, as well as cold quantities and figures and logic.
SECONDBORN [rising to the occasion eloquently] And who dares say that mathematics and reasoning are not passions? Mathematical perception is the noblest of all the faculties! This cant about their being soulless, dead, inhuman mechanisms is contrary to the plainest facts of life and history. What has carried our minds farther than mathematical foresight? Who has done more for enlightenment than Giordano Bruno, Copernicus, Galileo, Newton, Descartes, Rutherford, Einstein, all of them far seeing guessers carried away by the passion for measuring truth and knowledge that possessed and drove them? Will you set above this great passion the vulgar concupiscences of Don Juan and

Casanova, and the romance of Beatrice and Francesca, of Irish
Deirdre, the greatest bores in literature, mere names incidentally im-
mortalized by a few lines in a great poem?
MRS THIRDBORN. Hearts! What are hearts without brains? You
mean that they had glands: pituitary glands, adrenal glands, thyroid
glands, pouring hormones into their blood. Do you suppose that there
is no mathematical hormone? Our anatomists have not yet discovered
it; but it is there, undiscovered and invisible, pouring into our brains,
controlled by our enzymes and catalysts as surely as our appetites for
beef and brandy. La Rochefoucauld told you two centuries ago that
though the appetite we call love is in everybody's mouth very few have
ever experienced it. God is not Love: Love is not Enough: the appetite
for more truth, more knowledge, for measurement and precision, is
far more universal: even the dullest fools have some glimmer of it. My
wife never tires of playing bridge and solving crossword puzzles as she
tires of housekeeping. Her love for me is very variable; it turns to hate
in its terrible reaction: Mathematical passion alone has no reaction:
our pleasure in it promises a development in which life will be an intellectual ecstasy surpassing the ecstasies of saints.[28]

In the "Sixth Fable" of *Farfetched Fables* the characters engage in an
argument remarkably similar to the one in *Buoyant Billions*. Again, it
is a futuristic setting, and the creature who has advanced farthest
along the line of evolutionary development, Raphael, speaks of the
mathematical passion to the lesser advanced Maiden 4:

RAPHAEL. No. I stop short of your eating and drinking and so forth,
and of your reproduction methods.
MAIDEN 4. No passions, then?
RAPHAEL. On the contrary: intellectual passion, mathematical passion, passion for discovery and exploration: the mightiest of all the
passions. [7:465]

Shaw himself made his high regard for mathematics known, Stephen Winston claimed, in an interview in 1950. In reply to a question
concerning his characterization of Isaac Newton in *"In Good King
Charles's Golden Days"* (1939), Shaw made this revealing comment:

I wonder how Newton would have liked my play? He would have regarded my new-found interest in mathematics as a waste of time. And
yet to me, mathematics is the greatest of all passions and holds within
itself the key to the universe. I've obviously been on the wrong scent
all my life. It's never too late to commence.[29]

The change in Shaw's view of mathematics about 1920 applied as
well to the physical sciences so dependent upon mathematics. In the

preface to *Back to Methuselah* Shaw attempted to rescue physics and other "purer subjects of thought" from what he labeled the corruptions of Darwinian materialism:

> The physicists went further than the Darwinians. Tyndall declared that he saw in Matter the promise and potency of all forms of life, and with his Irish graphic lucidity made a picture of a world of magnetic atoms, each atom with a positive and negative pole, arranging itself by attraction and repulsion in an orderly crystalline structure. Such a picture is dangerously fascinating to thinkers oppressed by the bloody disorders of the living world. Craving purer subjects of thought, they find in the contemplation of crystals and magnets a happiness more dramatic and less childish than the happiness found by mathematicians in abstract numbers, because they see in crystals beauty and movement without the corrupting appetites of fleshly vitality. In such Materialism as that of Lucretius and Tyndall there is a nobility which produces poetry. . . .
>
> But the physicists found their intellectual vision of the world incommunicable to those who were not born with it. It came to the public simply as Materialism; and Materialism lost its peculiar purity and dignity when it entered into the Darwinian reaction against Bible fetichism. [5:317–18]

To what exact degree the First World War changed Shaw's feelings toward the physical sciences is difficult to say. As with the biological sciences, some change must have been brought about simply by the obsolescence of his nineteenth-century debate. Laudatory references to physicists and astronomers began to appear in Shaw's writing in 1920. Later, in the preface to *Buoyant Billions* he would single out for praise the physicist James Clerk-Maxwell, and in the play itself a character praises Ernest Rutherford, a major figure in the history of physics (7:310, 373).[30] When the future of man is recounted by the Commissioner in the "Fourth Fable" of *Farfetched Fables*, physicists and mathematicians are characterized as soldiers and servants of Creative Evolution:

> This briefly is the history of the epoch-making change in social organization produced by the ending of the food problem which had through all recorded history made men slaves of nature, and defeated all their aspirations to be free to do what they like instead of what they must. The world became a world of athletes, artists, craftsmen, physicists, and mathematicians, instead of farmers, millers, bakers, butchers, bar tenders, brewers, and distillers. Hunger and thirst, which had for centuries meant the need for bread and onions, cheese and beer, beef and mutton, became a search for knowledge of nature and power

over it and a desire for truth and righteousness. The supergorilla became the soldier and servant of Creative Evolution. [7:448]

In the preface to the play Shaw included mathematicians with poets, historians, philosophers, and playwrights as men "without whom civilization would not be possible." (7:385)

Archibald Henderson, in his 1956 biography *Bernard Shaw: Man of the Century,* wrote that Shaw "looked upon the whole realm of modern mathematics, physics, astrophysics, and astronomy . . . as a pretentious mental construct of fraud and imposture, to which he was incapable of giving credence."[31] This description is appropriate only if applied to Shaw prior to 1920, but it does not accurately characterize his thinking after that time. Not only did Shaw use mathematical thinking to depict advanced intelligence, he also relied on Einsteinian physics. In *Back to Methuselah* the perception of space-time is explained by Pygmalion to be a faculty that is instinctual to the infants of the future:

> You must remember that these poor devils [twentieth-century men] were little better than our idiots. . . . Why the Newly Born there knows by instinct many things that their greatest physicians could hardly arrive at by forty years of strenuous study. Her simple direct sense of space-time and quantity unconsciously solves problems which would have cost their most famous mathematicians years of prolonged and laborious calculations requiring such intense mental application that they frequently forgot to breathe when engaged in them, and almost suffocated themselves in consequence. [5:594]

Again in *Back to Methuselah* Shaw found the numeration and the terminology of physics and mathematics suited to describe the Life Force:

> THE ORACLE. You do not understand. I am not speaking of an agricultural field. Do you not know that every mass of matter in motion carries with it an invisible gravitational field, every magnet an invisible magnetic field, and every living organism a mesmeric field? Even you have a perceptible mesmeric field. Feeble as it is, it is the strongest I have yet observed in a shortliver.
> NAPOLEON. By no means feeble, madam. I understand you now; and I may tell you that the strongest characters blench in my presence, and submit to my domination. But I do not call that a physical force.
> THE ORACLE. What else do you call it, pray? Our physicists deal with it. Our mathematicians express its measurements in algebraic equations.

NAPOLEON. Do you mean that they could measure mine?
THE ORACLE. Yes: by a figure infinitely near to zero. [5:333]

Later in the scene, Napoleon asks as a test of power if The Oracle could "calculate what the mathematicians call vectors, without putting a single algebraic symbol on paper?" (5:536)

Beginning with *Too True to Be Good,* completed in 1931, Shavian frequency of references to astrophysics and physics greatly increased. In *Too True to Be Good* Shaw used the relativity theory of Einstein and the "uncertainty principle" of Werner Heisenberg to prompt The Elder, a mechanist and determinist, to despair over a universe in which spirituality and free will could no longer be precluded.[32] Here Shaw once more fought the nineteenth-century battle against materialism, but this time, ironically, he used the findings of contemporary physics in his argument. In Act III The Elder laments the loss of "rational Determinism":

Yes, sir: the universe of Isaac Newton which has been an impregnable citadel of modern civilization for three hundred years, has crumbled like the walls of Jericho before the criticism of Einstein. Newton's universe was the stronghold of rational Determinism: the stars in their orbits [*sic*] obeyed immutably fixed laws; and when we turned from surveying their vastness to study the infinite littleness of the atom, there too we found the electrons in their orbits obeying the same universal laws. Every moment of time dictated and determined the following moment, and was itself dictated and determined by the moment that came before it. Everything was calculable: everything happened because it must: the commandments were erased from the tables of law; and in their place came the cosmic algebra: the equations of the mathematicians. Here was my faith: here I found dogma of infallibility: I, who scorned alike the Catholic with his vain dream of responsible Free Will, and the Protestant with his pretense of private judgment. And now—now—what is left of it? The orbit of the electron obeys no law: it chooses one path and rejects another: it is as capricious as the planet Mercury, who wanders from his road to warm his hands at the sun. All is caprice: the calculable world has become incalculable: Purpose and Design, the pretexts for all the vilest superstitions, have risen from the dead to cast down the mighty from their seats and put paper crowns on presumptuous fools. [6:499–500]

Shaw employed the terminology and theories of Einstein in *Back to Methuselah, Geneva* (1938), *Buoyant Billions,* and *"In Good King Charles's Golden Days."* In *Geneva* world leaders are deceived by a report that the earth is changing its orbit and "jumping to the next quantum"

(7:157). The Quantum Theory, proposed initially by Max Planck and expanded upon by Einstein, has nothing to do with the orbit of the earth, but rather with the nature of radiation. Shaw knew this, but he used the term to advance the action of the play and to make an old point about people's credulity concerning science. As the Secretary at one point exclaims, "You have nothing to do but mention the quantum theory, and people will take your voice for the voice of science and believe anything" (7:164–65). In *Buoyant Billions* Secondborn (the character inspired by Archibald Henderson) makes general mention of the Einsteinian idea that time and space are relative to an observer's frame of reference, a principle set forth in Einstein's 1905 *Special Theory of Relativity:*

> My dearest: nothing in the world ever stays put for ten seconds. We can know it only relatively at any moment. Yet most people can think only absolutely. Relatively, variably, mathematically, they cannot think at all. [7:350]

In *Geneva, Buoyant Billions,* and *Farfetched Fables* Shaw explored two outgrowths of Einsteinian physics: atomic energy and atomic weapons. The issue of atomic energy and weapons is an important theme in Shaw's last three major plays, and in these plays we witness Shaw's admiration for practical science. Shaw felt that atomic weapons were so devastating that they would be banned by international agreement. This opinion, expressed in the postwar preface to *Geneva,* became the center of the action of the "First Fable." Shaw did not feel, however, that the advent of atomic weapons would eliminate war. Biochemical war he feared could take the place of atomic war, as it did in the "Second Fable." Here we see Shaw at the very end of his life still holding the biological sciences as the enemy of mankind—indeed, threatening its extinction.

In *Buoyant Billions* Shaw voiced an optimism about atomic power that was current in many scientific circles at the time. Atomic power, it was believed, could safely be used to build canals and be so controllable and plentiful that a small yearly fee would take the place of electric meters on homes. In *Buoyant Billions* the Son is the proponent of atomic power. He explains the benefits to his father:

> When atom splitting makes it easy for us to support ourselves as well as by two hours of work as now by two years, we shall move mountains or straighten rivers in a hand's turn. Then the problem of what to do in our spare time will make life enormously more interesting. No more

doubt as to whether life is worth living. Then the world betterers will come into their own. [7:320–21]

A moment later in the scene the Son tells of how the power of the atom would make the psychology of power beneficial to civilization:

FATHER. Power corrupts; it does not ennoble.
SON. It does if it is big enough. It is petty power that corrupts petty men. Almighty power will change the world. If the old civilizations, the Sumerians, the Egyptians, the Greeks, the Romans, had discovered it [atomic power] their civilizations would not have collapsed as they did. There would have been no Dark Ages. The world betterers will get the upper hand. [7:321]

Although Shaw in the preface to *Geneva* mentioned this only as a remote possibility, it was noteworthy that he felt atomic technology hinted at some future scientific discovery that might bring about global peace:

Victory might . . . win cities if it could repopulate them soon enough, whereas atomic bombing leaves nothing for anyone, victor or vanquished. It is conceivable even that the next great invention may create an overwhelming interest in pacific civilization and wipe out war. You never can tell. [7:43]

The Shaw who talked of science effecting world peace was indeed different from the Shaw of the late nineteenth and early twentieth centuries who ridiculed and berated the physical sciences. As further evidence of this we can recall Shaw's caustic remarks about the numeration and terminology of astrophysics and his conversation with Henry Perigal and compare them with his acceptance of astrophysics's procedures and terms as expressed at another point in the preface to *Geneva*. In a review of what was known at the time about the atom-splitting phenomenon, Shaw said, "That such [atomic] explosions have visibly occurred on other stars (called novas) is vouched for by our astronomers, who have seen them with their naked eyes and studied their photographs and spectrographs for years past" (7:21). One can just imagine the ridicule that spectrography would have drawn from a younger Shaw.

In the preface to *Farfetched Fables* Shaw even chided politicians for being "pre-Einstein":

None of our politicians seem to know that political action, like all earthly action, must take place in a world of four dimensions, not three. The fourth dimension is that of time. To ignore it is to be pre-Einstein which is as out of date as to be pre-Marx. [7:409–10]

Shaw also made the physicist Newton a principal character in "*In Good King Charles's Golden Days*," a play which deals with a number of significant issues in the history of physics. In the play much is made of the historically anomalous problem with the perihelion of Mercury, which was important in the Newtonian scheme because it could not be explained by his laws of motion.[33] The problem remained unsolved until Einstein's General Theory of Relativity gave reasons for the aberration. In the play there is also a discussion of the implications of the artist Kneller's observation about the basic geometric figure of the universe being a curve not a Newtonian straight line, which anticipates Einstein's notion that matter "curves" space.

Shaw at various other times in his writing referred to "whirling electrons" and other concepts of physics and astrophysics (5:334). And he made a mathematical operation of relativity, "the square root of minus x," a humorous point of confusion for the Black Girl in *The Adventure of the Black Girl in Her Search for God*, who interprets it to mean "the square root of Myna's sex."[34]

The idea that the great artist and the great scientist labored in the same field was a notion that has an interesting history in Shavian thought. In the preface to *Back to Methuselah*, in the section entitled "Artist-Prophets," Shaw claimed, imaginatively, that Beethoven intuited the makeup of the atom:

> Beethoven never heard of radio-activity nor of electrons dancing in vortices of inconceivable energy; but pray can anyone explain the last movement of his Hammerklavier Sonata, Opus 106, otherwise than as a musical picture of these whirling electrons? . . . I should much like to know what other storm than the atomic storm could have driven him to this oddest of all those many expressions of cyclonic energy which have given him the same distinction among musicians that Michael Angelo has among draughtsmen. [5:334–35]

In the play itself characters remark about the special relationship between art and science. In "The Gospel of the Brothers Barnabas," Franklyn says to Lubin,

> You are quite right: the poem is our real clue to biological science. The most scientific document we possess at present is, as your grandmother would have told you quite truly, the story of the Garden of Eden. [5:422]

Later, in "As Far As Thought Can Reach," Ecrasia pronounces,

> The artist divines by inspiration all the truths that the so-called scien-
> tist grubs up in his laboratory slowly and stupidly long afterwards.
> [5:592]

Einstein held similar opinions about the relationship of the artist
and the scientist. Archibald Henderson carried messages between
Shaw and Einstein that dealt with just this subject:

> In late December 1923, I paid a visit to Shaw at 10 Adelphi Terrace,
> just before leaving for Berlin to work on Relativity and Atomic Theory
> with Einstein. Pointing to the portrait hanging on the wall, he asked
> me if I would give Einstein a message for him. "Tell Einstein," he said
> solemnly, "that I value his portrait more highly than any other in the
> room, because"—and then a mischievous grin—"it is the only one I
> had to pay for." Shaw remarked to me: "Please give Einstein another
> message from me. Tell him that he doesn't resemble a scientist at all.
> The portrait suggests a musician, Beethoven or Brahms. Tell him I
> believe he is a musician in disguise, masquerading as a scientist." To
> this Einstein, after a hearty laugh, observed seriously: "It is fallacious
> to assume that a scientist cannot be an artist. You yourself are an ex-
> cellent illustration: the mathematician and the literary artist. Relativity
> is no bar to my playing on the violin in which I delight. In my opinion,
> after a certain level of technical skill is attained, science and art tend to
> coalesce, in esthetic, plasticity, and form. The greatest scientists are
> always artists, even if they have no avocation."[35]

This idea of the kinship between artists and scientists interested
Shaw to such an extent that he made it the major theme of "In Good
King Charles's Golden Days." Dan H. Laurence has pointed out that
Shaw's toast at the Ort-Oze dinner anticipated the play, and he has
suggested that it may have inspired it.[36] It seems just as likely that
Shaw also drew on ideas that he had dealt with in earlier plays and
prose works and on Einstein's own words, which revealed a remarkable agreement with his own and which themselves might have inspired the toast. That this subject was on Shaw's mind at the time of
the dinner can be confirmed by an exchange between Shaw and Einstein that took place there during informal conversation in which Einstein repeated the idea that he had expressed to Henderson in 1923.
Shaw raised the issue:

> "I'd like to write a play one day which consists entirely of an argu-
> ment between a religious person, an artist, and a scientist."

"Unfortunately, my friend," Einstein explained, "your religious person, your scientist, and your artist would never find time to argue, and besides they may be one and the same person."[37]

Some critics have written that in *"In Good King Charles's Golden Days"* Shaw displayed his life-long animosity toward science in general and physics in particular. It would be wrong to conclude, however, that Shaw's purpose was to ridicule all scientists in the person of Isaac Newton or to make artistic truth appear to be the single truth. As we have seen, Shaw in 1939, when he was writing this play, no longer felt the antipathy toward mathematics and physics that he once did, and so he was not on a mission to attack science. Shaw's goal was to correct what he felt was an imbalance in people's beliefs. In the preface to the play, Shaw spoke of the confrontation between Kneller and Newton as representative of the "eternal clash" between the artist and physicist, "a clash which is important and topical in view of the hold that professional science has gained on popular credulity since the middle of the nineteenth century" (7:204–5). What Shaw hoped to do was to disabuse the "popular credulity" by revealing that the artistic, religious, and scientific truth were of equal validity.

Although Shaw called Godfrey Kneller the "victorious antagonist" in his encounter with Newton, neither Kneller, nor George Fox, nor Newton was the winner in the sense of establishing a monopoly on the truth (7:205). For as Shaw had said elsewhere, "Idolatry of artists is as dangerous as idolatry of scientists" (*EPWW*, p. 190). As further evidence for this we have Shaw's own comments on the play and remarks made by the characters themselves.

Esmé Percy and Stephen Winsten once asked this question of Shaw:

> In *"Good King Charles"* Kneller seems to have the better of Newton in argument. Here, in *Buoyant Billions*, you go all out for the mathematician. Does it mean that you have changed your mind?

Shaw replied,

> I do not go all out for anybody or anything. I am a playwright, not a Soot or Whitewash doctrinaire. I give Newton his own point of view and Kneller his. There is neither change nor contradiction on my part. [7:376]

In *Everybody's Political What's What?* Shaw spoke about his dialectical device of establishing two opposed points of view to arrive at the truth:

> My method of examining any proposition is to take its two extremes, both of them impractical; make a scale between them; and try to determine at what point on the scale it can best be put in practice. [p. 162]

It was the device in operation in *"In Good King Charles's Golden Days."* Certainly, Shaw wanted to raise artistic and even religious truth to the same level as scientific truth—they would ultimately find agreement in the truth of Creative Evolution. The point that he hoped we would get from the play was expressed through Newton when he says, "This painter has one kind of understanding: I have another" (7:270). Louise expresses it more precisely:

> All I meant was that Mr Kneller and Mr Newton seem to mean exactly the same thing; only one calls it beauty and the other gravitation; so they need not quarrel. [7:279–80]

Shaw began *"In Good King Charles's Golden Days"* in November 1938. Earlier that year, it is clear, he had Einstein and his physics on his mind. To Lord Alfred Douglas, then a nearly forgotten poet, his days of Wildean notoriety long behind him, Shaw sent a book as a gift. The two had been in correspondence through the decade after a long hiatus resulting from Douglas's hostility. Now Douglas, lonely and eager for renewal of connections to the better parts of his past, had reached out to Shaw, and Shaw was trying to reawaken those talents in Douglas (a Catholic convert) which might still be dormant. The book was *The Evolution of Physics,* coauthored by Einstein. Speaking of the "revolution in physics which has taken place in our time," he said,

> You see, the whole Catholic philosophy is founded, on its scientific side, on Aquinas, who was founded on Aristotle, a pagan whose works were made virtually canonical in the thirteenth century. Nowadays a Catholic who is ignorant of Einstein is as incomplete as a thirteenth-century Dominican ignorant of Aristotle.
> The protest against scientific physics was led by Luther, Melanchthon and the Protestants generally. Religion without science is mere smallmindedness.[38]

If, then, something of Shaw's play is owed to Einstein, it was counterpart to Einstein's having already taken a small leaf from Shaw in penning a fragmentary playlet. In a letter seven years earlier (25 July 1931) congratulating Shaw on his seventy-fifth birthday, Einstein had referred facetiously to a happy new era in which the problem of world hunger was solved by giving ceremonial dinners. No doubt Einstein was sharing a joke here with Shaw about the dinner given ten months earlier at which Shaw delivered his toast. Einstein undertook a little dramatic writing to make his point:

> Here is yet another congratulation from someone who holds you in the highest affection, namely he who in his youth discovered the relativity theory and who in London you have praised in such exceedingly graceful terms.
>
> I congratulate you also that you have been permitted to witness this great era, the time of a new way in international politics, which is characterized by the following dialogue:
> A. We have easily overcome the difficulty of earlier ages. When people hunger, when apparently unconquerable differences between states threaten, ministers with great power hasten together and contrive a ceremonial dinner and. . . .
> B. (*Curiously*) And?
> A. Now, you insatiable people, you are not satisfied with this!?[39]

Einstein greatly admired *The Intelligent Women's Guide to Socialism, Capitalism, Sovietism, and Fascism.* He spoke of his appreciation for the book in a letter to his friend, fellow physicist Michelangelo Besso, (1873–1955) and in a letter to Mrs. Hedwig Fischer, "Here speaks the Voltaire of our time."[40] Although Einstein avoided giving commercial endorsements, he agreed in a letter to "Herr Wolff," probably Theodor Wolff, editor-in-chief of the *Berliner Tageblatt,* to the use of his name in the advertisement of the political tract: "I find the book by Shaw . . . so excellent and so important for political enlightenment in the fullest sense of the word that I gladly permit the use of my name for the purpose of spreading his influence. I have written to the publisher Fischer the same wish."[41]

Einstein's respect for Shaw's prose style was high. Einstein once compared Shaw's prose to Mozart's music: "There is not a superfluous word in Shaw's prose, just as there is not a superfluous note in Mozart's music. The one in the medium of language, the other in the medium of melody, expresses perfectly with almost superhuman precision, the message of his art and soul." Shaw, when told later of Einstein's remarks, said that no one had ever paid him a more gracious compliment. That it came from Einstein, he said, gave him "the greatest joy imaginable" and that nothing in the world could have delighted him more. When Einstein was told of the great pleasure his compliment gave Shaw, he replied, "I shall always treasure the hours I spent with Shaw. His heart is as great as his brain; he is a man without prejudgment or prejudices."[42]

Einstein also greatly admired Shavian drama. In reply to Shaw's toast, Einstein delivered a short address in which he praised Shaw and his dramatic method:

> You, Mr. Shaw, have succeeded in gaining the love and the joyful admiration of mankind by a path which for others has led to martyr-dom. You have not only preached to mankind morality but even dared to mock at what to others appeared unapproachable. What you have done can be done only by the born artist. From your box of tricks you have taken countless puppets which, while resembling men, are not of flesh and bone but consist entirely of spirit, wit and grace. And yet, in a way even more than ourselves, they resemble men and women and make us forget almost that they are not the creations of nature but only the creations of Bernard Shaw. You make these gra-cious puppets dance in a little world guarded by the graces who allow no resentment to enter in.
>
> Whoever has glanced into this little world sees the world of our reality in a new light. He sees your puppets blending into real people so that the latter suddenly look quite different from before. By thus holding the mirror before us, you have been able as no other contem-porary to effect in us a liberation and to take from us something of this heaviness of life. For this we are all grateful to you and also to fate—that with all our earthly ailments has also been granted to us a physician and liberator of the soul.[43]

In a greeting to Shaw on his eightieth birthday in 1936, Einstein wrote again of Shaw's special powers as a dramatist:

> There are few people with sufficient independence to see the weak-nesses and follies of their contemporaries and remain themselves un-touched by them. And these isolated few usually lose their zeal for putting things to rights when they have come face to face with human obduracy. Only to a tiny minority is it given to fascinate their genera-tion by subtle humour and grace and to hold the mirror up to it by the impersonal agency of art. Today I salute with sincere emotion the su-preme artist of this method, who has delighted and educated us all.[44]

Outside the drama, Shaw would comment on Einstein again a year after completing *"In Good King Charles's Golden Days,"* in a talk pre-pared for BBC Radio in June 1940 on what British war aims should be. The Second World War was in its tenth month, and France, in-vaded by Nazi troops, was crumbling. "I have a friend who is a Jew," the relevant segment began.

> His name is Albert Einstein; and he is a far greater human prodigy than Mr Hitler and myself rolled into one. The nobility of his charac-

ter has made his genius an unmixed benefit to his fellow creatures. Yet Adolph Hitler would compel me, the Nordic Bernard Shaw, to insult Albert Einstein; to claim moral superiority to him and unlimited power over him; to rob him, drive him out of his house, exile him, be punished if I allow a relative of mine to marry a relative of his; and finally to kill him as part of a general duty to exterminate his race. Adolph has actually done these things to Albert, bar the killing, as he carelessly exiled him first and thus made the killing impossible. Since then he has extended the list of reprobates from Semites to Celts and from Poles to Slavs; in short, to all who are not what he calls Nordics and Nazis. If he conquers these islands he will certainly add my countrymen, the Irish, to the list, as several authorities have maintained that the Irish are one of the lost tribes of Israel.

Now, this is not the sort of thing that sane men can afford to argue with. It is on the face of it pernicious nonsense; and the moment any ruler starts imposing it on his nation or any other nation by physical force there is nothing for it but for the sane men to muster their own physical forces and go for him. We ought to have declared war on Germany the moment Mr Hitler's police stole Einstein's violin. . . .

Einstein may never have seen Shaw's remarks. He could not have heard them because the Ministry of Information cancelled the broadcast before it was delivered. Cantankerous and paradoxical as always, Shaw had leavened his good sense with controversial matter about Nazi sympathizer Sir Oswald Mosley, and had noted Shavian affinities with Hitler—such as their vegetarian diets. The remarks were published obscurely[45] in 1948. In the process they became almost Shaw's last words on Einstein—*almost*, because in January 1950, in Shaw's 95th year, *Leader Magazine* asked famous men for their choices of "Man of the Half-Century," and his choices—predictably cantankerous—were Stalin, Einstein, and "one whom I cannot modestly name."[46]

Later that year came Einstein's last letter to Shaw, in his usual awkward English, wishing Shaw a speedy recovery from a broken hip incurred by a fall in the garden at Ayot St. Lawrence. The poignancy of the vision of the great physicist reading to his invalid sister is increased by our knowledge that Shaw would die from complications stemming from his accident. Einstein wrote from Princeton,

> I am enjoying so much reading again your dramatic works that I feel that strong wish to thank you for the beautiful hours you are giving me. I am thanking you also in the name of my invalid sister to whom I am reading every evening for an hour.
> Heartiest wishes for your speedy recovery.[47]

Einstein must have realized that Shaw would not recover. It was a generous gesture and the game of compliments would end with it. Yet it was not just a routine of fulsome exchanges so much in the German tradition. Einstein's feelings were genuine, and Shaw had profoundly enlarged his intellectual world through his encounter with Einstein. Without Einstein, later Shavian drama—and thought—would have been less in harmony with the twentieth century.

# Notes

All references to the plays and prefaces are from the Bodley Head edition of Shaw's plays and prefaces.

The two works listed below appear in the text and notes as *IWG* and *EPWW:*

Bernard Shaw, *The Intelligent Woman's Guide to Socialism, Capitalism, Sovietism, and Fascism* (London: Constable and Company, 1928).

Bernard Shaw, *Everybody's Political What's What?* (New York: Dodd, Mead, and Company, 1944).

1. Ronald W. Clark, *Einstein: The Life and Times* (New York: Avon Books, 1971), pp. 272–329. See specifically Eddington's letter to Einstein on 1 December 1919 (p. 304) and the account of the medals awarded to Einstein (p. 305).

2. Clark, pp. 295–97.

3. Clark, pp. 307–8.

4. Clark, p. 330.

5. Aylesa Forsee, *Albert Einstein: Theoretical Physicist* (New York: MacMillan Company, 1963), p. 88; Antonina Vallentin, *The Drama of Albert Einstein,* trans. Maura Budberg (New York: Doubleday and Company, 1954), p. 104.

6. Bernard Shaw, *Collected Letters 1911–1925,* ed. Dan H. Laurence (New York: Viking, 1985), p. 732.

7. T. F. Hickerson, "Mathematician and Man," in *Archibald Henderson—The New Crichton,* ed. Samuel Stevens Hood (New York: Beechhurst Press, 1949), pp. 154–55.

8. Archibald Henderson, *George Bernard Shaw: Man of the Century* (New York: Appleton-Century-Crofts, 1956), p. 262.

9. *Man of the Century,* p. 664.

10. Bernard Shaw, "Foundation Oration," in *Platform and Pulpit,* ed. Dan H. Laurence (New York: Hill and Wang, 1961), p. 150.

11. *Man of the Century,* pp. 765–66.

12. Archibald Henderson, *Relativity: A Romance of Science* (Chapel Hill: University of North Carolina Press, 1923).

13. *Man of the Century,* p. 765.

14. *Man of the Century*, p. 662.

15. See Albert Einstein, "What I Believe," in *Living Philosophies*, ed. Henry Goddard Leach (New York: Simon and Schuster, 1931), pp. 3–7.

16. Bernard Shaw, typewritten letter signed to Albert Einstein, 2 December 1924, Box 45 (33–241), in the Albert Einstein Duplicate Archive, Seeley G. Mudd Library, Princeton University. Quoted by permission of the Society of Authors.

17. Clark, p. 514.

18. Blanche Patch, *Thirty Years with G.B.S.* (London: Victor Gollancz, 1951), p. 105.

19. The toast was entitled by Warren Sylvester Smith "Religion and Science": Bernard Shaw, "Religion and Science," in his *Religious Speeches of Bernard Shaw*, ed. Warren Sylvester Smith (University Park: Pennsylvania State University Press, 1963), pp. 81–88.
A brief segment of the toast can be seen in the *NOVA* episode entitled "Einstein," produced by WGBH, Boston.

20. See, for example, the Elder's long speech in Act 3 of *Too True to Be Good* (6:499–501).

21. Bernard Shaw, "The Conflict Between Science and Common Sense," *Humane Review*, April (1900), pp. 9–10.

22. Bernard Shaw, *The Adventures of the Black Girl in Her Search for God*, in *The Portable Bernard Shaw*, ed. Stanley Weintraub (New York: Penguin Books, 1977), p. 657.

23. *The Adventures of the Black Girl, The Portable Bernard Shaw*, pp. 657–58.
Interestingly, Shaw linked this debate to the issue of the existence of ether, a substance propounded by Michael Faraday (1791–1861) to be the medium through which light is transmitted. An experiment in 1881 by Albert Michelson (1852–1931) and Edward Morley (1838–1923) called into doubt the existence of ether, and it was Einstein who resolved the question by recognizing as a universal law that the speed of light was a constant. That Shaw was aware of this issue is further evidence of his increased interest in physics, especially Einsteinian physics. For a discussion of the ether issue see Lincoln Barnett, *The Universe and Dr. Einstein* (New York: Bantam Books, 1948), pp. 40–45.

24. "Foundation Oration," p. 147.

25. Bernard Shaw, *Collected Letters 1898–1910*, ed. Dan H. Laurence (New York: Dodd, Mead, and Company, 1972), II, p. 762.

26. *The Adventures of the Black Girl in Her Search for God, The Portable Bernard Shaw*, p. 644.

27. Arthur H. Nethercot, "Bernard Shaw, Mathematical Mystic," *Shaw Review*, 12, No. 1 (1969), 3–26. Though Nethercot wrote of Shaw's changed attitude towards mathematics, he failed to consider Shaw's remarks to Stephen Winsten, to note the significance of Shaw's new outlook in the scheme of Creative Evolution, or to mention the influence of Henderson or Einstein. Nethercot did mention that as Shaw grew older references in his works to men such as Newton, Clerk-Maxwell, and Einstein increased, but he only spoke of them in passing in a footnote. He also failed to connect the mention of these *physicist*-mathematicians with Shaw's changed attitude toward the physical sciences.

28. See as a possible inspiration for this passage the following article by Henderson, which he said "strongly influenced" Shaw's thinking "about the predestined role of science in the future of the race" (*Man of the Century*, p. 662); Archibald Henderson, "Science and Art: An Approach to a New Synthesis," *American Scientist*, 34, No. 3 (1946), 453–63.

29. Stephen Winsten, *Shaw's Corner* (New York: Roy Publishers, 1952), p. 166.

30. "The professional biologists . . . raise problems; and genuine scientists must face them at the risk of being classed with Cagliostro instead of with Clerk-Maxwell and Einstein, Galileo and Newton, who, by the way, worked hard at interpreting the Bible, and was ashamed of his invention of the Infinitesimal Calculus until Leibniz made it fashionable." The speaker is Secondborn, 7:310.

31. *Man of the Century*, p. 26.

32. For a discussion of determinism and the uncertainty principle of Heinsenberg see Barnett, *The Universe and Dr. Einstein*, pp. 32–36.

33. Newton could not have been aware of discrepancy between his laws of motion and the orbit of Mercury because the means for observing the anomaly did not yet exist. Shaw rejoiced in the historical impossibility: see *BHP*, pp. 205–6. See also the toast, pp. 84–85. For a discussion of the perihelion of Mercury see Barnett, *The Universe and Dr. Einstein*, pp. 85–86.

34. *The Adventures of the Black Girl, The Portable Bernard Shaw*, pp. 657–60.

For a brief discussion of the pun see the note on page 636 of *The Portable Bernard Shaw;* Henderson, *Man of the Century*, p. 768; and Warren Sylvester Smith, "A Note on the Mathematical Pun . . . ," *Shaw Review*, 12, No. 1 (1969), 26.

35. *Man of the Century*, p. 765.

36. Bernard Shaw, *Shaw: An Exhibit*, ed. Dan H. Laurence (Austin, Texas: Humanities Research Center, 1977), item 138.

37. Stephen Winsten, *Jesting Apostle: The Life of Bernard Shaw* (London: Hutchinson, 1956), p. 179.

No source is given for this exchange.

38. Mary Hyde, *Bernard Shaw and Alfred Douglas: A Correspondence* (New York: Ticknor and Fields, 1982), p. 37. The book was Albert Einstein and Leopold Infeld, *The Evolution of Physics* (Cambridge: Cambridge University Press, 1938).

39. Albert Einstein, signed letter to Bernard Shaw, 25 July 1931, Box 45 (33-253), in the Albert Einstein Duplicate Archive, Seeley G. Mudd Library, Princeton University. The translation of the letter from German is my own.

40. Albert Einstein and Michelangelo Besso, *Albert Einstein-Michele Besso: Correspondence 1903–1955*, trans. Pierre Speziali (Paris: Herman, 1972), pp. 241–42, letter 93.

Albert Einstein, letter to Mrs. Hedwig Fischer, 1928 (quoted in P. de Mendelsohn's *The S. Fischer Verlag* [1970], p. 1164), Box 45 (33-246), in the Albert Einstein Duplicate Archive, Seeley G. Mudd Library, Princeton University. The translation from German of the remark to Fischer is my own.

41. Albert Einstein, typescript to "Herr Wolff," probably Theodor Wolff, 16 January 1929, Box 45 (33–248), in the Albert Einstein Duplicate Archive, Seeley G. Mudd Library, Princeton University. The translation from German is my own.

42. Richard Nickson, "The Arts and the Sciences: Bernard Shaw and Albert Einstein," *Independent Shavian*, 27, No. 3 (1979), pp. 8–9.

43. Albert Einstein, "They Say—" *New York Times*, trans. by *NYT*, 2 November 1930, Sec. 9, p. 2x.

44. Albert Einstein, *The World As I See It*, trans. Alan Harris (New York: Philosophical Library, 1949), p. 37.

45. "The Unavoidable Subject," first published in Anthony Weymouth's *Journal of the War Years (1939–1945) and One Year Later* (London, 1948); reprinted in Dan H. Laurence, ed., *Platform and Pulpit* (New York: Hill and Wang, 1961), p. 290. Shaw would publish similar material in "Notes by the Way" in *Time and Tide*, 12 October 1940, condensed as "Einstein, Hitler and Me" in *English Digest*, January 1941, but Einstein was three thousand miles away, in the U.S.

46. "Man of the Half-Century?" *Leader Magazine,* 7 January 1950, p. 8.

47. Albert Einstein, signed letter to Bernard Shaw, 20 September 1950, Box 45 (33–256), in the Albert Einstein Duplicate Archive, Seeley G. Mudd Library, Princeton University.

## Susan Albertine

# SHAW'S INTEREST
# IN HAROLD FREDERIC

One of Bernard Shaw's forgotten acquaintances in London at the turn of the century was Harold Frederic. In literary history Frederic endures chiefly as the author of a minor American classic, *The Damnation of Theron Ware* (1896). Shaw, however, knew and admired a very different figure, the controversial director of the London bureau of the *New York Times* from 1884 to 1898. The two men shared a remarkable number of social concerns, a convergence of interest we can see in their works. More to the point, the playwright appreciated the American writer's cleverness, his courage, and his politics. The very fact of their acquaintance helps to explain a side of literary London that has been largely overlooked.

The only surviving anecdote about the two men together reveals Shaw haranguing Frederic and their mutual friend Frank Harris about the bad business of eating meat. Significantly, all three writers appear as part of a self-conscious literary scene. According to Harris, Shaw refused to pose as a literary man:[1]

> I tried to cure him of this by inviting him to my *Saturday Review* luncheons at the Café Royal; but it was no use. He came a few times, being sincerely interested in the Café, in the waiters, in the prices, in the cooking: in short in the economics of the place; and he concluded that Harold Frederic and I ate too much meat, and that it was a waste of money to pay Café Royal prices for his own plateful of macaroni, which he could obtain elsewhere for tenpence. The fact that I paid for it made no difference whatever to him: he objected to a waste of my money just as much as of his own.

Shaw mentions these gatherings himself in the preface to his 1895 diary:[2]

> Frank Harris tried to establish a regular lunch every Monday for choosing members of the *Saturday Review* staff at the Café Royale. I

attended them for some time. Harold Frederic, Mrs. Devereux, Marriott Watson and others used to come. Oscar Wilde came once, immediately before the Queensberry trial, with young Douglas. They left in some indignation because Harris refused to appear as a witness—a literary expert witness—to the high artistic character of Wilde's book *Dorian Gray*. These lunches wasted my time and were rather apt to degenerate into bawdy talk. When a play called *The Home Secretary* was produced at the Criterion Theatre, I took the opportunity to protest against the attempt in the play to trade on the Anarchism bogey, my object being to call attention to some hard features in the case of Charles, "the Walsall Anarchist." Harris alarmed by this, cut the passage out of the article. This incident brought my growing impatience with the brag and bawdry of the lunches to a head; and I never went again. They seem to have fallen through afterwards.

Harris's editorial trimming and the "brag and bawdry" of the larger group, more than the economics, probably caused Shaw to drop out of the *Saturday Review* luncheons, but the incident in question is more interesting for what it says about attitudes toward writing. Shaw, the major artist, placed some value on his literary milieu (he attended some of the luncheons), but he also saw through the writer's public trappings. The distinction implied here is between the writer as working artist and the writer as popular figure. Of more immediate concern is the fact that Shaw knew Frederic and gave him a definite literary placement; he puts Frederic first in the group of *literati* mentioned.

The *Saturday Review* luncheons may have occurred rather late in Shaw and Frederic's acquaintance. Harris, for one, had known Frederic since perhaps 1884, a decade before the former took over the *Saturday Review:* "My wife was not, by any means, so important to me or to my mental growth as some of my friends, notably John Addington Symonds, Francis Adams, Grant Allen, and Harold Frederic. In the first ten years of my London life, friends meant more to me than any other influence, and notably such companions as these, who excited me intellectually. . . . From thirty to forty or so, Frederic grew as I grew."[3] Harris was not, however, the first person who could have brought Shaw and Frederic together. For if Harris was the most obvious connection between the two men, Shaw and Frederic had been moving in the same circles for five to eight years.

Frederic and Shaw became colleagues as journalists in the second half of the eighties. Frederic met T. P. O'Connor, for example, as early as 1884 and traveled together with O'Connor and Timothy Healy in Ireland that same year. According to Harris, Frederic had a "passionate belief in the justice of the Irish cause. . . . It is not too much to say that the 'New York Times' did more to arouse American sympathy with Ireland from 1884 to 1890 than any other journal."[4] Shaw would have noticed this kind of work, not necessarily in the *New York Times* but in the many English journals where Frederic also published. O'Connor himself provided another link since Shaw wrote for the *Star* beginning in 1888 and continuing into this century.

A third important professional connection between Frederic and Shaw came by way of William T. Stead, editor of the *Pall Mall Gazette,* soon after Frederic's arrival in London. Frederic and Stead were initially on good terms, and in 1885 Frederic contributed his "Saunterer in the Labyrinth" essays on prostitution to the *Gazette* as part of the "Maiden Tribute" campaign.[5] But on 8 August 1885, between the two installments of the "Saunterer," the *Gazette* picked up the Sir Charles Dilke scandal to run as a kind of exemplum during the "Maiden Tribute." This was a shade more righteous than Frederic could stand. Although he agreed with Stead that child prostitution was a serious problem, Frederic defended the province of adult prostitutes. He thought such women had a necessary place in the social hierarchy. He was unwilling, moreover, to watch in silence as the reputation of his friend Dilke was destroyed by yellow journalism. By 7 September 1885, Frederic was attacking Stead in the *New York Times:* "He [Stead] is still dominated by that essential instinct of Puritanism to control other people for their own good—that instinct which shut up all the playhouses under the Lord Protector, which burned the witches at Salem, which founded the Salvation Army, which makes every English city a desolate horror on Sunday."[6]

Shaw, as David H. Bowman notes in "Shaw, Stead, and the Undershaft Tradition," was also working for Stead in 1885.[7] On the subject of Stead and the "Maiden Tribute," Shaw had this to say: "Nobody ever trusted him after the discovery that the case of Eliza Armstrong in the Maiden Tribute was a put-up job, and that he himself had put it up."[8] Hence, not only were Shaw and Frederic connected professionally as early as 1885, but Shaw must have known about Frederic's very public fight with Stead. The noisy feud continued for years, intensifying in the early nineties when Dilke sought reelection to Parliament after his self-imposed exile. Acrimonious remarks were set in print by both sides; Stead attacked Dilke and Frederic, the "henchman," and Frederic, defending Dilke, attacked Stead.[9] The "Saunterer in the Labyrinth" was a sensation in its own right because its anonymous author admitted his relations with prostitutes. Shaw, well attuned within the world of journalism, must have known the identity of the man of the world who wrote so candidly about the question of the hour, and he could hardly have missed the "Saunterer." In any case, Frederic was also publishing signed pieces in the *Gazette* in 1885.[10] Although Shaw and Frederic, as fellow contributors, were not necessarily introduced to each other this early—nor is it clear that either had actually met Stead at this point—they were likely to read each other's work.

When Frank Harris took over the *Saturday Review* in 1894, he got Frederic to come along. Frederic had written for Harris's *Fortnightly Review*, and his articles began to appear in the *Saturday Review* in 1895.[11] Shaw, of course, was there at the time. The milieu of literary London also brought the two together. Both worked extensively in the British Museum. Both are listed among the guests in society columns.[12] Both could be found at the National Liberal Club, which Frederic joined in 1886. Curiously enough, though, the most compelling evidence of the acquaintance appears after Frederic's death. An unpublished letter sent by Shaw to Mrs. Edward Pease on 8 May 1899, about seven months after a stroke killed Frederic, shows that Shaw had been watching the other man closely. Mrs. Pease, the wife of the secretary of the Fabian Society, was a friend of Cora Crane. Shaw writes:[13]

> Dear Mrs Pease
>     I have already paid my subscription to Mr Fisher; but I expressly empowered the trustees to use their discretion as to giving some or all of it to the Kenley children if they thought fit, as the death of Mrs Frederic, and the taking over of the girls by the family in America, has lightened the legitimate strain on the fund.
>     Perhaps, if Mrs Crane were to apply to the trustees for a share, they might let her have something—they can give her my fiver at any rate without asking leave.
>
> > Yours sincerely
> > G. Bernard Shaw

The circumstances of the letter are these. At the time of his death, Frederic had two households: in London his wife, Grace, and her children (four of six survived childhood); in Kenley, Surrey, his mistress, Kate Lyon, and three children. From about 1890, Frederic divided his time between the two homes, working strenuously to support both. And while discreet, he did not keep his mistress and her family secret. When Stephen and Cora Crane came to meet him in 1897, he found them a home nearby in Surrey, where he and Kate Lyon became their friends. During Frederic's final illness, beginning in the summer of 1898, Cora Crane took in Kate Lyon's children, the "young Barbarians," as Henry James called them.[14] Ruth, the daughter of Grace Frederic, came from London to care for her father. In his last months, when partial paralysis kept Frederic from writing, his secretary John Scott Stokes helped with proof and the weekly cables to the *New York Times.*

After Frederic died on October 19, Stokes and Cora Crane undertook to raise money for the children in Surrey. America's leading foreign journalist had died deeply in debt. To further complicate matters, Kate Lyon, a Christian Scientist, faced possible manslaughter charges because she and her Christian Science healer had withheld medical care against the wishes of Frederic's legal family and friends, including Cora Crane, Stokes, and Frank Harris—but, she maintained, with the dying man's consent. "He believes 'Christian Science' will help him, and he wants it."[15] Doctors and Christian Science practitioners were repeatedly called and dismissed in the confusion over the best way to care for Frederic, while he insisted on smoking and drinking as usual. Toward the end, when doctors once again were admitted, it was too late.

Kate Lyon's manslaughter hearing, which ended in acquittal, was heavily publicized. It sparked a scandal that surfaced in the press as a debate between Christian Science and medicine. Articles appeared in both Great Britain and the United States in the *Christian Science Journal,* the London *Times,* the *New York Times,* the *Saturday Evening Post,* the *Saturday Review,* and elsewhere. More publicity came from notices requesting aid for Frederic's children, particularly after Grace Frederic's death of cancer on 18 March 1899. Two funds, then, were organized, one for each set of children.

Shaw saw and, to a certain extent, participated in all this. As the letter to Mrs. Pease relates, he had donated five pounds to the fund for the London children, believing that the trustees of that fund would send money on to the Surrey children. He therefore declined Mrs. Pease's request. The following August, Cora Crane, in narrow financial straits herself, approached Shaw again on behalf of the Surrey children. Shaw wrote in response: "We have three very expensive orphans on hand already—parents alive in every case. My impulse is to repudiate all extra orphans with loud execrations. For the moment I can just persuade myself to part with another five pounds since the last one apparently went to the wrong address. I should simply take them out into the garden and bury them."[16] Frederic, no believer himself in the usual forms of philanthropy, would have comprehended this reply, although no one, including Shaw, denied that the children needed help. Shaw's second donation brought his total to ten pounds, not singularly generous, but useful.

Years later Shaw was still thinking about Frederic and the Christian Science scandal. From the preface to *The Doctor's Dilemma* (1906): [17]

> In short, the doctor needs our help for the moment much more than we often need his. The ridicule of Molière, the death of a well-informed and clever writer like the late Harold Frederic in the hands of Christian Scientists (a sort of sealing with his blood of the contemptuous disbelief in and dislike of doctors he had bitterly expressed in his books) . . . all these trouble the doctor very little.

Significantly, Shaw followed more than the newspapers and casual acquaintances might have provided. He read at least a few of Frederic's eight novels. Almost a decade after Frederic's death, Shaw was interested enough to offer the plausible explanation that Frederic had turned to Christian Science because he could not believe in the power of medicine. Shaw was correct about the skepticism and contempt regarding doctors in Frederic's novels. Witness Dr. Ledsmar in *The Damnation of Theron Ware* and the impotent physicians in *Gloria Mundi.* Indeed, Frederic's doubts were an extension of his attitude toward all modern science. While there is no evidence that he professed Christian Science, he trusted the practice further than he did professional medicine because Christian Science gave him more freedom. As his daughter Ruth remarked, "He tolerated whichever superstition gave him the greater scope to struggle or to die in his own way."[18]

Shaw and Frederic were attracted to Christian Science, not as believers but as doubters in the power of physical science. Their doubts about the forces of determinism and positivism had similar effects in that both men were prompted to examine and dramatize the religious reaction to evolutionary thought, specifically in evangelical Christianity and in such fundamentalist organizations as the Salvation Army. Neither had any use for traditional churches and formal philanthropy, yet both were extremely concerned about social morality and questions of reform. They were drawn to many of the same particular issues, public sanitation, for example, and prostitution and financial buccaneering. Finally, the great dispute between capitalism and socialism became for each writer a matter of urgency. Coincidences these, but fascinating in themselves. They give a certain body to the forgotten nuances of liberal and radical thought at the time. They also slightly alter the picture we have of each writer in question. The comic realist or naturalist from upstate New York appears quite another figure in the company of Shaw, while Shaw himself seems even more comprehensive and observant for what he knew about Frederic.

# Notes

1. Frank Harris, *Bernard Shaw* (New York, 1931), pp. 291–92. Austin Briggs, Jr., tells the same anecdote in *The Novels of Harold Frederic* (Ithaca, N.Y., 1969), p. 7.

2. Bernard Shaw, preface to the 1895 diary. The quotation is taken from the forthcoming *Bernard Shaw: The Diaries, 1885–1897,* ed. Stanley Weintraub (University Park, Pa., 1986). I am grateful to Professor Weintraub for supplying the passage.

3. Frank Harris, *My Life and Loves* (New York, 1963), pp. 601, 606. Harris, according to his account, met Frederic at the home of Sir Charles Dilke, probably between 1884 and 1886, since he mentions the meeting while recalling his years with the *Evening News* (1883–86) and since Frederic's friendship with Dilke dated from about the time of the Dilke scandal, beginning 1885. See Harris, *My Life and Loves,* pp. 325–26.

4. Frank Harris, "Harold Frederic. Ad Memoriam," *Saturday Review,* 86, 22 October 1898, 527.

5. Two unsigned articles appeared in the *Pall Mall Gazette:* "Two Views of the 'Maiden Tribute': I.—From a Saunterer in the Labyrinth," 18 July 1885, p. 2; and "Musings on the Question of the Hour.—I. By a Saunterer in the Labyrinth," 10 August 1885, pp. 1–2. These essays have been attributed to Frederic, and they bear the imprint of his style. The correct listings are missing, however, from Thomas F. O'Donnell, Stanton Garner, and Robert H. Woodward's *Bibliography of Writings By and About Harold Frederic* (Boston, 1975). The *Bibliography* gives instead references to the "Saunterer" in the *Pall Mall Budget* (B65 and B68). Since the *Budget,* a weekly compilation of pieces from the better-known *Gazette,* is not available on microfilm in North American libraries for the dates in question, the *Gazette* listings are useful. The *Gazette* is accessible on microfilm.

6. "Mr. Stead and His Work," by H.F., *New York Times,* 7 September 1885, p. 5.

7. David H. Bowman, "Shaw, Stead, and the Undershaft Tradition," *Shaw Review* 14 (1971), 29–32.

8. Quoted by Frederic Whyte in Whyte's *Life of W. T. Stead,* 2 vols. (New York, 1925), 1, p. 304.

9. See, e.g., Frederic's *The New Exodus: A Study of Israel in Russia* (1892), in *Major Works of Harold Frederic,* vol. 3 (Westport, Conn., 1969), p. 112; and "The Methods of the Dilke Persecution," *Welsh Review,* 1 (March 1892), 471–84. See also [William T. Stead], "What Answer Has Ananias?" *Review of Reviews,* 5 (March 1892), 256–57.

10. See, e.g., "The New American Administration," *Pall Mall Gazette,* 6 March 1885, pp. 3–4. This reference corrects the date given in O'Donnell, Garner, and Woodward's *Bibliography,* p. 337.

11. See O'Donnell, Garner, and Woodward, eds., *Bibliography,* p. 22.

12. See, e.g., William H. Rideing, "Stories of a Famous London Drawing-Room," *McClure's Magazine,* 33 (August 1909), 388.

13. T.L.S., Shaw to Mrs. Edward Pease, 8 May 1899. Quoted by permission, Stephen Crane Papers, Rare Book and Manuscript Library, Columbia University, and the Society of Authors.

14. Letter from Henry James to Cora Crane, 4 September 1899, in Henry James, *Letters, Volume IV, 1895–1916*, ed. Leon Edel (Cambridge, Mass., 1984), p. 117.

15. Paraphrased letter from Kate Lyon to Mrs. Mills, in *The Correspondence of Harold Frederic*, ed. George E. Fortenberry, Stanton Garner, and Robert H. Woodward (Fort Worth, 1977), pp. 483–84.

16. A.L.S., Shaw to Mrs. Cora Crane, 25 August 1899. Quoted by permission, Stephen Crane Papers, Rare Book and Manuscript Library, Columbia University, and the Society of Authors. Stanley Weintraub mentions this letter in his chapter on Frederic, which includes a complete account of Frederic's death and the manslaughter hearings, in *The London Yankees: Portraits of American Writers and Artists in England, 1894–1914* (New York, 1979), p. 136. Passages from the letter appear as well in *Stephen Crane: Letters*, ed. R. W. Stallman and Lillian Gilkes (New York, 1960), p. 190.

17. *The Collected Works of Bernard Shaw*, vol. 12 (New York, 1930), pp. 64–65.

18. Paul Haines, "Harold Frederic," unpublished Ph.D. diss., New York University, 1945, p. 230. Taken from a 1935 interview with Ruth Frederic.

## Stanley Weintraub

# A JENNIFER FROM AUSTRALIA. EDITH ADAMS, HER HUSBAND, AND *THE DOCTOR'S DILEMMA*

During Easter weekend in 1893 Shaw picnicked with friends in Surrey, and noted for the first time in his diary[1] the names of Francis William Lauderdale Adams, a poet, and his strikingly attractive Australian second wife, Edith Goldstone Adams, an actress. (Adams's first wife had died.) The laconic reference suggests that Shaw had met the Adamses before, through Henry and Kate Salt, who lived near Tilford, and with whom he was holidaying in the country. A novelist and poet best known for his politically radical *Songs of the Army of the Night,* he had returned from Australia (where he had gone in 1882) to publish in London in hopes of being more widely known before the coffin lid closed over him. He was suffering from tuberculosis, which was now so far advanced that there was little expectation of a cure.

Francis Adams, Frank Harris recalled in *My Life and Loves,* had been "really my first good English friend." Galway born, Harris had gone to America but had returned to London to take up journalism and politics. In Hyde Park, where Harris spoke on "introducing some Socialist measures in English life," Adams had come up to the speaker's area afterwards and introduced himself, and they became friends. Then Adams went to Australia, returning five years later when Harris was editor of the *Fortnightly Review.* Harris offered him some work, but was distressed at his condition, and unimpressed by the pretty wife. (The editor of the *Fortnightly* had a yen for teenage girls.) "I managed to help him to go to Egypt. I told him he should live in the desert above Assouan, or in some high place such as Davos. . . ."

Adams and his wife returned from Egypt in 1893 with his health having further deteriorated. He could not afford to live abroad any longer, and had no hope. He had even tried to kill himself, he confided to Harris, but his courage had failed him. He would go back to Margate with Edith. Harris preached courage, and gave him a short story he had written on the subject.

Shaw heard, and thought, nothing of the Adamses for months after their meeting. While Adams declined further at the seaside, G.B.S. returned to music reviewing and to writing his first plays, for one *World* music column going for the first time to the Star and Garter in Richmond, where the Richmond Orchestral Society was performing. The terrace of the Star and Garter would later be the setting of the second act of his *Doctor's Dilemma,* in which he would place, it seems, the Adamses among a covey of admiring physicians. He would dine at the Star and Garter again the next month with James Brown, the orchestra's director, somehow the setting remaining in his subconscious along with the tubercular poet and his adoring wife.

Early in September it was all over for Adams. Although the tubercular Louis Dubedat in Shaw's play would expire on stage, in the presence of his wife and several doctors, and with a challenge on his lips, the end for Adams was even more theatrical, and far more trying for the dying man's wife. Adams was about to go for a drive in the restorative sea air when one of the hemorrhages he feared came on. Returning to his room he told Edith that the blood was from his lungs, and that he was dying. He gave her a message for Harris, and asked for his revolver. Certain that he was in fact dying, she gave him the gun. He put the barrel in his mouth, already red with his blood, and fired. The bullet went through his head into the ceiling.

At a hearing before a Margate magistrate, Mrs. Adams was charged with being more than a witness: indeed, she was an accessory before the fact. Nevertheless, she was let off. When Shaw saw her again she was staying with the Salts in Surrey. "After dinner," he noted on 2 October, "took a walk with Mrs. Francis Adams, who told me a good deal about herself." On the sixteenth in London he saw—at different times—both Frank Harris and Edith Adams, and noted, "In the morning I had been delayed in getting to work by having to answer a letter from Walter [Gurly] about her." The inference must be that he had been seeing so much of her (however unrecorded) that his physician uncle was curious about the new lady in his life. On the twenty-fifth he noted, "Leave Ms. of F. Adams' *Tiberius* at the Democratic Club for Mrs. Adams." She was seeking someone to edit for publication her late husband's verse drama, and although Shaw had little interest in it, he retained considerable interest in her.

Eventually the editing would be undertaken by sixtyish widower William Michael Rossetti, whose interest, possibly, was entirely in the flaming radicalism of Adams's verses. But one aspect of the future *Doctor's Dilemma* was already beginning to incubate here—the personable, tubercular artist (here a poet) whose work, questionable in merit, will be posthumously promoted by a beautiful, loyal young widow in whose matrimonial prospects the professional men around her dying husband are interested. Shaw had already visited one of the future play's settings. A dozen years would pass before the conscious impetus to the play would come through Shaw's friendship with research physician Almroth Wright, who was working on a possible tuberculosis cure.

Early in 1894 Shaw was still interested, noting in his diary that he discussed Edith Adams with May Morris. He was still then involved with Florence Farr, the "Louka" of his *Arms and the Man* production that spring, and if that intimacy had not complicated Shaw's interest in the young widow, perhaps his biography would have taken a different turn. (He later wrote that "experienced" women always interested him more than innocent ones.) Nevertheless, there would be a matrimonial future for Edith Adams. In a church in Hampstead in 1897, she married London landscape painter Frank Dean. William Michael Rossetti gave the bride away.

Is Edith the beautiful Jennifer Dubedat of Shaw's 1906 play? Shaw makes Jennifer a Cornishwoman, suggesting exotic origin less remote than Australia; little else can be pointed to other than the circumstantial evidence of the diaries. Later, possibly having second thoughts about the noble attitudes which the young woman had struck, Shaw wrote to Cathleen Nesbitt, who was playing Jennifer in a 1923 London production, "Jennifer is a sort of woman whom, I, personally, cannot stand, enormously conceited, morally patronizing to everyone, seeing herself always in some noble, devoted, beautiful attitude, never looking facts in the face or telling herself or anyone else the truth about them for a moment, and making even her husband's death a splendid opportunity for taking the centre of the stage."[2]

No other person out of Shaw's life so suggests Jennifer, while Louis Dubedat's disease (and profession) may have come not only from Francis Adams—an artist of a different sort—but from Aubrey Beardsley, whom he knew, or from Dante Gabriel Rossetti, whose amoral charm with artistic patrons was notorious, and parallels that of Dubedat. Edward Aveling's unscrupulous charm with women, and with lenders of money may have also been in the back of Shaw's mind. Still, Shaw's characters were often an amalgam of real life and imagination, and it is remarkable that in the years of his encountering the fascinating Adamses—both of whom may reappear in the Dubedats—he would also be introduced to the setting in which part of his play occurs. The creative process is a complex one. By the time that Shaw wrote *The Doctor's Dilemma* he may even have forgotten some of its sources in his early years as a playwright.

# Notes

1. *Bernard Shaw: The Diaries* (University Park, PA, 1986), ed. Stanley Weintraub, is the major source, on the dates noted. Frank Harris's *My Life and Loves* (1926) and William Michael Rossetti's *Some Reminiscences* (1906) furnish further background.

2. Shaw to Cathleen Nesbitt, 28 April 1923, in *Collected Letters III: 1911–1925* (New York, 1985), ed. Dan H. Laurence, 823–24.

# Katherine Lyon Mix

# LAURENCE HOUSMAN AND
# BERNARD SHAW

Bernard Shaw and Laurence Housman, younger brother of poet
A. E. Housman of *A Shropshire Lad*, were well known to each other,
and to London literary circles, by the middle 1890s. Shaw had come
to London from Dublin in 1876, and Housman from Worcestershire
in 1887. Housman intended to study art, but soon abandoned his
black-and-white illustrating for a free-lance career as a writer. For
both men, drama soon became the preferred medium, but Shaw,
nearly ten years older than Housman, was an established playwright
while Housman was still publishing fairy tales.

In 1946 Shaw wrote to Housman, who had apparently been
troubled by some misunderstanding, "As to the fancied offence, it is
widely off the target. Our cordial relations for forty years have never
been clouded for an instant. Charlotte would say the same if she were
available."[1] Shaw's wife had died in 1943.

Shaw had underestimated the length of their friendship, which had
begun in the nineties when both were members of the Bohemian
group that met at the home of Edith Nesbit, the poet, and her Fabian
Socialist husband Hubert Bland. It was Edith who introduced Housman to Shaw when she took him to the City Temple to hear Shaw in
informal debate with Belfort Bax.[2] In the discussion which followed
Housman said if the working class were paid higher wages they
wouldn't know how to use them properly. Shaw so demolished him
that he never made such a statement again, but at the moment he
didn't like Shaw.[3]

During the 1890s both men wrote busily but both escaped the
mantle of the *fin de siècle* though Shaw had an essay "On Going to
Church" in the *Savoy* and Housman two drawings in the *Yellow Book*.
The Wilde scandal affected them differently; Shaw drew up a petition
to the Home Secretary for a mitigation of Wilde's sentence while
Housman was discreetly silent. However, it has been said that in the

Lawrence Housman
Sketched by G B S.
13 10 10

Pencil sketch of Laurence Housman by G.B.S., dated 13 October 1910. Reproduced by permission of the Iconography Collection, Harry Ransom Humanities Research Center, University of Texas at Austin.

last year of Wilde's life Housman and Shaw, dining at the Café Royal, took up a collection for Wilde, and Housman carried the money to Paris to pay Wilde's debts.[4]

By then Shaw as a new playwright had already suffered from the Lord Chamberlain's banning of *Mrs Warren's Profession* from presentation on the stage. In 1902 Housman began his own dramatic career with a mystery play, *Bethlehem*, which was also banned by the censor, not for any indecency but because the Holy Family could not be portrayed in the theater. Housman was furious and at once joined the band of dramatists—among them Shaw, Barrie, Galsworthy, and Sutro—who were actively protesting the Lord Chamberlain's censorship.

Shaw's plays were usually produced by the Stage Society until in 1904 Harley Granville Barker and John Vedrenne assumed management of the Court Theatre in Sloane Square as a venue for Shaw's plays. Granville Barker was a talented young actor and producer. Housman had seen him as Eugene in *Candida* and so admired him that he had asked for an introduction, which led to Barker suggesting that they write a play together. *Prunella or Love in a Dutch Garden,* a fantasy play, was the result. Barker borrowed the money from Professor Gilbert Murray to produce it at the Court, where it lost money at every performance. Shaw liked *Prunella,* but he advised Housman to write his next play without Barker.[5]

He did just that, though he had Barker's advice and approval when he brought to light *The Chinese Lantern.* Barker and Vedrenne had now taken over the Haymarket and Shaw's *Getting Married* was doing well there. However, Shaw thought that younger men not so well known, like Housman and Masefield, should also be given a chance, and so *The Chinese Lantern* was announced and *Getting Married* withdrawn. Shaw thought, he wrote to Vedrenne, that "something more fantastic" than his own plays, or Barker's or Pinero's, would be "safer"—Housman's, for example. But Housman's new play was even a worse fiasco than his first. Shaw counted up the cost in pounds and pence, in time and effort, and the *Lantern* was extinguished.[6]

About this time Barker had written his own play, a political tragedy called *Waste.* It had been promptly banned because of its mention of abortion. For the play to be copyrighted it had to have a public reading and this was given on 28 January 1908 in the morning at the Savoy with a distinguished but largely amateur cast: Mrs. H. G. Wells, Mr. and Mrs. Bernard Shaw, Mr. and Mrs. H. Granville Barker (Harley had now married the actress Lillah McCarthy), William Archer, and Laurence Housman as the hero, Henry Trebell.[7]

Housman had found no difficulty in the licensing of his plays *Prunella* and *The Chinese Lantern,* but when he gave Gertrude Kingston his four-act play *Pains and Penalties* to open her little theater on John Street in 1910, matters were different. The play was a vindication of the honor of Queen Caroline, whom George IV had divorced for adultery. In Housman's version the king and his mistress, Mrs. FitzHerbert, are the offenders and the queen is innocent. Housman believed this had been the true situation, but the censor would have none of it, decreeing that relatives of the present Royal Family could not be presented on the stage. No arguments of Housman moved him. The play had one performance by the Pioneer Players; in the interval after act one, a group of embattled playwrights passed a motion against the newly appointed censor, who had written a play in which a character called Mr. Bleater had written a play *Sewage.*[8] Shaw called *Pains and Penalties* a "chronicle play," saying it was hundreds of years since a chronicle play had been written for the English stage.[9]

Dramatists, critics, and men of the theater so bedevilled Parliament on the censorship issue that eventually a Parliamentary Committee was appointed to hear complaints. Sessions dragged on day after day. Housman and Shaw fought shoulder to shoulder until Housman proposed a King's Proctor who would advise a manager as to the propriety of a play he was considering. Shaw was definitely opposed. He argued that no individual would have the legal knowledge to advise on all subjects,[10] and the King's Proctor never appeared.

Play censorship was not the only problem stirring controversy in the first decade of this century. Votes for Women was turning the British public into Suffragettes and Anti-Suffragettes. Housman joined the men's branch of the Women's Civil and Political League and threw himself wholeheartedly into the fight. He spoke, wrote, devised strategy, and was arrested for the cause. Shaw was more restrained. He did sign a petition and said he thought women were particularly fitted to be voters,[11] but he refused to speak for them. However, when women prisoners who refused to eat were being forcibly fed, he took the platform at Kingsway Hall on 23 March 1913 with the subject, "Torture by Forcible Feeding is Illegal." But he explained he meant for all prisoners, not merely women. He began, "I am not a suffragette speaker," going on to say he had become hardened to that reproach having heard it so often at home and from his friend Mr. Laurence Housman.[12]

On another occasion Housman persuaded him to come to a meeting in honor of Mr. Wicks, who had been arrested for failure to pay his wife's inhabited dwelling tax, a Suffragist ploy. Housman knew

Shaw's appearance would ensure a good audience. However, Shaw had no sympathy for Mr. Wicks, declaring that if his wife violated the law in that manner he would divorce her. Mr. Wicks was aghast and Mrs. Wicks was reduced to tears. Housman tried to clear the atmosphere by saying he didn't think Shaw really meant it, but privately he thought he did, every word of it.[13]

Votes for Women faded into the background with the outbreak of war in 1914. Housman, too old for military service, became secretary of a home for Belgian refugees. Shaw contributed money to the home but thought the government should bear the cost, not the public. Housman was not a pacifist at the beginning of the war but he gradually became one. In World War II he was a declared pacifist and worked with the Peace Pledge Union, but he did not subscribe to the armed pacifism of Shaw. He worked to free conscientious objectors while Shaw came out for compulsory military training. Both sympathized with the enemy. Housman rejoiced when he heard that Shaw had said, "Men must learn to be kind and just to those they most properly hate."[14] Both were horrified by the use of the atom bomb. Shaw wrote Housman of the need for "brains, and character and moral courage. . . . If the Japs had had a leader with these the Hiroshima atrocity would have lost us the war. All it produced was a paroxysm of terror everywhere. World cowardice!"[15]

Between and during the wars both men continued to write plays but tried other fields as well, Shaw in philosophy and politics and Housman in fiction. Each seemed aware of the other's current publications. In 1914 Shaw wrote to Housman about his novel, *The Royal Runaway*, a story of the abdication of the king of the mythical country of Jigalo. After praising the contents Shaw added that he thought the novel was too flimsy a form for so serious a subject. Though some novels are "more precious than others . . . they are all drawing-room comforts . . . and the effect you produce is a little that of slipping a lighthouse under the tasteful subduing shade of the standard lamp."[16] In Housman's copy of the book in the Library at Street is inserted a clipping from the *Evening Standard* containing an article by Bernard Shaw, "The King, the Constitution and the Lady." It was a satirical account of the circumstances leading up to the abdication of Edward VIII.

In 1945 Shaw wrote Housman about his newly published *Back Words and Fore Words*, which included excerpts from his writing between 1893 and 1945, saying, "I might try a collection of samples myself. It hasn't been done before, has it? It is decidedly appetizing."[17] But Shaw had already sent Housman something of the kind,

*Short Stories, Scraps and Shavings* (1931). Housman found the contents "unequal" but thought the book had some good things in it.[18]

He was much impressed with Shaw's *The Adventures of the Black Girl in Her Search for God.* Though he thought the book was "flippantly written," he was almost in complete agreement with Shaw's final summing up.[19] Shaw, he said, "is one of our most useful men—spiritually and prophetically."[20] And again, "Shaw was the most fundamental Christian of all of us."[21] But Housman was often critical of Shaw's style and language, saying that he nearly drove him frantic with the "foolish things he says or the foolish way he says wise things."[22] He disliked his "verbal exaggerations which were sometimes almost silly."[23] He thought Shaw's repeated use of the word "bloody" had done the language a real disservice; the word had lost its ability to shock.[24] But he admired the way Shaw used laughter as a weapon. Under cover of laughter he had said some very wise things. At the judgment seat Shaw could tell the Lord that he had taught men to laugh at themselves. "And the man that can laugh at himself," Housman concluded, "has not lost his soul."[25]

From 1925 to 1934 Housman carried on a correspondence with the Reverend R. R. L. Sheppard of St. Martin's in the Fields. These letters were published after Sheppard's death as *What Can We Believe?* Sheppard had asked Housman to write a pageant for the 300th anniversary of St. Martin's. In it Housman showed damning scenes of the historical Church but never belittled Christianity. Shaw saw the pageant and declared he had never expected to see the Church put on the white sheet and so confess its sins.[26]

In his letters to Sheppard, Housman often mentioned Shaw, once saying, "Of living men the one I most believe in is Bernard Shaw."[27] Shaw's belief in Housman was not so openly stated but Housman treasured every kind word Shaw gave him. In the days of the Court Theatre he was just coming out of *Man and Superman,* still laughing, when he met Shaw and congratulated him on the play. Shaw then praised *Prunella;* Housman was pleased until he wondered if Shaw was only returning his compliment.[28] Once he overheard Shaw saying that what Housman really suffered from was the British public's dislike of intellect. Housman pressed him for an explanation and Shaw said, "Don't you know it yourself? You've got all Barrie's qualities but unfortunately you've got intellect as well." Housman hoped it meant Shaw preferred him to Barrie.[29]

That conversation occurred at a luncheon at the Shaws' when T. E. Lawrence was also a guest. After the meal, Lawrence told Housman he would like to talk to him about *Green Arras,* Housman's first book of poems. The poet waited in happy anticipation until Mrs. Shaw reminded Lawrence that he was going to help them buy a motor car and they must be off. So the moment was lost.[30]

Housman seemed to be familiar with meals at the Shaws'. At least he said he could remember Shaw's before- and after-dinner volubility, though he could seldom recall what he had said.[31]

Financially, Shaw made more money from his plays than Housman from all his writing. Shaw was aware of his friend's less prosperous condition. When Housman asked him if he would mind if he sold some of the books Shaw had given him, Shaw replied, "Why shouldn't you? Nothing would give me more pleasure than to hear you had sold every scrap of writing of mine you possess, printed or written, at the top of the market and had made some cold cash out of them." Then he added, "But don't blow it all on the Save Europe nonsense. It can't even save Street."[32] Housman was now living in the Quaker village of Street in Somerset.

The Bible often claimed the critical attention of both men. In December 1937 the *London Mercury* printed an essay on "The English Bible" by Laurence Housman. He praised the Bible as literature and regretted that the present generation was so ignorant of it, but he admitted it was difficult to read with its disfiguring marginal references, outmoded style of printing, and meaningless chapter divisions. The next month the *Mercury* contained a letter from Bernard Shaw to Laurence Housman on "How to Print the Bible." Housman, he said, had left uncontradicted the modern complaint of every sentence in the Bible being a numbered paragraph. Shaw considered older and more recent printings of the Bible, finding some fault with each. He preferred the old biblical style, with every sentence an epigram or a statement of fact, and he asked Housman to join him in denouncing the revival of the forty-year-old Vulgate.

Housman had the last word with a letter to the editor of the *Mercury* written in biblical style with short, numbered sentences and marginal references. He was sorry to differ from Shaw, who was the older and better man, but if Shaw thought this letter was improved by its biblical and Jacobean form, he didn't. He was "Faithfully yours" with a reference to Revelation 2:10.

Housman was quite sincere in calling Shaw the better man. He told a German scholar, Anna Rudolph, that all modern writers had been influenced by Shaw and he was among that number, especially during his thirties. He wholly agreed with Shaw about the moral compromising of modern society. Shaw had a lively conscience and was absolutely courageous in saying what he believed to be the truth.[33]

Housman sometimes specified the influence of Shaw on his own writing. It was Shaw's *Androcles and the Lion* and seeing O. P. Heggie as the saintly tailor that inspired him to write his *Little Plays of St. Francis.*[34] Beginning in 1925 the St. Francis plays were given every year by the Dramatic Club of the London University College. In 1933 Housman wrote *Nunc Dimittis, An Epilogue,* suggested, he said, by Shaw's Epilogue to *Saint Joan.* Shaw was always being held up to him as an example. If Shaw could write an Epilogue, why shouldn't he?[35]

In the performance of *Nunc Dimittis* at University College, Housman played his own death scene, attended by a doctor and a nurse. The producer had asked Shaw to play the doctor, but he refused, saying he might be mistaken for God and that would detract from Housman's glory.[36] In the play, St. Francis enters, and Housman tells him of his literary friends, two mobsters named Shaw and Drinkwater who went about seeking people to write about. He punned that Drinkwater didn't but the other man did. Housman said he had taken Saint Francis to save him from Shaw, who was looking for another saintly being to follow St. Joan. Shaw couldn't have written about St. Francis; he would have made him Shaw. Shaw had taken Joan to save her from Drinkwater. Housman loved Shaw; he was a wonderful man, but he couldn't stand fools.[37]

After the success of Housman's play *Victoria Regina,* he did a new version of the *Epilogue,* into which he introduced the queen. Again Shaw's name is brought up, the author telling the queen that he wrote about her to save her from Shaw, who would have made her Shaw. The queen does not know who Shaw is. Housman identifies him as the greatest playwright since Shakespeare. The queen says he was not alive in her day. He was, says Housman, but he was a Socialist.[38]

Years passed. Shaw wrote to Housman, "I am no longer the man you saw last time. A dotard of 89⅚ forgets everything in ten minutes except what happened fifty years ago."[39]

When Housman was eighty, Shaw was ninety and his neighbor Stephen Winsten planned to honor the day with a book of appreciations from his friends. Housman began his contribution with the statement, "Bernard Shaw is the most devastating influence that has befallen my country, from the nineties of the last century up to the present day." But it had been a beneficent influence. He had forced people to laugh and listen to him. The well-educated mind of the twentieth century was largely Shaw's production. Housman himself was different from knowing him, and he recalled the debate in the City Temple. He compared him to Shakespeare, Socrates, and Voltaire, but he could not resist a mention of Shaw's "bad taste," "gratuitous exaggerations," and use of "worn-out clichés." He especially emphasized Shaw's fight for the recovery of moral and social values that had become defective under the veneer of Christianity. At first Shaw had been entirely secular in his approach, but in the Preface to *Androcles and the Lion* he openly championed Christianity. The Humanist had come to the rescue of Christian realism.[40]

Shaw died in 1950 at the age of ninety-four. Housman died in 1959. He was ninety-four.

# Notes

1. Shaw to Housman, postcard, 30 May 1945, Harry Ransom Humanities Research Center, University of Texas at Austin.

2. D. L. Moore, *E. Nesbit, A Biography* (London, 1933), p. 122.

3. Stephen Winsten, ed. *G.B.S. and the Victorians* (London, 1946), p. 57.

4. R. P. Graves, *A. E. Housman Scholar Poet* (Scribner's New York, 1980), pp. 131–32.

5. Housman to his sister Clemence, undated letter, sold at Sotheby's in 1968, location unknown.

6. Shaw to J. E. Vedrenne, letter, 22 May 1908, in *CL*.

7. C. B. Purdom, *Granville Barker* (London, 1956), p. 76.

8. Ibid., p. 27.

9. G.B.S. in *The New Statesman*, London, 3 May 1913.

10. Shaw, *The Shewing-up of Blanco Posnet*, preface.

11. Rodelle Weintraub, ed. *Fabian Feminist: Bernard Shaw and Woman* (Penn State Press, 1977), pp. 248–54.

12. Ibid., p. 229.

13. L. Housman, *The Unexpected Years* (London, 1936), p. 246.

14. *G.B.S. and the Victorians*, p. 55.

15. Shaw to Housman, postcard, 17 May 1946, Harry Ransom Humanities Research Center, University of Texas at Austin.

16. Shaw to Housman, letter, 22 August 1914, quoted in *Sotheby Catalogue* (London, 1968), p. 162.

17. Shaw to Housman, postcard, 30 May 1945.

18. L. Housman, *What Can We Believe?* (London, 1939), p. 227.

19. Ibid.

20. Ibid., p. 194.

21. Ibid., p. 227.

22. Ibid., p. 225.

23. Ibid., p. 227.

24. *Unexpected Years*, p. 215.

25. L. Housman, *Preparation of Peace* (London, 1940), p. 246.

26. *Unexpected Years*, p. 281.

27. *What Can We Believe?*, p. 225.

28. Housman to Clemence; see note 5 above.

29. *Unexpected Years,* pp. 312–13.

30. Ibid.

31. Ibid., p. 172.

32. Shaw to Housman, 17 May 1946, HRC (Texas).

33. Anne Rudolph, *Die Dichtung von Laurence Housman* (Breslau, n.d.), p. 31.

34. *Unexpected Years,* p. 204.

35. Ibid., p. 300.

36. Ibid.

37. L. Housman, *Nunc Dimittis, An Epilogue* (Privately printed, 1933) reprinted in L. Housman, *Back Words and Fore Words* (London, 1945), pp. 238–9.

38. New Version *Nunc Dimittis* (Privately printed, University College Dramatic Society, 1940), p. 43 ff.

39. Shaw to Housman, 30 May 1945, HRC (Texas).

40. *G.B.S. and the Victorians,* pp. 55–58.

# Bert Cardullo

# THE MYSTERY OF *CANDIDA*

Bernard Shaw subtitled *Candida* (1894) "A Mystery," and Elsie B. Adams was the first to take this to mean that it is "a modern mystery play of the Madonna and Child, which will be performed in the modern equivalent to the medieval cathedral, the theatre where the catholic religion of Creative Evolution lives."[1] Candida is the name of a first-century Neapolitan saint recognized by both the Roman Catholic Church and the Church of England; Marchbanks raises the Candida of the play to the level of the Virgin Mother in his mind, and both he and Morell are children to her, the one to be educated for passage into the mysterious night, according to Shaw the "true realm of the poet,"[2] the other to be coddled within the sanctuary of marriage. The truth about Candida, however, as Prossy says in Act I, is that "she's got good hair and a tolerable figure,"[3] and is "very nice, very good-hearted" (1:523). Her name in secular usage (our word *candid* comes from the Latin *candidus*, "white, bright") suggests that she is not a figure of mystery, but of accessibility: she is open in her knowledge, and openly knowable. The eighteen-year-old prodigal Marchbanks, in need of an illusion with which to fall in love and embrace as his own, poeticizes her, only to discover at the end of the play that the woman he has enshrined as an earthly variant of Titian's Virgin is rather an efficient homemaker and caring wife, participant in a relationship in which she needs her husband (for her defense, livelihood, and dignity, as he puts it) as much as he needs her. Realizing that there is no glorification of woman possible in marriage, Marchbanks chooses to live freely outside the stultifying, compromising happiness of its bonds and attain exaltation through devotion to his art.

This is the "secret in [his] heart" (1:594) that Shaw refers to in the last stage direction, and of which Candida and Morell are ignorant. She knows that Marchbanks "has learnt to live without happiness" (1:593); she does not know that he predicates his ability to create great art on his unhappy existence, on the frustrations and tensions in it that he will simultaneously transfigure and defuse in his work.

She cannot perceive this, since she has no real interest in art and how it is made. *Candida* is a modern mystery to the extent that it celebrates the birth of a poet's art. Just as the medieval mysteries focused on the life, death, and resurrection of Christ, the play centers on the life and death of the boy Marchbanks and his rebirth as a man, as an artist. The mysteries juxtaposed paganism against Christianity, temporal happiness against eternal peace; *Candida* juxtaposes life against art, marital comfort against self-dramatization or self-transmutation. Candida and Morell, unbeknownst to them, are Marchbanks's spiritual mother and father; they are comparable in their ignorance to Joseph, if not to Mary. For moral reasons as well as for practical theatrical and artistic ones, Shaw had Candida leave her two children behind, ill, when she returns to London: he was an outspoken critic of the exploitation of child actors; always a careful theater man, he was keeping his cast to a manageable size by excluding the children; and, as long as their existence was established, the children were not needed on stage—they would not be useful to this drama as Shaw conceived it. The effect, however, of their exclusion, as opposed to Shaw's reasons for it, is to emphasize Candida's and her husband's role as *Marchbanks's* parents. On the surface it appears that the dramatist made Morell a pastor partly out of irony: the man of the cloth fathers, not his likeness, not a servant of God, but a man of letters. In fact, to return to Adams's equation of the theater with a modern cathedral, Morell fathers a modern Jesus, an artist-genius who discerns "the distant light of the new age" and "keeps on building up his masterpieces until their pinnacles catch the glint of the unrisen sun."[4] Morell himself is the one to point out that art has something in common with religion: "I well know that it is in the poet that the holy spirit of man—the god within him—is most godlike" (1:542). As the servant of the new catholic religion, Creative Evolution, it will be Marchbanks's role, in Adams's words, "to represent through his art a vision of a world not yet evolved" (p. 432).

By depicting the artist as a Christ figure and presenting his birth in the form of a mystery play, Shaw pays homage to the Middle Ages in addition to arguing for Creative Evolution as the religion of the twentieth century and for artists as its prophets. The Middle Ages, he believed, created the last great art before the Renaissance because it provided "an iconography for a live religion";[5] with the Renaissance came religious skepticism and a resultant decline in art. Shakespeare, Shaw writes,

> could not become the conscious iconographer of a religion because he had no conscious religion. He had therefore to exercise his extraordi-

nary natural gifts in the very entertaining art of mimicry, giving us the famous "delineation of character" which make [*sic*] his plays . . . so delightful. Also, he developed that curious and questionable art of building us a refuge from despair by disguising the cruelties of Nature as jokes. . . . He would really not be great at all if it were not that he had religion enough to be aware that his religionless condition was one of despair.[6]

"Ever since Shakespear," Shaw continues, "playwrights have been struggling with the same lack of religion" (5:336); he includes among them the two giants of his own time, Ibsen and Strindberg, who "refused [their audiences] even the Shakespearian-Dickensian consolation of laughter at mischief, accurately called comic relief."[7]

Although *Candida* is a modern mystery play of the Madonna and Child, it both imitates and stretches the form of the medieval mystery. There are also what I shall call secularly mysterious aspects of the play, over which many critics have puzzled and which they have taken as evidence for its subtitle. Shaw carefully interweaves secular and sacred mystery in *Candida*; he introduces mysterious elements into the action, raises questions about the plot, the answers to which come or are underlined, paradoxically, in the fulfillment of the play's sacred mystery.

Marchbanks introduces the first element of literal mystery into the play: we want to know what this eighteen-year-old dishevelled aristocrat is doing in the home of the Reverend and Mrs. James Morell. They have children of their own and are busy enough looking after them and Morell's congregation; why would they take a stranger in? In response to Burgess's question about Marchbanks's identity, Candida says, "Oh, Eugene's one of James's discoveries. He found him sleeping on the Embankment last June" (1:533–34). For what has Morell discovered Marchbanks? What plans does he have for him? It should be clear from their confrontation before lunch in Act I that the pastor wishes to domesticate Marchbanks, to set an example for him, to demonstrate marriage and the family unit as the ideal state in which to live; Morell may not have been conscious of his purpose when he first brought the young man into his house, but he seems to be conscious of it by the time Candida and Eugene return to London. Morell tells Marchbanks at one point, "I'm very fond of you, my boy; and I should like you to see for yourself what a happy thing it is to be married as I am" (1:539); and at another, "Some day, I hope and trust, you will be a happy man like me. You will be married; and you will be working with all your might and valor to make every spot on earth as happy as your own home" (1:542).

Ironically, Marchbanks falls in love with the pastor's wife; equally ironically, he learns through his relationship with her and her husband that marriage is not for him. That he elects at the end of the play to live the solitary life of an artist instead of ever taking a wife is the final indication that his entire education in the Morell household has tended toward making this choice: it was laid before him there (and there is no evidence that he had considered marriage before meeting the Morells), he discerned it, and he made his decision. Now that his education is complete, he may leave. Just as Christ's mission was to go to earth and incarnate the sacred mystery that is God, Marchbanks's will be to plunge into the night and intimate through his art the mystery that is a perfect world. In order to do this he must, like Christ, remain single: marriage must not be allowed to interfere with his idealization of women, love, and beauty, which is in the service of his vision of a future world.

The second element of mystery in the play concerns the rivalry between Morell and Marchbanks for Candida's love. The drama would appear to lie, as in conventional romantic comedy, in that rivalry. But there can be little question that Candida's love is not someone's for the taking. As she says in Act II:

> Ah, James, how little you understand me, to talk of your confidence in my goodness and purity! I would give them both to poor Eugene as willingly as I would give my shawl to a beggar dying of cold, if there were nothing else to restrain me. Put your trust in my love for you, James; for if that went, I should care very little for your sermons: mere phrases that you cheat yourself and others with every day. [1:565]

The play is a mystery to the extent that Marchbanks is never a serious contender for Candida's love, yet manages to precipitate a spiritual crisis in the Morell marriage. This occurs because the pastor misunderstands the nature of his wife's love for him, believing that "it was [in the pulpit] that I earned my golden moment, and the right, in that moment, to ask her to love me" (1:578). He thinks that Candida married him for his vocation; and that she is bound to him, in goodness and purity, out of duty and obligation. Thus, when Marchbanks implies toward the end of Act I that Candida merely tolerates the moralist and windbag in her husband, Morell feels that his marriage is threatened, that he may lose his wife to the young poet. Uncannily, as if in anticipation of this crisis in his marriage, Morell has telegraphed *before* the play to the Guild of St. Matthew to say that he will not speak for them on the evening of the day Candida comes home. The telegram from the Guild that he responds to in Act II is their urgent request that he change his mind; his reply here is not his initial breaking of the speaking engagement, as a result of his clash with Marchbanks in Act I, as is often thought, but a reiteration of the earlier cancellation.

Aside from being mysterious in the secular sense, the trouble in the Morell marriage adds up to a religious mystery. The Roman Catholic and Eastern churches recognize marriage as one of seven sacraments (actually called mysteries in the latter church), which are acts, ceremonies, or practices distinguished from all others in Christian rites as having been instigated by Christ as the visible means by which Divine grace is sought and conferred. The Church of England, of which Morell is a clergyman, officially accepts only two sacraments, baptism and Holy Communion; nevertheless, it recognizes marriage, as the following declaration by the Anglican bishop in *Getting Married* indicates: "To me there is only one marriage that is holy: the Church's sacrament of marriage."[8] Morell gives marriage the quality of a sacrament when he says to Lexy in Act I, "Ah, my boy, get married; get married to a good woman; and then you'll understand. That's a foretaste of what will be best in the Kingdom of Heaven we are trying to establish on earth" (1:521). He says virtually the same thing to Marchbanks later in the same act: "[In marriage] you will be one of the makers of the Kingdom of Heaven on earth" (1:542). By the end of the play the Morell marriage has been reborn, reconfirmed; it has found its true identity in the charity and humility espoused by Christ. In Candida and James's final embrace—their sacred union—the secular mystery of their marital crisis is absolutely dispelled.

Burgess introduces the third element of mystery in *Candida*: we want to know why he is visiting his daughter and her husband for the first time in three years. He says that he has come out of "family sentiment" (1:529); that he wants to make up the quarrel he had with James over the low wages he, Burgess, was paying his workers. Morell does not believe him and finally declares, "Come now: either take your hat and go; or else sit down and give me a good scoundrelly reason for wanting to be friends with me. Thats right. Now out with it" (1:531). But Burgess does not give him a good scoundrelly reason; he avoids the issue by flattering his son-in-law, by saying that he now thinks more highly of clergymen than he once did and has come to tell James so. Burgess is telling the truth: he does think more highly of clergymen, but only because they have been gaining influence in the business world. He wants to reconcile with Morell so that the latter will introduce him to some big jobbers. Morell suspects this, and we learn it when Burgess is invited to hear him speak before the Guild of St. Matthew (James decides to give the talk after all) and declines to go until the pastor says that he can meet the chairman there, who is on the Works Committee of the County Council and has

some influence in the awarding of contracts. Candida's father treats
this man, Lexy, and Prossy to a champagne supper after Morell's
speech, virtually assuring that he will receive favorable treatment in
the future. Burgess leaves his daughter's house, then, having
achieved exactly what he came there for. The irony of this is that he
has been encouraged in the pursuit of her husband's friendship and
its advantages by Morell himself. He has been encouraged, that is, in
the open and honest pursuit of his capitalistic deviltry by a Christian
Socialist. Morell tells Burgess, "So long as you come here honestly as
a self-respecting, thorough, convinced scoundrel, justifying your
scoundrelism and proud of it, you are welcome. . . . I like a man to
be true to himself, even in wickedness" (1:530–31). Like Marchbanks
and like the Morell marriage, Burgess himself is reborn at the end of
*Candida*—not as a repentant Christian, but as a confirmed devil. He
is comparable to the devil figures in the medieval mysteries, as I in-
tend to demonstrate, but unlike them he gets no comeuppance. In
the gradual reassertion of his deviltry, Burgess clears up the mystery
of his sudden appearance in the Morell home.

In addition to being a mystery figure in his own right, Burgess
forms together with Lexy and Prossy the "realistic" triangle in the
play to Marchbanks's, Morell's, and Candida's "mysterious" triangle.
In this role the former three are not so different from the realistic
figures in medieval mystery plays, the purpose of whom was three-
fold: (1) precisely to provide an element of realism with which audiences seeking diversion as well as instruction could identify; (2) to put
the figures of the mystery in perspective; and (3) to place the devil in
the comic-realistic guise of at least one character. Alfred Turco, Jr.,
has described the "mysterious" triangle in *Candida* as follows:

> Morell embodies genial affection and vigorous dedication to a goal,
> marred by lack of awareness concerning his true position in both home
> and pulpit. Candida exemplifies maternal insight and household wis-
> dom divorced from appreciation of such higher matters as her hus-
> band's socialism or her suitor's poetry. While Marchbanks is undeniably
> a weak personality in some respects, the contrasts to Morell's sentimen-
> tality and Candida's mundaneness underscore his comparative tough-
> ness of mind and force of imagination.[9]

The "realistic" triangle in the play could be described in contrasting
terms. Lexy idolizes Morell and, ironically, enables us to take the latter seriously, for all his pontificating, because he, Lexy, is a pale, comic
imitation of his mentor. The unmarried Prossy is in love (from a distance) with Morell, and for this reason is able to see her "rival" with

piercing eyes: as she says, "[I] can appreciate [Candida's] *real* qualities far better than any man can" (1:523; emphasis mine). Burgess obviously does not worship Morell—he wants to use him; and his very earthy and earthly presence in his daughter's home is in effect an argument against the idealization of her by both her husband and Marchbanks. Burgess, Lexy and Prossy form, I hasten to add, a triangle by default. In contrast with the Marchbanks-Morell-Candida triangle, there is no love among its members. Prossy tells us that Lexy thinks her "dowdy and second rate enough" (p. 523), and Burgess believes that both of them, as employees of his son-in-law, should be kept in their place.

The devilish Burgess, as the Christlike Marchbanks's opposite in the play, deserves discussion in greater detail. Jacob Adler, sensing the mystery of Marchbanks's disruption of the Morell household, has said "Shaw's whole story is very close to much ado about nothing." He adds that "the presence of a character [Burgess] who feels this way himself is disarming."[10] Burgess's response to Morell's sermonizing, Marchbanks's "poetic horrors" (which he gets when he realizes that Candida does menial chores along with the servants), and his daughter's independence of mind, is to think that all three characters are mad, since they grossly overstate their complaints or opinions. He thus functions as a comic devil who cannot take the "mysteries" unfolding before him seriously, or who simply does not understand them. Burgess is funny precisely because he combines equal amounts of ignorance and arrogance in the same character. Like the devil figures of medieval mystery plays, who often were composites of the worst sins that the audience could commit, he is a stand-in for any audience of *Candida,* from Shaw's day to our own, as his name indicates: *les bourgeois* identify with Burgess. That is not to say that we identify with his point of view on the action completely—we cannot, the most important reason for this being that he is not onstage at the crucial moments in the Marchbanks-Morell-Candida story. What he does is drain off our own devilish disbelief in the feasibility of Marchbanks's assault on the Morell marriage. As Adler put it, "Paradoxically enough, the audience can take the events [on stage] more seriously, precisely because Burgess [himself] does not."[11] He pulls us back from the action, so that we can observe it for the insights it contains into marriage—of male and female on one hand, and of the artist and his muse on the other.

If Burgess pulls us back from the action, represents the comically objective point of view on it, Marchbanks takes us into the action, personifies subjective submersion in it. Their opposition is reinforced, paradoxically, by their similarities: both are outsiders—Burgess by virtue of having been estranged from his daughter and her family for three years—and both are alone. Marchbanks is estranged from his own family and has been living outdoors; Burgess has been living by himself in the house he once shared with Candida (he never mentions his wife, who we may assume is dead, or any other family members). The two men are at opposite ends of the play's social ladder, however, the young aristocrat at the top and the old Cockney at the bottom. And they pursue mutually exclusive interests: the one, art for humanity's sake; the other, commerce for money's sake. When they meet for the first time, Marchbanks nearly runs away from Burgess, so dissimilar are they in motive, temperament, appearance, and social station. Their very names tell us how different they are. Marchbanks (originally Marjoribanks, shortened by Shaw to what would be heard in normal pronunciation) has been sleeping on the Embankment, and "in [his] garments he has apparently lain in the heather and waded through the waters" (1:535). Marjoribanks also would have offered upper-class echoes to Shaw's audiences, as the name was a familiar one in Victorian life, in both society and government. That Eugene was the nephew of an earl would have been acceptable from his name, blurred, however, by production change. Burgess is clearly Marchbanks' opposite in origin, a Cockney elevated by money into a petty bourgeois. While Burgess dismisses what he cannot understand about his daughter and her husband as madness, Marchbanks takes Morell and Candida very seriously and finally penetrates to their core. He is utterly sincere, and completely without humor; Burgess, on the other hand, is insincere and likes a good laugh. Ironically, Marchbanks forgets, in his worship of Candida, that she is a Burgess—her father's daughter, and so named before she acquired through marriage a new surname. It would not have occurred to Eugene that the Virgin Mother herself was of lowly birth, but it would have occurred to Shaw.

Perhaps as a deliberate Shavian paradox, *Candida* employs the form of a mystery play to present three "faiths": those of marriage, art and capitalism. It even makes room for an additional faith nearly heretical to true religion: worship of another mortal, practiced by Lexy and Prossy toward Morell. The play is hardly a vindication of Victorian marriage, as was believed by its original audiences, but neither is it a total rejection of marriage as an institution in favor of the solitary pursuit of an artistic vision. *Candida* is not an apology for Burgess's capitalism, either, but it is also not a denunciation of his money-grabbing in favor of selfless devotion to work for another. Rather, the play's balanced, humanitarian view stresses simultaneously the necessity of the comparative safety and restricted bliss of domestic life for some, the unchecked freedom to plumb the depths of holy, artistic night for others; and the need for some to live their lives in the service or imitation of another, for others to dedicate their energies to self-aggrandizement, to surrounding themselves with material comfort. As Elsie B. Adams has written, "Religion to Shaw does not signify orthodoxy or sectarianism. [His] Creative Evolution encompasses all sincerely held beliefs, including the Christian Socialism of Morell, the revolutionary doctrine of John Tanner, the Catholicism of Saint Joan, even the capitalism of Andrew Undershaft" (pp. 431– 32, note). Shaw believed that the drive of the will was toward ultimate good. Thus any sincere manifestation of it, even if it appeared evil on the surface (as capitalism does to many), would contribute to the improvement of the human condition. Artists like Marchbanks may be in the vanguard of Creative Evolution, but they are not the only soldiers in its army. Hence, in addition to Marchbanks, the Morell marriage and Burgess are reborn at the end of this mystery: the poet, the pastor, and the businessman have each learned to live in self-knowledge instead of self-deception.

# Notes

1. Elsie B. Adams, "Bernard Shaw's Pre-Raphaelite Drama," *PMLA*, 81 (1966), 437. Hereafter cited by page number in the text. Shaw has the following to say about Creative Evolution in his Preface to *Back to Methuselah:*

> What hope is there then of human improvement? According to the Neo-Darwinists, to the Mechanists, no hope whatever, because improvement can come only through some senseless accident which must, on the statistical average of accidents, be presently wiped out by some other equally senseless accident.
> But this dismal creed does not discourage those who believe that the impulse that produces evolution is creative. They have observed the simple fact that the will to do anything can and does, at a certain pitch of intensity set up by conviction of its necessity, create and organize new tissue to do it with. [5:267]
> Creative Evolution is already a religion, and is indeed now unmistakably the religion of the twentieth-century, newly arisen from the ashes of pseudo-Christianity, of mere scepticism, and of the soulless affirmations and blind negations of the Mechanists and Neo-Darwinians. [5:332]

2. Shaw says this in his letter to the Rugby boys, dated 8 March 1920, about the "secret" of Candida. The letter is quoted in full in George A. Riding, "The *Candida* Secret," *The Spectator,* 185 (Nov. 17, 1950), p. 506. Riding's article is anthologized in Stephen S. Stanton, ed., *A Casebook on "Candida"* (New York: Thomas Y. Crowell, 1962), pp. 166–69 (the phrase "true realm of the poet" appears on p. 168).

3. Bernard Shaw, *Plays Pleasant* from *The Bodley Head Shaw,* 1. All further quotations from the plays and prefaces are from the Bodley Head edition and will hereafter be cited by volume and page number in the text.

4. Bernard Shaw, Preface, *Plays Pleasant* (1:374).

5. Preface, *Back to Methuselah* (5:333). The next three references in this paragraph are to this preface.

6. Dropped from *The Bodley Head Shaw* text. See London: Constable and Co., Ltd., 1921, pp. lxxxii–lxxxiii.

7. Dropped from *The Bodley Head Shaw* text. See London: Constable and Co., Ltd. 1921, p. lxxxiv.

8. Bernard Shaw, *The Doctor's Dilemma, Getting Married,* and *The Shewing-up of Blanco Posnet* (3:598).

9. Alfred Turco, Jr., *Shaw's Moral Vision: The Self and Salvation* (Ithaca, NY: Cornell University Press, 1976), p. 103.

10. Jacob H. Adler, "Ibsen, Shaw and *Candida,*" *Journal of English and Germanic Philology,* 59 (1960), p. 57 (both quotations).

11. Ibid.

# J. Scott Lee

# COMIC UNITY IN
## *ARMS AND THE MAN*

Early criticism of *Arms and the Man* has had an enduring effect on subsequent discussion of the play. William Archer's review specified many of the grounds of critical investigation. Although most critics have since disagreed with Archer's conclusions, problems he posed have yielded fruitful insights.

Archer's central problem is, does *Arms and the Man* have a particular nature? To Archer, most of the play is not a comedy but an extravaganza: that is, a play whose parts and probabilities are wildly unconnected to form and reality:

> Let [the playgoer] rather look for a fantastic, psychological extravaganza, in which drama, farce, and Gilbertian irony keep flashing past the bewildered eye, as in a sort of merry-go-round, . . . If one could think that Mr. Shaw had consciously and deliberately invented a new species of prose extravaganza, one could unreservedly applaud the invention, while begging him in the future to apply it with more depth and delicacy. But I more than suspect that he conceives himself to have written a serious comedy, a reproduction of life as it really is. . . .[1]

The line of argument that Archer follows is that the play is divided against itself. To him the parts of the play do not cohere as a unified whole comedy. The first act he sees as satire on war. The last two acts become crude psychological "character presentation" which is neither "'romantic comedy' or coherent farce."[2]

Shaw answered some of these points in his defense of the play, "A Dramatic Realist to His Critics." Shaw's concern, however, was not how the comedy unified various parts of the play. Rather, he showed how the comedy pervasively operated through many scenes of the play as a clash of ignorance and knowledge: "The comedy arises, of course, from the collision of the knowledge of the Swiss with the illusions of the Bulgarians."[3] Shaw concludes his defense by appealing

to the knowledge he possesses over and against the ignorance of critics as the principle of the comedy:

> [The] above will, I hope, suffice to show that what struck my critics as
> topsy-turvey extravaganza, having no more relation to real soldiering
> than Mr. Gilbert's *Pinafore* has to real sailoring, is the plainest matter
> of fact. . . . I claim that the dramatic effect produced by the shock
> which these realities give to the notion of romantic young ladies and
> fierce civilians is not burlesque, but legitimate comedy, none the less
> pungent because . . . the romantic young lady was on the stage and the
> fierce civilians in the stalls.[4]

Archer's description of the two different materials of war and
"character presentation" provided topics which critics have contin-
ually addressed. Shaw's arguments have been used to construct a
unity for the play on the basis of the relation of romanticism/realism
or ignorance/knowledge.[5] The unity constructed is usually not a
comic unity. Berst's essay, for example, illustrates this argumentative
development: "The tightly knit humor of incident and character in
*Arms and the Man* has tended to obscure the more inclusive range of
Shaw's artistic achievement in the play."[6] For Berst what is central to
the achievement is the play's "synthesis of psychological insight." The
comedy *serves* this unifying function by bringing out stages of the synthesis in each character. On the whole, criticism has dismissed without
rebuttal Archer's main objection that the play was not a *whole romantic
comedy unified in its parts*. Did Shaw write a comedy in which character
and incident are unified in and by ridiculous romantic action? Archer's question still remains.

We can divide *Arms and the Man* into two sections which reflect potentialities for the action and the comic action itself. The first section
is an extended "prologue." It runs to the point in Act II when Sergius
and Louka are alone. The second is the comic action proper. It begins
with Sergius's advance towards Louka. It is obvious that there are two
romances in this play. However, Sergius's action is *not* that of making
love, though making love is necessary to his action. His action is,
rather, a proof of his bravery, honor and superiority as a man. Raina
does make love to Bluntschli. Their comedy is essentially Bluntschli's
recognition and acceptance of Raina's overtures. These two stories
are linked by the breaking of the match between Sergius and Raina.
Yet, they are separate and different because one is a story of romantic
love and one is not.[7]

The prologue provides the comic potentialities which differentiate
these stories. This constitutes one of two reasons why the play has

unity in its comic actions, for without the prologue it is almost impossible to see why Sergius, Raina and Bluntschli act the way they do. The other reason involves the discoveries by characters which serve to complete the comedy of each story. These two lines may not only be differentiated by why the participants act, but how those actions are achieved. The discoveries made by Sergius and Bluntschli are central to this, because the comic unity of *Arms* is two-fold, depending upon two different romances. One of these is less unified than the other.

*Arms and the Man* opens as Catherine brings word to Raina of her fiance's successful cavalry charge. Raina shares her thoughts with her mother:

> CATHERINE. Oh, if you have a drop of Bulgarian blood in your veins, you will worship him when he comes back.
> RAINA. What will he care for my poor little worship after the acclamations of a whole army of heroes? But no matter: I am so happy! so proud! . . . It proves that all our ideas were real after all.
> CATHERINE [*indignantly*] Our ideas real! What do you mean?
> RAINA. Our ideas of what Sergius would do. Our patriotism. Our heroic ideals. Oh, what faithless little creatures girls are! When I buckled on Sergius's sword . . . it came into my head just as he was holding me in his arms and looking into my eyes, that perhaps we only had our heroic ideas because we were so fond of reading Byron and Pushkin, and because we were so delighted with the opera . . . Real life is so seldom like that! indeed never, as far as I knew then. . . . Yes: I was only a prosaic little coward. Oh, to think that it was all true! That Sergius is just as splendid and noble as he looks! that the world is really a glorious world for women who can see its glory and men who can act its romance! What happiness! what unspeakable fulfillment!

Shaw opens the play as Sergius's action confirms Raina's romantic disposition.

"Intensely conscious" Raina has been undergoing a process of reflection for some time. The pre-war promise of Sergius's character is part of that process. She has used the "tangible" evidence of her fiance's looks, her experience and her imagination to decide what the world is like. She has sought to widen her thinking as her station and sex permit. Trips to Vienna and Bucharest, reading Pushkin and Byron, and the impact of war have activated her imaginative sensibilities.

Sergius's charge marks a difference between men and women. Raina seems to accept that the lot of women is to praise glorious deeds. But what she says suggests she would have it another way. She fears her praise of Sergius will be worth little compared to the praise of heroes who have fought. Her life has had little contact with heroic action except in literature and opera. The disparity between art and her prosaic life cause her worse doubts about what life is like. Happily, Sergius's charge seems to prove her ideas correct. Unable to participate in heroic actions, Raina contemplates them and their agents. Thus, she takes pride and fulfillment in the thinking which steered her through doubts to the right conclusions.

Raina is an emotional, thoughtful romantic, open to the action of life's romance. She honors Sergius in so far as he shares the same outlook on life and has done deeds which warrant that outlook. This esteem is a sign of Raina's heroic love of Sergius. Yet, if action is as important to Raina in life's romance as she indicates, it is likely that action would carry great weight in a love romance too. Long before Sergius comes home, Shaw gives Raina the opportunity to experience how important action is. Raina saves a Serbian officer not once, but twice. In the second chance, Raina's desire for romance comes alive in comedy.

Bluntschli climbs up to Raina's balcony to escape the Bulgarian soldiers. First he uses his (empty) revolver to gain Raina's cooperation. Next he uses Raina's embarrassment over her state of undress to keep her quiet. When it becomes clear that the Bulgarians will enter Raina's room, Bluntschli offers her cloak to her and warns her not to look. Raina responds to Bluntschli's kind gesture and hopelessness with a kindness of her own. She hides him.

> THE MAN [*sincerely and kindly*] No use dear: I'm done for. [*Flinging the cloak to her*] Quick! wrap yourself up: they're coming.
> RAINA. Oh thank you. . . . [*anxiously*] What will you do?
> THE MAN [*grimly*] The first man in will find out. Keep out of the way; and dont look. It wont last long; but it will not be nice.
> RAINA [*impulsively*] I'll help you. I'll save you. . . . Here! Hide behind the curtains.

After the search of the room, Raina is left alone with Bluntschli. He must stay for a few moments. Yet, the awkward fact is that he is the enemy. Bluntschli supplies the polite manners to accommodate the situation. His politeness provokes Raina's gentility and makes conversation between them easier. Bluntschli begins to speak of the Bulgarian cavalry charge. It is here that the comedy begins to arise, which shapes Raina's and Bluntschli's romance.

When Raina is exposed to the wider experience of Bluntschli, he comes off as the wit and she the butt. This is more than a collision of his knowledge and her ignorant illusions:

> RAINA [*eagerly turning back to him, as all her enthusiasm and her dreams of glory rush back on her*] Did you see the great cavalry charge? Oh, tell me about it. Describe it to me.
> THE MAN. You never saw a cavalry charge, did you?
> RAINA. How could I?
> THE MAN. Ah, perhaps not. No: of course not! Well, it's a funny sight. It's like slinging a handful of peas against a window pane: first one comes; then two or three close behind him; and then all the rest in a lump.
> RAINA [*her eyes dilating as she raises her clasped hands ecstatically*] Yes, first One! the bravest of the brave.
> THE MAN [*prosaically*] Hm! you should see the poor devil pulling at his horse.
> RAINA. Why should he pull at his horse?
> THE MAN [*impatient of so stupid a question*] It's running away with him; of course: do you suppose the fellow wants to get there before the others and be killed?

True, Raina is ludicrous through a natural ignorance. But aside from asking questions, she could hardly be expected to do anything about her ignorance. However, Raina *makes herself* ridiculous by how she *acts* when she cherishes the illusion of the "One" against Bluntschli's metaphor of the peas. The heart of the comedy is Raina's romantic *sincerity*—her tenaciousness of thought and feeling: "*her eyes dilating as she raises her clasped hands ecstatically.*" Her sincerity depends on her attachment to romantic, heroic action which has confirmed her disposition. When the comedy only attacks her ignorance, Raina *does* nothing that is foolish. But the sincerity of her disposition *leads her* to a ridiculous grand-opera posture. Then the comedy makes clear that her action is foolish because her whole romantic character is involved, not just her ignorance. This is important because Shaw now has in hand the possibility that Raina's "illusions [will] lead her into a great deal of pretty nonsense."[8]

Bluntschli continues to speak from his "professional point of view." He unintentionally insults Sergius as he explains that Sergius's charge was suicidal. Raina resolves that Bluntschli must go. However, Bluntschli is exhausted. He might fall from her balcony. Worse, he might be shot. It is these considerations which make Raina act:

> RAINA [*anxiously*] But if you fall?
> THE MAN. I shall sleep as if the stones were a featherbed. Goodbye.

> RAINA [*rushing to stop him*] Stop! [*She seizes him recklessly, and pulls him quite around*]. Theyll kill you. . . . [*clinging to him*] Theyre sure to see you: it's bright moonlight. I'll save you. Oh, how can you be so indifferent! You want me to save you, dont you?

Raina's kindness comes to Bluntschli's aid again.

Yet, Bluntschli is still the enemy. Now Raina's manners overcome the difficulty:

> RAINA. Come away from the window. . . . Please! [. . . *She releases him, and addresses him patronizingly*]. Now listen. You must trust to our hospitality. You do not know in whose house you are. I am a Petkoff.

Raina's lengthy demonstration of trustworthiness follows. All her experience, passion and thought enter into the proof. These are supposed to secure Bluntschli's trust:

> RAINA [*affectedly*] I tell you these things [about her father's military rank, the stairs of the house, possession of a library] to show you that you are not in the house of ignorant country folk who would kill you the moment they saw your Serbian uniform, but among civilized people. We go to Bucharest every year for the opera season; . . . I thought you might have remembered the great scene where Ernani, flying from his foes just as you are tonight, takes refuge in the castle of his bitterest enemy, an old Castilian noble. The noble refuses to give him up. His guest is sacred to him.

Raina's romanticism pushes her to a concluding statement which is contrary to the facts of this night's events: ". . . if instead of threatening me with your pistol as you did you had simply thrown yourself as a fugitive on our hospitality, you would have been as safe as in your father's house."

Of course, this conclusion is comic. The elaborate proof that supports it exposes Raina as one who takes for granted absurdly irrelevant social distinctions, stories, events and moral obligations. What makes this evidence of trustworthiness absurd is that Raina has saved Bluntschli already. She has offered to save him again. What more does she need to do? But, the comedy of the proof goes further than irrelevance to the situation. The incredible notion of hospitality allows Raina's disposition to act in concert with her kindness. Raina yearns to act life's romance. This is the chance. The fundamental absurdity of the comedy is that in painstakingly proving that she will save Bluntschli, Raina obscures for herself the basis upon which she is acting—her *kindness*. Her kindness to Bluntschli and his kindness to her make romance possible. Raina's absurdly romantic character makes a comic romance nearly inevitable.

When Catherine and Raina speak of Sergius in Act I he sounds like a successful, head-strong, and courageous patriot. His handsome looks suggest to them a fiery officer. An aristocrat, Sergius enjoys the engagement of a beautiful young woman of his station. Raina adores his portrait and honors him in person. Her mother strongly approves of him. In sum, Sergius seems an admirable man who is accustomed to hearing his praises sung.

In Act II Sergius returns from war. He is as we might expect. But he has an additional trait that afflicts some who expect extensive praise. Sergius is a devotee of epideictic judgment. He is concerned with whether people and actions of this world are honorable, not whether they are successful. Sergius's concern surfaces as soon as he enters the Petkoff's garden. Catherine brings up the cavalry charge:

> SERGIUS [*with grave irony*] Madam: it was the cradle and grave of my military reputation.
> CATHERINE. How so?
> SERGIUS. I won the battle the wrong way when our worthy Russian generals were losing the right way. In short, I upset their plans, and wounded their self esteem. Two Cossack colonels had their regiments routed on the most correct principles of scientific warfare. Two major-generals got killed strictly according to military etiquette. The two colonels are now major-generals; and I am still a simple major. . . . I have only waited for the peace to send in my resignation.

Success and honor have parted company in Sergius's travels. Sergius comes home, his honor unrecognized by the professionals who are his military superiors.

Sergius has succeeded in action without aid of knowledge. Experts have failed. His bravery is undeniably admirable. And, to Sergius, his bravery overcame all the correct principles. Thus, he has come to think that courage is not only honorable, but the only relevant consideration in a practical, dangerous situation. Sergius's war experience causes him to conflate epideictic and deliberative judgment. Sergius is an idealist, a man who possesses virtue *without consideration for practical contingencies*. This makes him comic. He almost invariably acts counter to practical concerns.

The distinction between Sergius's idealism and Raina's romanticism is important. The difference between the two shapes their respective comic actions. Raina seeks romance through heroic action. That is why she gave Bluntschli her elaborate proof. Sergius looks for virtuous character in action. That is why anyone who acts professionally is something of a coward and tradesman to him. He sees the skill and misses the virtue; "I have no ambition to shine as a tradesman." This difference between the two lovers begins to work against their heroic romance almost as soon as Raina enters the garden.

Petkoff and Sergius have encountered Bluntschli at the war's end. An exchange of horses for prisoners had acquainted them with Bluntschli's skills. Sergius relates the general outline he has learned of Bluntschli's escape from his cavalry charge. The picture Sergius draws is different from what Raina has in mind:

> Oh yes: quite a romance! He was serving in the very battery I so unprofessionally charged. Being a thorough soldier, he ran away like the rest of them, with our cavalry at his heels. To escape their sabres he climbed a waterpipe and made his way into the bedroom of a young Bulgarian lady. The young lady was enchanted by his persuasive commercial traveller's manners. She very modestly entertained him for an hour or so, and then called in her mother lest her conduct should appear unmaidenly. The old lady was equally fascinated. . . .

In one absurd stroke Sergius innocently obliterates the forced entry, the kindness Raina and Bluntschli shared, the fantastic romantic hospitality, Raina's bravery, and her defense of Sergius's honor. For this he substitutes a coward with a glib tongue. Raina is gullible and, perhaps, indiscreet. Catherine's years have not improved her wisdom. No wonder Raina later wishes to shock his propriety. Sergius *is* a walking sense of propriety, hopelessly unrequited in action and myopic about everybody else's.

Shortly after this the Petkoffs leave the garden to the two lovers. Sergius's character shapes the romance that follows. This is heroic romance as Sergius conceives it. Romantic love, as Raina thinks of it, is squeezed out:

> SERGIUS [*hastening to her*] Am I forgiven?
> RAINA [*placing her hands on his shoulders as she looks up at him with admiration and worship*] My hero! My king!
> SERGIUS. My queen! [*He kisses her on the forehead*].
> RAINA. How I envied you Sergius! You have been out in the world, . . . I have had to sit home inactive—dreaming—useless—doing nothing that could give me the right to call myself worthy of any man.
> SERGIUS. Dearest: all my deeds have been yours. You inspired me. . . .

RAINA. When I think of you, I feel I could never do a base deed, or think an ignoble thought.
SERGIUS. My lady and my saint! [*He clasps her reverently*]
RAINA [*returning his embrace*] My lord and my—
SERGIUS. Sh-sh! Let me be the worshipper, dear. You little know how unworthy even the best man is of a girl's pure passion.
RAINA. I trust you. I love you. You will never disappoint me, Sergius.

Unable to speak of her one heroic action, Raina can only wish for some action that would ennoble her. Sergius's idealism pushes the romance to comic destruction. His concern with character so constricts the affair that acts of love are impossible! The romance is absurd for this reason. But it is comically self-destructive in relation to its participants' desires. Raina is in exactly the same position as when she learned of Sergius's charge. All she can do is sing his praise. Sergius is no better off. He wants honor. But the romance forces him to subordinate his worth to Raina's. Thus he turns to Louka in relief. With her, at least, his superiority is unquestionable.

Sergius takes Louka's hand after Raina leaves. This act by Sergius immediately provokes characteristic thoughts:

> SERGIUS [*coming clear of the table and drawing her with him*] I am surprised at myself, Louka. What would Sergius, the hero of Slivnitza, say if he saw me now? What would Sergius, the apostle of the higher love, say if he saw me now? . . . Do you consider my figure handsome, Louka?

Unchecked by speculation, he slips his arm around her waist. This is done without regard that they can be seen from the house. Louka sensibly points this out. Sergius's propriety rises to chasten her:

> LOUKA [*plaintively*] I may have been seen from the windows: Miss Raina is sure to be spying after you.
> SERGIUS [*stung: letting her go*] Take care, Louka. I may be worthless enough to betray the higher love; but do not you insult it.

Sergius tries to kiss her. At that point Louka reveals Raina's "indiscretion" because the chastening is presumptuous and the love-making insincere:

> LOUKA [*avoiding him*] No: I dont want your kisses. Gentlefolk are all alike: you making love to me behind Miss Raina's back; and she doing the same behind yours.

Louka's revelation does not make Sergius angry with Raina. His primary concern is to avenge the slight to his honor that Raina's transgression represents:

> SERGIUS [. . . *with deep bitterness*] [I am] a coward: jealous, like all cowards, Louka.
> LOUKA. Yes?
> SERGIUS. Who is my rival? . . .
> LOUKA. I dont know. I never saw him. I only heard his voice through the door of her room.

He becomes angry with Louka because she cannot tell him who his rival is. To vent his frustration he accuses her of eavesdropping. The action of Sergius's quest for honor begins with this insult and Louka's retort:

> SERGIUS. Damnation. How dare you?
> LOUKA [*retreating*] Oh, I mean no harm: youve no right to take up my words like that. The mistress knows all about it. And I tell you that if the gentleman ever comes here again, Miss Raina will marry him, . . . I know the difference between the sort of manner you and she put on before one another and the real manner.
> *Sergius shivers as if she had stabbed him.*

Prior to this moment Sergius acts out of relief, lust and "chivalric" jealousy. His turn to Louka strikes him as different than an abstract exercise of virtue; but his speculations do not stop him from acting. He finds his actions enjoyable, his qualifications suitable. He can reflect on these romantic actions just as he reflects on the worthiness of everybody else's actions and qualifications. He is the only judge.

Now Louka's speech challenges Sergius's real motivation. She calls his action to account. Sergius acts to prove his honor. Thereafter, he uses his strength, tongue, chivalry and station with Louka. But Louka calls all of these into question:

> LOUKA [*her eyes filling with tears in spite of herself*] No: I want my hurt made well.
> SERGIUS [*sobered by her tone*] How?
> *She rolls up her left sleeve; clasps her arm with the thumb and fingers of her right hand; and looks down at the bruise. Then she raises her head and looks straight at him. Finally, with a superb gesture, she presents her arm to be kissed.*

Sergius refuses. The scene ends seriously. Louka is in painful dignity, Sergius rudely crossed. But her steadfast ability to call his honor into question, facilitated by her attractions, brings Sergius back to her in Act III. All the elements of a comedy are there except an overriding absurdity because Sergius has provoked Louka through his habitual concern with honor.

He provides the absurdity in his return to her. Louka's challenge of his honor reversed the relative advantage Sergius enjoyed over her on account of his superior social position. With a little time to think, Sergius has reformulated the incident in the garden. Now the bruising has become part of his love-making:

> SERGIUS. Shall I cure it?
> LOUKA [*instantly withdrawing herself proudly, but still not looking at him*] No. You cannot cure it now.
> SERGIUS [*masterfully*] Quite sure? [*He makes a movement to take her in his arms*].
> LOUKA. Dont trifle with me, please. An officer should not trifle with a servant.
> SERGIUS [*indicating the bruise with a merciless stroke of his finger*] That was no trifle, Louka.

Sergius is trying to regain his superiority, his honor, by making love to her. This converts the seriousness of the previous scene to the comic action of this scene. In his heroic romance with Raina, Sergius must accept the "unworthier" position because the romance precludes action that would make him noble. He turns to Louka and insults her. Thus, he loses the upper hand with her. She challenges him to measure up. Thus far he has failed to do so. Now, Sergius decides he has taken an action (making love) which will make a difference in his nobility. But what hope does Sergius have of regaining his honor when the judge he appeals to is the plaintiff?

Louka is merciful. She will grant him clemency if he will admit they are equal. He will not stoop to apologize. So, Louka decides to prove their equality. She picks for her proof the one ground on which Sergius prides himself—bravery. She gets him to admit that the poor men, like her father, are just as brave as the rich like himself. But this is not brave enough for Sergius. He proposes for Louka a formula for bravery that only he could come up with: "Oh, [*fervently*] give me the man who will defy to the death any power on earth or in heaven that sets itself up against his own will and conscience: he alone is the brave man." Louka supplies him with such a test. She supposes that she were the Empress of Russia. She declares she would marry any man she chose, no matter what anyone thought. Then, Louka dares him to do the same. Her dare has as much substance as his formula;

but Sergius does not fix on that. Yet, surprisingly he picks what looks like a practical consideration as a barrier to the test—his engagement. But this is an objection to the qualifications of the judge, Louka, not a practical difficulty!

> SERGIUS [*bounding up*] You lie: it is not so, by all the stars! If I loved you, and I were the Czar himself, I would set you on the throne by my side. You know I love another woman, a woman as high above you as heaven is above earth. And you are jealous of her.

Louka sweeps this away by revealing that Bluntschli is his rival. Reminded again of Raina and her inferior position, she now wants Sergius to propose marriage to her before Bluntschli and Raina are affianced. She wants the satisfaction of raising herself to Raina's station as positive proof of Sergius's sincerity:

> LOUKA. . . . She will marry the Swiss.
> SERGIUS [*recoiling*] The Swiss!
> LOUKA. A man worth ten of you. Then you can come to see me; and I will refuse you. You are not good enough for me. [*She turns to the door*].
> SERGIUS [*springing after her and catching her fiercely in his arms*] I will kill the Swiss; and afterwards I will do as I please with you. . . . I will not be a coward and a trifler. If I choose to love you, I dare marry you, in spite of all Bulgaria. If these hands ever touch you again, they shall touch my affianced bride.

Sergius joins the opportunities to defy death and to defy all other earthly powers. What is funny here is not just Sergius, but the whole action. He has accepted as a test of his honor and courage a dare to marry. Recall, for a moment, King Edward VIII, who abdicated his throne. He was not trying to test his courage by marrying; he was only following his love, for which stubborn courage was required. Sergius has the cart before the horse. He has made an additional comic mistake. He has expanded Louka's dare far beyond its original bounds in his decision to duel Bluntschli. This commits him to a test against a man far better equipped to fight than Sergius is.

These two absurd mistakes join all the potentialities of his character to the action. Some of the unity and beauty of the comedy begins to reveal itself through those mistakes. The part of the prologue which involved Sergius now becomes necessary for the comedy instead of satire on war or heroics. Without the charge, without Sergius thinking success and honor had parted, without his desire to have his honor acknowledged, without his concern for character, without his hopeless heroic love, without his flirtation with Louka, none of this would have been possible or comic.

However, the beauty of Sergius's comic pursuit of honor depends on more than the consonance of these potentials with the action. The action has taken on a ridiculous inevitability that is far more complex than Sergius's plans. There are three points on which his test of bravery and honor depends. He must have a duel. He must act out of a noble reason. He must survive to marry Louka. In these three points we can see how the *comedy* shapes events in the play. If there is to be a comedy and if Sergius is to survive, it is not likely he will fight Bluntschli. Were Bluntschli killed, that would destroy the comedy, not to mention Raina's and Bluntschli's romance. But also, were Sergius to survive as Bluntschli indicates he would, then Sergius would have ignobly failed the first part of his test:

> BLUNTSCHLI . . . No harm will be done: Ive often acted as a sword instructor. He wont be able to touch me; and I'll not hurt him.

This too would destroy the comedy. How does Shaw preserve the comedy and still allow Sergius to prove his honor and bravery? The solution is to thwart the duel. The only way to do this is to nullify Sergius's noble reason without nullifying its nobility in his eyes. No reason, no duel, no loss of honor:

> SERGIUS. . . . Bluntschli: you knew our relations; and you deceived me. It is for that I call you to account, not for having received favors *I* never enjoyed.
> BLUNTSCHLI [*jumping up indignantly*] Stuff! Rubbish! I have received no favors. Why the young lady doesnt even know whether I'm married or not.
> RAINA [*forgetting herself*] Oh! [*Collapsing onto the ottoman*] Are you?
> SERGIUS. You see the young lady's concern, Captain Bluntschli. Denial is useless. You have enjoyed the privilege of being received in her own room, late at night—
> BLUNTSCHLI [*interrupting him pepperily*] Yes, you blockhead! she received me with a pistol at her head. I'd have blown out her brains if she'd uttered a cry.
> SERGIUS [*taken aback*] Bluntschli! Raina: is this true?
> RAINA [*rising in wrathful majesty*] Oh, how dare you, how dare you.

Before this Bluntschli threatened to ruin the nobility of Sergius's quest by proposing, out of kindness, to gratify Sergius not by fighting to the death—but by exhausting him in the fight. Undaunted, Sergius pressed on. Here, he attacks Bluntschli on a point of honor in which he feels superior. He has been deceived. With this in mind Sergius tries to test Bluntschli's character by forcing him to duel. Raina's reaction confirms Sergius's thinking. He pushes on and comes to face his own ignorance of the incident. Bluntschli confirms he used desperate tactics to save himself. Sergius's noble reason vanishes, but not because Bluntschli is guiltless of deception. What Sergius recognizes from Bluntschli's revelation he states shortly after:

> I refuse to fight you. Do you know why? . . . You shall hear the reason . . . my professional. The reason is that it takes two men—real men—men of heart, blood and honor—to make a genuine combat. I could no more fight with you than I could make love to an ugly woman. Youve no magnetism: youre not a man: youre a machine.

Bluntschli's desperate action with Raina makes the Swiss completely unworthy of a duel. Sergius discovers Bluntschli's skills and tactics as the whole of the Swiss' character. He absurdly eliminates Bluntschli's kindness in offering not to kill Sergius, the courage Bluntschli shows in accepting the duel, and his confidence in doing so. Sergius does this because his conception of bravery excludes the possibility of a courageous man, possessing these skills and other virtues, acting confidently in a fashion other than the outcome Sergius foresees. To Sergius, a brave man's function is to face death regardless of any other human or practical concerns. The professional, skillful man evidently acts to avoid death when he could so easily inflict it. Sergius knows he is willing to face death. So, Sergius not only excludes character from his judgment of Bluntschli—discovering in him not a man, but a machine—in addition Sergius discovers his own soul. His "superiority" to Bluntschli as a man is the difference which accounts for the actions each takes: ". . . it takes two men—real men—men of heart, blood and honor—to make a genuine combat."

Sergius's discovery is a true and probable comic reversal of his action. The whole ground of the challenge was to prove himself the better man. Now with the bald facts of Bluntschli's action and "character" Sergius draws the conclusion that he is already the courageous man and no duel is necessary. His conclusion is comic. But what is even funnier is the whole preposterous way he proves his superiority—not by a duel as he planned, but by refusing to fight! With his honor secure in the face of death, he need only touch Louka's hand to complete the test.

Sergius's romance proves his manhood through an absurd pursuit of honor and courage. Raina's romance of Bluntschli culminates when he discovers she is a woman who has been making love to him. Looked at this way, the action of their romance is two incidents. One incident is composed of a series of revelations by Raina which Bluntschli fails to understand. The other incident is his discovery when he learns she is twenty-three.

There are simple reasons why he misses what she has been doing. She is engaged. He thinks she is seventeen. Until his discovery Bluntschli takes Raina seriously as an adult takes a child. He constantly seeks to enhance her pleasures and reduce her pains. This unconscious, unaffected concern on his part is the foil for Raina's comic frustration in trying to get Bluntschli to take her seriously as a lover. But if Raina's attempt to make love and Bluntschli's later discovery of her pursuit is comic, these reasons are not enough to cause much mirth. The fact is that Raina's absurd attempt to make love makes it impossible for Bluntschli to see the truth. Yet, what makes his discovery comic is that he, of all people, ought to have recognized Raina's overtures.

With Bluntschli's return Raina begins to make love to him. Wherefore? Sergius's sense of propriety has made mincemeat out of her saving Bluntschli. Their heroic romance is starved for action. She has seen Sergius and Louka flirting. Finally, she has given and received kindnesses with Bluntschli. Archer had objected that Raina too quickly transferred her affections. Shaw replied to him in a letter:

> "Did Raina love Sergius and then *transfer* that love to Bluntschli; or did she, after imaginatively living up to an ideal relation with Sergius, and conceiving a sub-conscious dislike for him under the strain, fall in love for the first time with Bluntschli?" Mrs. Archer will tell you that the latter is the true solution, and that it is writ large in the play. . . .[9]

Yet, subsequent criticism has tended to see a transfer of loyalty by Raina from Sergius to Bluntschli in Act III.[10]

But the way she goes about making love to Bluntschli is far closer to Shaw's view of her. She begins by revealing that the escape incident is known and then continues:

> But they dont know it was in this house you took refuge. If Sergius knew he would challenge you and kill you in a duel.
> BLUNTSCHLI. Bless me! then dont tell him.
> RAINA. Please be serious, Captain Bluntschli. Can you not realize what it is to me to deceive him? I want to be quite perfect with Sergius:

no meanness, no smallness, no deceit. My relation to him is the only really beautiful and noble part of my life. I hope you can understand that.

BLUNTSCHLI [sceptically] You mean you wouldnt like him to find out that the story about the ice pudding was a—a—a You know.

RAINA [wincing] Ah, dont talk of it in that flippant way. I lied: I know it. But I did it to save your life. He would have killed you. That was the second time I ever uttered a falsehood. [*Bluntschli rises quickly and looks doubtfully and somewhat severely at her*] Do you remember the first time?

BLUNTSCHLI. I! No. Was I present!

RAINA. Yes; and I told the officer who was searching for you that you were not present.

BLUNTSCHLI. True. I should have remembered it.

RAINA [*greatly encouraged*] Ah, it is natural that you should forget it first. It cost you nothing: it cost me a lie! A lie!!

Raina is making love to Bluntschli by making it look as if she is saving him again. She knows the power of the noble attitude in romance with other men—it worked. She has used heroic "action" to save Bluntschli before. Making love to him by saving him is too much to resist. But her strategy is not that simple. She is more noble than that. To protect Bluntschli she will sacrifice her perfect love and principles of truthfulness—her character—in one selfless romantic *act*. In short, she is making herself even more worthy of Bluntschli than her original simple act of saving him. That is why she is greatly encouraged when she misses his irony. She sees a chance to emphasize her nobility. Raina *has no* romantic loyalty to Sergius; she is positively casting him adrift. She is completely out of Sergius's world. He makes love for the sake of nobility. Raina makes herself noble for the sake of love.

This episode is the romantic's culmination of romance like the *Ernani* episode in Act I was the romantic's culmination of war. But Raina's act *of kindness* in Act I was not ridiculous; only her character and reasoning were. Here her act of making love is ridiculous through both its means and consequences. Instead of securing Bluntschli's love, she supposes that she earns only his ingratitude:

> *Bluntschli, quite touched, goes to the ottoman with a particularly reassuring and considerate air, and sits down beside her.*
> BLUNTSCHLI. My dear young lady, dont let this worry you. . . . Now what are the two things that happen to a soldier so often that he comes to think nothing of them? One is hearing people tell lies [*Raina recoils*]: the other is getting his life saved in all sorts of ways by all sorts of people.

> RAINA [*rising in indignant protest*] And so he becomes a creature inca-
> pable of faith and of gratitude.

Raina's love-making directs Bluntschli's attention to the apparent remorse she feels over her loss of character. Bluntschli responds to the
remorse, and not to the "sacrifice" she is making. The strategy becomes absurdly worthless. So, she decides to rely exclusively on her
character by forcing Bluntschli to see that her lie was for his sake:

> RAINA . . . Oh, I see now exactly what you think of me. You were not
> surprised to hear me lie. To you it was something I probably did every
> day! every hour!

But the absurdity of her statements force Bluntschli to concentrate
on what she says, not what she is doing. He pushes her to the point
where the only thing she can do is defend her "character":

> BLUNTSCHLI . . . When you strike that noble attitude and speak in
> that thrilling voice, I admire you; but I find it impossible to believe a
> single word you say. . . .
> RAINA [*standing over him, as if she could not believe her senses*] Do you
> know what you said just now? Do you know what you said just now?
> BLUNTSCHLI. I do.
> RAINA [*gasping*] I! I!! [*She points to herself incredulously, meaning "I,
> Raina Petkoff, tell lies!" He meets her gaze unflinchingly. She suddenly sits
> down beside him and adds, with a complete change of manner from the heroic
> to a babyish familiarity*] How did you find me out?

Everything she has done has worked against her purpose. As with
Sergius, her heroic love has left her incapable of acting life's romance.

Pleasant consequences, unforeseen by Raina, emerge from this failure. She learns, to her surprise, Bluntschli treats her seriously:

> RAINA [*wonderingly*] Do you know, you are the first man I ever met
> who did not take me seriously?
> BLUNTSCHLI. You mean, dont you, that I am the first man that has
> ever taken you quite seriously?
> RAINA. Yes: I suppose I do mean that. [*Cosily, quite at ease with him*]
> How strange it is to be talked to in such a way!

But, reflection on her disastrous efforts causes her to rebuke herself.
To her relief she learns that Bluntschli does not despise her, but truly
admires her:

> RAINA. . . . [*Discouraged*] . . . I suppose, now youve found me out, you
> despise me.
> BLUNTSCHLI [*warmly, rising*] No, my dear young lady, . . . I'm like all
> the rest of them: the nurse, your parents, Sergius: I'm your infatuated
> admirer.
> RAINA [*pleased*] Really?
> BLUNTSCHLI [*slapping his breast smartly with his hand, German fashion*]
> Hand aufs Herz! Really and truly.
> RAINA [*very happy*] But what did you think of me for giving you my
> portrait?

Raina mistakenly thinks progress has been made. But the questions
about the picture prove no more fruitful in advancing her love.
Forced to admit that she wrote something on the back of it, Raina
reaches a low point in her love-making efforts:

> RAINA [*vexed almost to tears*] Oh, to have done such a thing for you,
> who care no more—except to laugh at me—oh!

No wonder she finally gives up with "Oh, I wish I had never met you."
   All her efforts comically delay Bluntschli's discovery of her love for
him. Yet, her failures are the basis on which he discovers this later. At
the point of the discovery Bluntschli says: "If you were twenty-three
when you said those things to me this afternoon, I shall take them
seriously." It seems to me that there are only three things which Raina
said which could possibly overcome the image of Raina "full of fairy
princes" that Bluntschli entertains. The first is her delight in being
taken seriously. The second is her pleasure in his admiration. The
third is her dismay in supposing he is laughing at her. Each of these
involves a sense of kindness extended and received between them.
Taken at their true value they reveal to Bluntschli that a romantic like
Raina makes love by heroic manners, by ruffled feathers, and by giving a shared token of their danger.
   What is ultimately comic about Bluntschli's discovery, then, is that
the supreme romantic Bluntschli needs to be told how old a woman
is before he recognizes a romantic action. To him romance is joining
the army, climbing a balcony, taking a peek at Raina. These are boys'
tricks in an adult world:

> BLUNTSCHLI. . . . [I am] a vagabond, a man who has spoiled all his
> chances through an incurably romantic disposition, . . . I went into the
> army instead of my father's business. I climbed the balcony of this
> house when a man of sense would have dived into the nearest cellar. I
> came sneaking back here to have another look at the young lady. . . .

But when confronted with a woman trying to make love in a child's manner, Bluntschli cannot see the obvious:

> BLUNTSCHLI. . . . Do you suppose I am the sort of fellow a young girl falls in love with? Why look at our ages! I'm thirty-four: I dont suppose the young lady is much over seventeen. . . . All that adventure which was life and death to me, was only a schoolgirl's game to her—chocolate creams and hide and seek. Heres the proof! [He takes the photograph from the table]. Now, I ask you, would a woman who took the affair seriously have sent me this and written on it "Raina, to her Chocolate Cream Soldier: a Souvenir"? . . .
> RAINA [*going to the table to face him*] I quite agree with your account of yourself. You are a romantic idiot. . . . Next time, I hope you will know the difference between a schoolgirl of seventeen and a woman of twenty-three.[11]

The two lines of action of this play differ substantially in the comic unity they attain. They also differ in what each requires for comic completion. In Act I Raina's absurd claim that Bluntschli should have thrown himself at her feet merged her kindness, heroic manners and romantic disposition by means of the comedy. The ridiculous attempt to make love to Bluntschli depends on this. But neither the prologue, nor Raina's attempt, carry sufficient force in themselves to provoke his recognition of Raina's love-making. Shaw relies on a disguised "deus ex machina" to make the discovery possible:

> CATHERINE. Louka: you have been telling stories.
> LOUKA. I have done Raina no harm.
> CATHERINE [*haughtily*] Raina!
> LOUKA. I have a right to call her Raina: she calls me Louka. I told Major Saranoff she would never marry him if the Swiss gentleman came back.
> BLUNTSCHLI [*rising, much surprised*] Hallo!

The reason Shaw must use this device is that the comedy of Raina's romance has rested on her self-defeating manner. Why construct the comedy this way? Because the very basis of the romance—their shared kindness in Act I—is all that is necessary for the romance to happen once Raina begins to make love. Without the self-defeating manner Raina would quickly conquer her man. Once Shaw was committed to a comic romance, he could only delay. He exhausts the inherent potential by the end of Bluntschli's and Raina's interview in Act III. Thereafter, he uses the challenge of Sergius, Louka's listening, and Petkoff's discovery of the picture to put off Bluntschli's dis-

covery.[12] Totally thwarted, there is nothing Raina can do unless someone clues in Bluntschli to what is going on. In effect, his memory
needs to be jolted. Thus, when Bluntschli makes his discovery it
comes through Louka's and Sergius's romance, not through the efforts of either Raina or Bluntschli. The unity then, is achieved by his
character—his memory and boyishness—not by the action of the romance. That boyishness brought him back to Raina. But it has had
nothing to do with her frustration in getting him to take her seriously.
In consequence the comedy is reduced.

If this seems picky, or dubious, compare it to Sergius's and Louka's
romance. There you can see a couple of deeds which generate and
require Sergius's discovery in order to complete the action. These
deeds are Sergius's acceptance of Louka's absurd challenge and his
extension of it to dueling Bluntschli. These actions force Sergius to
discover his superiority as a man. Raina's attempt to make love to
Bluntschli does not force him to see that she is serious.

Sergius's discovery that he is brave and that all he needs to do is to
acknowledge this himself is conditioned by his character. The discovery of Bluntschli is made by his memory after Louka points out what
the situation is. Sergius's discovery depends on his memory of the
charge, his sense of honor, his reasoning of what would be *most*
brave—his entire idealistic character. The discovery takes place because he is in a battle of wits with Louka. All this serves his struggle
to redeem his honor in Louka's eyes. The discoveries that he is a better man than Bluntschli and engaged to Louka by a touch of her hand
are comically dependent on the action he is undertaking—not merely
who he is. The consequences of these discoveries are truly preposterous. Sergius proves his bravery by not fighting, and his superiority by
being equal. The magnitude of his comic romance with Louka—its
preposterousness—is greater for having been achieved in an action
unified by and uniting all the elements that go into making the
comedy.

Shaw's achievement in *Arms and the Man* was considerable. In Sergius and Louka he took traits of character that would normally stymie
action and used them to produce a comic action. This action allows
Sergius to achieve what he most desires—recognized honor. In *Arms*
Shaw imitates a world of men and women who are actuated by desire,
but who require more than its satisfaction. These characters, whatever lights they are guided by, are required to think things through
to get their rewards. They have habits which condition their thought.
Such is the case in their inclinations to romantic and idealistic folly.
They have motives which are, in part, a key to future developments

of Shavian comedy in later plays. Look at Sergius. His motive is not just to be brave, but to be brave in a particular and foolish way. His motive entails his experience and a view of life which is woefully out of proportion to any practical consideration. In other words, it is preposterous. Raina is different. Her motive is not preposterous. But what she thinks will best serve her motive, her talent for heroics, is absurdly contrary to her romantic aspirations as anything could be.

So, if the quality of Shaw's comedy is preposterous, it is so based upon the values these characters hold and the valuelessness of the romantic actions they take. That valuelessness depends on *doing* what they *think* they are good at: on Sergius's undertaking a proof of bravery when he is already a humanly brave soul, on Raina's undertaking a heroic romance with Bluntschli when all she needs is her kindness. Shaw's defense of the play speaks to this:

> I demand respect, interest, affection for human nature as it is and life as we must live it even when we have bettered it and ourselves to the utmost. . . . I shall continue to put [men and women] on the stage as they are to the best of my ability, in the hope that some day it may strike [the audience] that if they were to try a little self-respect, and stop calling themselves offensive names, they would discover that the affection of their friends, wives and sweethearts is not a reasoned tribute to their virtues, but a human impulse towards their very selves.[13]

To put this another way, the comedy and humanity of this play, and later Shavian comedies, depends on the folly of doing something well, so thoroughly, that the characters almost lose sight of what most touches "their very selves." This is an especially benign yet revealing comic vision. And it requires a unity to see its beauty.

# Notes

1. William Archer, "Arms and the Man," *The Theatrical 'World' of 1894* (London: Walter Scott, 1895), pp. 110–11.

2. Ibid., pp. 116–17.

3. George Bernard Shaw, "A Dramatic Realist to His Critics," *Shaw on Theatre*, ed. by E. J. West (New York: Hill and Wang, 1958), p. 23.

4. Ibid., p. 34.

5. Archibald Henderson continued the distinction between the first and last two acts by referring to two points of view to be taken on the play. *George Bernard Shaw, His*

*Life and Works: A Critical Biography* (Cincinnati: Stewart & Kidd Co., 1911), p. 310. Bentley takes up the argument of romanticism. *Bernard Shaw* (London: Methuen & Co., 1960), p. 168. Martin Meisel merges the conventions of military romance with the common sense of Bluntschli. *Shaw and the Nineteenth Century Theatre* (Princeton: Princeton University Press, 1963), p. 194.

6. Charles A. Berst, *Bernard Shaw and the Art of Drama* (Urbana, Illinois: University of Illinois Press, 1973), p. 26.

7. The reader will, of course, notice that the breaking of the match between Louka and Nicola is not mentioned as a story line. The reasons are two. First, Louka would marry Sergius whether or not she was engaged to Nicola. Their engagement makes no difference to her actions at all. For example, in Act III she is listening at the door to Sergius, Raina, and Bluntschli because "My love was at stake." Further, Nicola knows she would make a match with Sergius: "I've often thought that if Raina were out of the way, and you a little less of a fool and Sergius just a little more of one, you might become one of my grandest customers, . . ." (Act III). Second, Nicola's primary concern is to start a shop in Sofia. The only step he actually takes toward this is accepting Louka's romance with Sergius. Nicola's story, if it is to be called that, is nothing more than maintaining his character as a servant in order to succeed in business. The primary function of Nicola in the play is to show us his character so that we can see that, truly, Louka has the qualities which enable her to rise. Nicola has no such pretensions. Hence, he does not mourn Louka's loss.

8. Shaw, *Shaw on Theatre*, p. 39.

9. George Bernard Shaw, *Collected Letters 1874–1897*, ed. by Dan H. Laurence (London: Max Reinhardt, 1965), p. 429.

10. Berst sees Raina "clinging to the last vestiges of her heroic romance with Sergius" at the beginning of Act III. Bentley sees a "decisive turn" with Raina's remark, "How did you find me out?" in which "Raina passes over for ever from Sergius' world to Bluntschli's." *Bernard Shaw*, p. 167.

11. Many commentators have pointed out that Raina and Sergius are disillusioned. But, in fact, though the Bulgarians constantly run up against one reality after another, they continue to act romantically or idealistically. As Shaw points out (*Shaw on Theatre*, p. 36):

> And so the idealist in my play continues to admit nightly that his bull terrier, which will fight as fiercely as a soldier, will let himself be thrashed as helplessly by the man in authority over him. . . . The observation is made in the play in a manner dramatically appropriate to the character of an idealist who is made a pessimist by the shattering of his illusions. His conclusion is that "life is a farce." My conclusion is (different).

To the end of the play this is true. What is Sergius's test of bravery and acceptance of Louka if not a romantic fulfillment of his idealistic test of honor? What is Raina's tearing up of the photograph in Bluntschli's face, if not romantic anger over treating her attempts to love him as if they were juvenile? The fact is that of all the people who are disillusioned, Bluntschli is the most thoroughly. Only he acts forthrightly on the basis of his discovery of what is going on.

12. Elder Olson has pointed this out in *The Theory of Comedy* (Bloomington, Indiana: Indiana University Press, 1968), p. 121.

13. Shaw, *Shaw on Theatre*, pp. 38–39.

Paul Sawyer

# THE LAST LINE OF
# *ARMS AND THE MAN*

*Arms and the Man* is unique among Shaw's plays in several respects: 1) it was the first of his plays to be produced in a commercial theatre; 2) it was the first of his plays to be acted in America; 3) it is the only one to be translated into Basic English; and 4) it is the only Shaw play to be printed with three different final curtain lines. This brief note will address itself to the last "respect."

Since *Arms and the Man* was written to order and in some haste to comply with Florence Farr's desire to present a new play by Shaw in a season of "New Dramatists" at London's Avenue Theatre, in 1894, it is not surprising that Shaw was not completely satisfied with the ending of the play, which opened on April 21. Of course Shavian revisions—substantial deletions, accretions, and less lengthy rewordings—are quite frequent as Shaw worked on editions or new performances of his plays. But in no other play did he tinker so much with the last line.

The original last line is "What a man! What a man!" It is found in Shaw's handwritten copy of the play now in the British Museum. It is also in a typescript of the play, on the title page of the first act on which Shaw has written his name; this typescript is now in the possession of the Beinecke Rare Book and Manuscript Library of Yale University. This copy of the play was obviously made for acting and each act has a tattered wrapper around it. It is this last line ("What a man! What a man!") that appears in the first printed version of the play in Volume II of *Plays Pleasant and Unpleasant* published by Grant Richards in 1898.

For 27 years after the initial publication of the play, and 31 after its initial production, the same line served as the basic ending, but obviously Shaw was not happy with it. The typescript-promptbook for the Theatre Guild production of *Arms and the Man* in New York in 1925, now part of the Billy Rose Theatre Collection of the Performing Arts Research Center of the New York Public Library, reveals this displeasure. In it the second exclamatory sentence of "What a man! What a man!" is crossed out by hand and the first has a superscripted asterisk handwritten after it, and slightly to the right of this asterisk is another handwritten asterisk and underneath it is handprinted CURTAIN with three underlines. This abbreviated last line was never incorporated into any printed version of the play, indicating that, like the tag line it replaced, it did not meet Shaw's always exacting and often protean standards.

The next printed transformation of "What a man! What a man!" occurred in the *Collected Edition* 1930–1932 published by Constable, for which Shaw made hundreds of revisions. This text (as we are told in the Bodley Head edition, vol. 1, p. 5) without alteration was reset and published in 1931–1932 as the Standard Edition. Here the last line becomes "What a man! Is he a man?" And this new version is also printed in the competing edition of Shaw's work issued about the same time, the *Collected Works*, Ayot St. Lawrence edition, 1930. Four years later Odhams Press of London reproduced this text as *Complete Plays* and, of course, "What a man! Is he a man?" recurs.

But Shaw was still not content, and in a subsequent alteration of the Standard Edition he made a typographically small but inflectionally and emphatically very large change: "What a man! Is he a man?" becomes "What a man! Is he a man!" The second exclamation mark of the original last line has replaced the question mark, and the doubt about whether Bluntschli is really a human being is converted into a confident assertion of Bluntschli's extraordinary capability. It seems clear that this third ending more closely approaches the meaning of the original ending than the second one does. As early as 1950 in the Penguin edition of the play and 1951 in Dodd Mead's *Seven Plays by Bernard Shaw*, this *final* final ending is given.

It is this version—"What a man! Is he a man!"—which is found in the last printing, authorized by Shaw himself, of *Arms and the Man* in the *Standard Edition*. This version is part of what is now accepted as the definitive text, and appears in the authoritative Bodley Head Edition first published in 1970. But a large number of texts of *Arms and the Man*, many of them used by students, incorporate the earlier endings. For example, New American Library's Signet Classic *Plays by George Bernard Shaw* (no date, but the foreword by Eric Bentley is copyright 1960) carries the "What a man! What a man!" ending, as does *Playreader's Repertory: Drama on Stage*, edited by White and Whiting (Scott Foresman, 1970). Dodd Mead's *The Theatre of Bernard Shaw*, edited by Alan Downer (1961), has "What a man! Is he a man?" even though ten years before the Downer book was published the same publisher had used "What a man! Is he a man!" in its *Seven Plays by Bernard Shaw.* The reason for the persistence of the earliest ending is readily apparent: money. The first ending has been in the public domain in America for many years, since until the recent changes in the law, copyright material was protected in the United States for only 56 years, including renewal, rather than for the lifetime of the author plus 50 years, as at present. Hence, publishers could reproduce the play as originally printed in 1898 without cost. The continued use of "What a man! Is he a man?" can be explained by the easy availability of old plates with this ending, and the loophole in the law. Now required, of course, for the third and final ending as published in the *Bodley Head* text is the permission of the Shaw Estate and its publishers, and at least a courtesy fee not for these lines but for the entire play.

Nevertheless, in the last decades the third ending has been making progress and appears in such substantial editions of the play as the Penguin, the Bobbs-Merrill, and the *Composite Production Book* of *Arms and the Man* compiled and edited by Bernard F. Dukore (Southern Illinois University Press) in 1982.

# Holly Hill

# SAINT JOAN'S VOICES: ACTRESSES ON SHAW'S MAID

In 1934, Shaw wrote: "It is quite likely that sixty years' hence, every great English and American actress will have a shot at 'Saint Joan,' just as every great actor will have a shot at Hamlet."[1] Shaw's prediction began to come true almost immediately. Since 1936, when Katharine Cornell played the Maid on Broadway and Wendy Hiller at the Malvern Festival, only a partial list of notable Joans in English language productions includes Eileen Atkins, Zoe Caldwell, Frances de la Tour, Judi Dench, Uta Hagen, Barbara Jefford, Gemma Jones, Lauri Kennedy, Roberta Maxwell, Siobhan McKenna, Joan Plowright, Lynn Redgrave, and Kim Stanley.

It is much too late to interview such actors as Richard Burbage, David Garrick, Henry Irving, Edwin Booth, and John Barrymore to attempt a full record of actors' approaches to *Hamlet*. It is none too soon to begin such a study of *Saint Joan*. While Katharine Cornell and Shaw's original Maids—America's Winifred Lenihan and Britain's Sybil Thorndike—are gone, most notable interpreters of his Joan are still active. Four of Britain's most acclaimed Maids—Dame Wendy Hiller (Malvern Festival, 1936), Barbara Jefford (Old Vic and international tour 1960–62), Judi Dench (Nottingham Playhouse, 1966), and Eileen Atkins (Prospect Theatre Company at the Old Vic and on tour, 1977–78) granted me interviews in England during July 1983.

Whether the actresses were speaking directly to or wandering from a point, their responses to some twenty questions touched upon a range of subjects: the historical and Shaw's Joan, Shaw himself and his work, acting technique, theatre history, dramatic theory, changing cultural standards, theatrical anecdote, and personal revelation. Because I found comparison and contrast of answers even richer than each individual interview, I have arranged the following material as if it were an exchange rather than separate recordings of ideas and experiences.

# Interest in Shaw's and/or the Historical Joan

Joan of Arc has a place in the childhood memories of all four actresses. Wendy Hiller recalls being aware in her girlhood of Saint Joan as a historical figure alongside others such as William the Conqueror, Nurse Edith Cavell, and Robert the Bruce; Eileen Atkins remembers a prized book about Joan, Florence Nightingale, and stormy-seas heroine Grace Darling; Judi Dench recalls buying a statue of Joan as a child when her parents took her to Rheims and told her about Shaw's play. Of the four, however, only Barbara Jefford had an attachment to both the real and dramatized Joan from childhood:

> My very first memory of her was when I was about four. My mother, who was a frustrated actress, I think, belonged to some sort of Dramatic Society. One of the speeches she had to do was "You promised me my life; but you lied." I remember following her around the house as she practiced the lines. I had a very pronounced lisp when I was small, and they tell me I used to recite that speech with all my *s*'s missing. I grew up with it, not really knowing what it came from or was about. But as soon as I became conscious that I wanted to be an actress, *Saint Joan* was one of the roles I wanted to play.
>
> Also, at a very early stage of my career, I came into contact with Sybil Thorndike, who used to talk about how Shaw had insisted on every single line being given its absolute weight, how frustrating that was, and how the very first night he went away they took almost half an hour out of the running time. I think knowing Sybil was also an inspiration.
>
> I lived with Joan for such a long time. I had the date of her death in my diary for years. I have a lot of books about her, and not only from the period when I started to study her seriously because I knew I was going to play the part. Some of the books date from my teens and student days. I think my girlhood vision of her was a very romantic one, partly because of the pictures that were about of various actresses playing her.

# Reactions to Other Actresses' Interpretations

Though Wendy Hiller received a letter from Sybil Thorndike congratulating the twenty-two-year-old actress for being chosen to play the Maid and warning her to "'get away from the stained glass image'" and "'make her an ordinary girl,'" she comments: "I should imagine that I must have fallen into the trap that three-quarters of the Saint Joans do and falling all ethereal. Nonsense, nonsense, nonsense." While she never saw Sybil Thorndike's Joan and never discussed it with her even when they later played together in the film of *Major Barbara*, her perspective on the role over the decades is informed by readings from the play by its British originator:

> I've heard Sybil, who was quite unique, and the only actress of her time who could play it. And again and again I've heard her do a couple of speeches—the cathedral, the trial. And I've thought, "No, I don't think this would do for now."
>
> Because Sybil at one time, you know, though nobody could have admired her more than I, was mannered in her speech. Compared to actresses in the sixties, seventies, and eighties, she was very mannered. She was superb for her time, but with fashions and with everybody recreating in her own decade, I think she would be considered mannered now. Sybil never said "God." She always said "Go/oo/od." She always made it into three syllables.
>
> Everything changes, except that everything can be contradicted. Somebody's given me a record of the voice of Ellen Terry doing "the quality of mercy" speech. Now hers is a completely unmannered delivery. It might be a woman of the eighties. The speed that she uses is not as we think of Edwardian and Victorian actresses dwelling and lingering and trailing away. No, none of that. There is Ellen Terry fairly beating along with enormous vitality in the voice, and such beautiful, crisp phrasing. That is a revelation. She is not mannered. Darling Sybil—at that time I think she was a little mannered, and I think it was a good deal of her husband's influence—dearest Lewis—who had a very strange way of producing. He used to produce entirely by sound from behind a screen and used to make everybody follow his speech rhythm. And that might have been Lewis's influence. I never dared ask Sybil.

"Stained-glass," romanticized portrayals of Joan distressed Barbara Jefford and Judi Dench and almost kept Eileen Atkins from playing the Maid. Miss Jefford remembers "people going for the poetic and the saintly side too much. I've seen ladies play it who couldn't possibly have withstood what she had to physically." One of Judi Dench's reasons for accepting the role was that "I believe so strongly that she was a presumptuous, jumped-up girl. Actually amazingly presumptuous. I don't think I played any of it in an acceptably lyric, compassionate way."

Posing in a mock-sentimental attitude of piety, Eileen Atkins comments that:

I was terribly put off by that idea of it in productions of *Saint Joan* I'd seen when I was at school. I'm sure she was terrific in her own way, but I was bored by the idea of someone whom I saw as so goody-goody. I was offered it five, if not seven times before I did it. I turned it down because there seemed to be nothing to do with anything I might believe in myself. I did play, when I was very young, Shakespeare's Joan, and I did it out of perversity because she is such a bitch that I was really pleased to be doing another kind of Saint Joan, screaming as she's taken to the stake.

# How Each Actress Came to Play Joan

Miss Atkins relates that:

When I was thirty-five I was offered Shaw's Joan at a very good festival. I turned it down flat, saying I was now far too old, really. And then when I was thirty-nine they thought the Old Vic was going to be lost forever. Running it then was a friend of mine, Toby Robertson, a terrific and now a much maligned director. Nobody could have made the Vic work at that time because there wasn't a penny to spend on it, and the National and the RSC were determined that no classical company was going to go in there. I knew that was going on and I was very fond of Toby, and he said, "I'm really in a state. I need a play to open the season. Would you do a play for me?" And I said, "All right. I trust you, Toby. I trust you'll think of something and I'll almost certainly do a play for you."

The next thing I knew he'd rung me and said, "We've settled on *Saint Joan,*" and I nearly died. I said, "Toby, I've turned that down five-six-seven times. I hate it, and now I really am too old." And he replied, "Oh, rubbish. Absolute rubbish," and I couldn't do anything because it was a *fait accompli*. Then I said I'd do it only if they cut the line "How old are you?" in the first scene. I can't remember whether it was seventeen or eighteen, but it was a horribly young age. I remember sitting in the audience when a certain actress said that line and I died of shame for her, and he said, "All right, we'll cut that."

Judi Dench was asked to play Joan and several other roles when actor-director John Neville, with whom she had acted at the Old Vic, took over the artistic direction of the Nottingham Playhouse. Barbara Jefford, who joined the Vic as leading lady in 1957 when they were

still producing only Shakespeare, was invited to play both Joan and
Rosalind in 1960 by Artistic Director Michael Benthall. Wendy Hiller
was invited by Shaw himself to act at Malvern after Shaw had seen
her make her West End debut in *Love on the Dole,* a play by her future
husband, Ronald Gow:

> G.B.S. had seen me in London, and I was playing *Love on the Dole* in
> New York when I had a cable: Was there any chance of my coming
> over and playing Saint Joan for his eightieth birthday, which Barry
> Jackson was celebrating with the Malvern Festival? It was tiny as festi-
> vals go now, but I think it had the highest reputation. It would be like
> the Italian Spoleto at its height, or like Edinburgh for music. I was
> released from *Love on the Dole*—which I shouldn't as it was doing very
> well—and when I got on the boat to come home I got another cable:
> Would I also play Eliza Doolittle? So that was two plays of Shaw.

# Researching the Role

Except for Barbara Jefford, none of the actresses did research on
Joan. Said Judi Dench: "I never do that for anything, or I just fall up
the hole in the middle. I simply get so confused that I want to take
the best of everybody. In a way, then you don't do something very
instinctive. It's probably very arrogant of me to say that." Eileen Atkins concurred: "I only ever go from the script. I'm not somebody
who has ideas about a part separately and then fits them on. I don't
do readings outside or anything like that. I just take the script and do
it and think 'Now what is Shaw trying to say through her?'"

Wendy Hiller would not have had time for research if she'd
wished it:

> There were several plays done at the Malvern Festival, with a month's
> rehearsal. Not a month's rehearsal for each but for all, which one took
> entirely for granted. Young people look at me and obviously don't be-
> lieve me when I tell them it was six rehearsals and, if you were lucky,
> you got through half a dress. One day when I said "G.B.S., we've only
> had six rehearsals," he said, "Well, it's a very good play, dear. If you
> can't have six weeks, six will do." In other words, "Get on with my play
> and shut up." You see, he was a man of the theatre entirely practical.
> Entirely practical. I think he'd be rather staggered at the self-

indulgence of sitting around and talking about what you feel. His attitude was "I have written a play. Get on and do the best you can with
*my* play, and I want to hear every word."

I had never even seen Sybil. She'd been the great one. Then the play
had been done and knocked about a bit, and when they asked me to
do it at Malvern I was the first sort of big public one, so that was a
hideous responsibility. I was sensible enough to know that I'd got that
on my shoulders and round my neck. But as for starting talking about
what Saint Joan meant to the Catholic Church, to the medieval
Church, to the Church now, and how she stood in history, don't talk
nonsense. I had six rehearsals, and I had to get on with *Pygmalion*, too.
In other words, I was doing a job, and you don't sit around and talk
and indulge yourselves.

# Rehearsals

When asked what she recalled about the Malvern production, Dame
Wendy replied:

Don't be silly dear, nothing. It was 1936. The thing was learn your
lines, where you were going to move, not bump into the furniture—
well, there wasn't much—not bump into anybody else, and get on with
it. Fortunately the wonderful actor Ernest Thesiger had played the
Dauphin in Dame Sybil's great production, and he was with us. So he
just went on, if you know what I mean, which was a wonderful center-
piece because he knew exactly and wasn't going to alter one jot or tittle
and why should he? And we got on with it as best we could.

*Saint Joan* was very blessed and we did a word rehearsal in an empty
swimming bath, supervised by G.B.S., who told me to hurry up and
get on with it, there was no time to try and act with it. Then we managed half a dress rehearsal, but it went on too long so G.B.S., who had
brought out his great big gold watch and timed the Inquisitor's speech
as he always did, snapped it shut and went home. He came up to me
and said in his beautiful Dublin accent: "I didn't mean to be rude,
Wendy. There's so little time, and I've got to get back for lunch."

Judi Dench recalls the Inquisitor's speech well, confessing that:

We did a terrible joke. Harold Innocent played the Inquisitor. Do you
know his work from the National? A big man. He likes his voice a lot,

and we suspected he was listening to it a bit. And about two days before we opened—this is a terrible, terrible story—the company got together and asked John Neville to call a rehearsal of the trial in costume. So he did.

We ran up to the Inquisitor's speech, where Harold always started getting slower and slower. About three lines into the speech, Job Stewart, who was playing de Stogumber I believe, took from underneath his cassock a very small flask and a couple of cups and poured out some hot coffee and passed it along. And Ronnie McGill, who was playing the Bishop of Beauvais, got from underneath his costume an enormous piece of purple knitting and started to knit. And I just remember hearing a thud—it was John falling on the ground he laughed so much. Harold was frightfully cross, frightfully cross, and then we all laughed and he was wonderful about it and has told the story often. Everybody kind of apologized and he did do the speech marvelously well.

Eileen Atkins, shocked to learn that she had agreed to play *Saint Joan*, was further distressed to learn that Toby Robertson was not going to direct it:

> He'd got a director, John Dove, who didn't want to direct me, because most of the new young directors hate directing anyone who's very experienced and want to bring in one of their young girls from up North. So he didn't want to do it with me, and I didn't want to do it with him, and I didn't want to play it at all anyway. And as soon as we started on the play we were all crazy about it and each other and everything. In fact, once I started working on it I couldn't believe it.

# Aspects of Production

Miss Atkins relates that:

> The production was pretty awful the first time out, and my god we toured one-night stands all over Europe for two weeks. You had to tour for the Prospect Theatre Company, which was Toby Robertson's group, to get funding. Its brief was as a touring company, and it wasn't really supposed to come into London and play the Old Vic at all—when it appeared to be challenging the National and RSC its funding was cancelled altogether.

Before all that happened, however, we just shoved on *Saint Joan* and
many in the supporting cast were not good. Then we toured and it was
still a mess and the sets weren't right. All the same it was a success and
Toby said, "Please come back next season and do it again."

So I said well, yes, but John Dove said he didn't want to do it. I rang
him up and just gave him hell. I said, "How many times are you going
to get this opportunity in your life to have messed up something and
then get the chance to do it again? How dare you not do it again." He
was sort of browbeaten into the second production. Yes, just as Joan
might have done. Absolutely. The awful thing is that you do sort of get
like the parts you're playing. There is no doubt. The second season we
did it and it was a lot better. I was better the second time around.

In addition to John Neville's inspirational direction, Judi Dench recalls of her Nottingham production:

Patrick Robertson did the costumes and they were very, very workman-
like. They looked like people had worn them. My armor looked bat-
tered about and worn. If I were to do it again now I would want that
even more so, and that again is playing against that aura of all very
shining and precise. In our terms, now, I would want her to wear jeans
and armor made up from something like tin cans, and a bit of old
metal tied on somewhere. I somehow feel that that would be more
what it should be about.

The set was very, very black; very, very simple indeed. The same set
that we did *Measure for Measure* on. We never brought the curtain
down. It was very stark, and that was a wonderful help. Ronald Hines
played Warwick. It was a marvelous performance—very solid. It gave
the impression that you couldn't move him. The more in the play you
give the impression that people stand firm, then somehow the bigger
the battle.

Barbara Jefford praises her director, Douglas Seale:

He had made his name, I think, in a marvelous production of the
*Henry VI*s which we did at the Vic. I played Margaret. After that we
did *Saint Joan* together, and it was a wonderful bonus for me to have a
director whom I admired and had worked with before. I was given
every possible help I could have. I had an outstanding cast to play
with—Alec McCowen was the Dauphin and was absolutely splendid.
We had several changes of cast on the various tours. There was a great
deal of experience about, and I also had a certain amount of experience myself, and it was something I had longed to do for most of my
life.

We had a wonderful set by Leslie Hurry which was, as far as I remember, very simple. The cathedral was suggested by just a great big stained-glass window and a lot of candles. The Trial scene—I suppose there is only one way of doing it and that is to have them all up on one side of the stage in great tiers. I wouldn't call it stylized in the Granville-Barker sense. I would call it simple. There was nothing to get in the way of the actors. The form was minimal.

We played the Kingfisher scene, I remember, very, very close to the edge of the stage when we were at the Vic, but then in other places we had to rejig the whole thing. In Dubrovnik we played in one of the forts, and we played the Kingfisher scene up twenty-five steps on a battlement and one had to rush up there and rush down again. I played Joan on and off for about two years. After the Vic we toured to the U.S. and we also went to Russia, Poland, Yugoslavia, and Czechoslovakia.

One of the high spots was playing her at the Herod Atticus Theatre in Athens, which was stupendous. Quite wrong for the play really, because a lot of it is very personal with people talking to each other. It's very difficult, if you're in that sort of auditorium, not just to stand and deliver. We simply had to bellow at each other and kind of work out a way of talking to Dunois, for instance, or to the Dauphin, but at the same time give it a huge amount of power. The last time I played the part was in Cairo outside at the temple by the Pyramids, with the Sphinx in the background and guns being shot off because it was Mohammed's birthday. So when I was being condemned to death they were shooting guns in the air celebrating in the distance.

# Shaw's Stage Directions

The actresses gave great attention to Shaw's stage directions. Barbara Jefford recalls:

> Douglas Seale wasn't at that time by any means a traditionalist. He's a very quicksilver, very offbeat chap. I remember we kicked it around. It's almost a challenge when things are so specifically put down. Shaw is very specific in his instructions, so that it almost makes you feel bolshie about it and you want to do the opposite. You do and you rehearse and that's what rehearsals are for. We did try—especially when we were re-rehearsing it for touring—doing it some other ways, and we'd come back to the way Shaw had said to do it. It was best.

Shaw's stage directions were virtually the only guidance Wendy Hiller had in her harried six days of preparation for *Saint Joan:*

Except being told at the word rehearsal to get on with it, the only direction I had was a letter from G.B.S. I must be one of the last actresses alive who spoke to him and got a whole lot of correspondence talking about the part. He wrote and ticked me off right, left and center, quite beautifully. But he waited until after the first night because he knew I had no time to do anything.

He told me exactly what I did wrong, how I did it wrong, and why I did it wrong. And within the performances I had left, I tried to put it right. He said to get on with it. She was a peasant girl. She knew exactly what she was doing. She was practical. She was down-to-earth. I remember he put it frightfully funnily and then finished up saying, "Now I can't rewrite *Saint Joan* for you, dearest." He was a dear. He was absolutely wonderful to me. He obviously loved me, but jolly well had to tick me off because I wasn't playing his part right.

Dame Wendy, who sometimes reads Shaw's letter in special performances such as benefits or a program tailored for her by Michael Meyer, disclosed that she had a rejoinder to it. With a self-mocking tone and expression, she explains:

You know how we are at twenty-two—frightfully wise—so when he'd written me this long letter telling me I was making all these mistakes, I thought, "G.B.S. can't realize how difficult this part is, and anyway I'm off the stage for all that long time, and it's not really consistent, you see." So I dropped him a note and asked if I could go round to see him in the hotel at Malvern, and I went round and Charlotte and I talked for a bit. She was a darling, and said, "Now you want to talk to my husband, so I have some letters to write."

There we were in the sitting room and he said, "Now, Wendy, now what's the trouble? Did my letter upset you?" "Well," I said, "G.B.S., I do know what you're getting at and I know you're quite right. But," I said, "you know it's not consistent that character of yours." Twenty-two years old. Can you believe it?

"Well, my dear," he replied, "I'm sure you're probably right." He must have been laughing at me. Can't you imagine? He must have been laughing and laughing. He really must. I think I asked him one or two questions and went back and tried to get on with it. You see, it's very strangely placed, Saint Joan, and I didn't find it nearly as easy as Eliza Doolittle. I just longed for more rehearsals in *Joan*, and I felt I'd landed on Eliza, although I didn't know how to phrase it. I felt more comfortable on *Pygmalion* nights, though I think I got better in *Saint Joan*. Well, I couldn't have gotten worse.

If I'd had six rehearsals with G.B.S., I might have been heaps better. I should think I was pretty shocking, but I happened to be the right age, looked right, was sturdy, wasn't a West End actress. I was the next best thing, do you know? He had to put up with me. And he put up with me and he was a dear friend. He wasn't gentle, but he never would consciously hurt anybody. He never hurt me, no matter how crisp he was with me. But he just ticked me off good and proper and he gave me about six points which I suppose I put right within my limits of being twenty-two and having no director and having to get *Pygmalion* on, too.

# Interpreting Joan: Basic Approaches

An analytic approach to the character may compartmentalize Shaw's Maid into Joan the country girl, the soldier, the precocious intellectual, the saint and visionary. While able to distinguish these facets of the character for the purpose of discussion, the actresses found difficulty with no particular facet, nor any sense of conflict between them. Judi Dench expressed the most forceful personal vision of the Maid:

I played up the arrogance of her. I just feel that her assumptions are very, very arrogant. To assume, for instance, that Dunois is not leading the army correctly. Before a certain period, everyone believed that she was so saintly, that she was recognized as a saint right away. In actual fact, in the end, they have a very good case against her. What they say is quite right. She surely can't believe that she's not going to be burnt and not going to be imprisoned. She's naïve. She's amazingly naïve.

I think she's an uncomfortable person, like some people who are fighting for the right are very, very uncomfortable and not easy to be with. I don't think that people felt easy with Joan. I think they thought "she's an arrant nuisance, and she must somehow be got rid of." There are many pointers to that in the play, but I don't ever think that's been played up enough.

Barbara Jefford comments in the same vein:

I think the quote about Joan that I came to realize was probably the most important one is that "saints are very difficult to live with." She is a difficult person. She's always doing the wrong thing, saying the wrong thing at the wrong time. But this is because of her absolute conviction that what she's doing is right. She's an awkward person to everybody in the play and, finally, because of her intractable way of going about things, she is rejected by everybody.

I'm a very simple soul. I go straight down the line. I believe what the dramatist says. I don't mean to say I don't think about it, but it seems to me that in that sense she's not a complex but a simple character. Because anybody with such a one-track mind, who can go through battle and go literally through fire, has to be simple. And this is one of the words that Shaw uses a great deal. This is what they're always accusing her of not being. They're always accusing her of being devious. I don't believe that she is. I don't know, I find that when I'm an actress approaching a part, that if a character is simple, then you've got to think about her in a simple way. If she's devious, you've got to become devious and your whole attitude towards rehearsals and towards your director changes—if you're playing a more difficult and devious person you become more difficult and devious when you're working. It sounds arrogant, but at the time I played Joan she seemed perfectly natural to me. And I was given the right circumstances and every possible help I could have.

While avoiding a sentimental picture of Joan, Eileen Atkins found a different key to her character:

One of the things that affected me is a very funny thing, but it was crucial to my interpretation. I would call myself extremely religious but I don't go to any particular church. I'm fascinated by all of them. I have no particular religion but I have a sort of—I don't know—but how many people do you get to observe who have a kind of religious ecstasy, or feel they're in touch?

I have a very great friend who's a very weird man. Well, I'm saying he's very weird but he's an excellent clairvoyant. Now he's extremely fat, very unprepossessing to look at. He comes from the north of England and he's very practical. He will say to me [in a deep, throaty voice with a North Country accent], "I've put the potatoes on to boil, love, and you come up over the steam as Charlotte Brontë. Now it will come into your aura and you'll be offered Charlotte Brontë." And I say, "No, Kenny, if I were offered any of those Brontë sisters it may have been Emily but not Charlotte," and he'll get very angry if I don't believe him. And he's nearly always right.

He is clairvoyant. He does believe in spirits, but it is immensely practical. And one of the things I thought for Joan when she speaks to God is that to her God is very present; He is absolutely real. Therefore she doesn't have to go into another voice or suddenly go all holier than thou and all that. He's there and He's someone who talks to her and helps her.

Wendy Hiller believes that the basic qualities she brought to Joan were:

> Youth. Vitality. Enormous vitality. A peasant quality. And, when you consider what I said to G.B.S., I was as stupid as she. That's why I was right for her. That's how she did it, you see. Her youth and inexperience. And that's how I did it. How could any actress of, say, thirty-five, have come from America knowing they were going to do *Saint Joan* on six rehearsals? No, no. Gibber, gibber, and hysteria.

# Joan the Country Girl

In the British stage tradition of using regional accents for lower-class characters, each actress settled upon a dialect. Dame Wendy chose a "slight North Country. That's because I am North Country. I think it's best when done in a slight Irish accent, because G.B.S. was Irish. It's sheer poetry, all of it. Written in a wonderful rhythm. You can't leave out a syllable." Barbara Jefford "did it with a West Country accent because I come from the West of England and it all fitted very well. Absolutely down to earth: [in the accent] 'I'm a soldier.' She wanted to be treated like a man." Also following her native dialect, Judi Dench

> played her with a Yorkshire accent, which is where I come from, and it's a very brusque accent indeed, very much to the point. It gives in a way—I'm not saying Yorkshire people are intolerant, but the way I played her didn't leave much room for tolerance.
>
> It worries me a bit actually, accents. It worried me that a French girl should have an English dialect. There's no way Joan could come on speaking in a standard English accent. Therefore what do you do? Then you get the soldier coming from Hell at the end, usually Cockney. That just worries me. It always has. I don't know what the answer is.

Eileen Atkins came by her accent circuitously:

> I remember that when Alec Guinness came to see it, he was very nice about my performance, but he said, "I wish you could say the last line

without that accent." And I said, "Well, you can't suddenly drop your accent." I played her with a sort of Midlands country accent, which seemed suitable for her, but I think some people didn't like me being so prosaic about it really.

Most Joans play it with either Irish—because Shaw was Irish—or Mummerset. Even though Shaw was Irish, I see no link with the accent. Siobhan McKenna fair enough, she is Irish, but I think Sybil chose it too. Most English actresses play it in a sort of Mummerset— not an exact Somerset but a mummer's Somerset. It means anything really west, which to our English ears is country life.

I started out knowing it had got to be an accent and trying to see just by reading what he'd written what came off the page. I was going over the Trial scene speech on top of a bus one day, I remember, and I was suddenly absolutely convinced it had to be Glaswegian. What was attracting me about the Glaswegian is its extreme aggressiveness. It suddenly felt right for her because it was a loose accent but it had attack, whereas the Mummerset which everybody was expecting me to do was all kind of rooley. I couldn't get any kind of attack on it, and I knew she was an attacker.

So I turned up at rehearsal and said, "Right, I'm doing it Glasgow." And the director very carefully didn't say anything, and I stuck with it for ages. At the end of two weeks, I said, "You know, it's not altogether right, is it?" and he answered, "No. I'm very relieved you said that."

The whole company used to laugh at me because they said I was so addicted that I kept the Glaswegian for one line: "I will dare and dare and dare again." That's because I could get hold of a word and really shove it, and you can't on a posh English or a rolling Mummerset. So really the accent comes out of trying what will suit you best as an actress. The Midlands country accent still has attack because all Northerners have more attack than Southerners. When you're playing a part you just keep going back saying "Why can't I get that right? It doesn't sound right." You go back and think how they're thinking and suddenly it all did seem to jell and I settled on Midlands. Not the industrial accent but the country one, because they do have tremendous hardiness.

Hardiness is a quality cited by several actresses as necessary for Joan. Not only, comments Barbara Jefford, does the role demand "a tremendous vocal range because she has such a lot to say," but:

> She's got to be sturdy physically and I think give an impression of physical strength. She was still a woman, but her strength became superhuman because she was imbued with divine power. I truly believe that. Otherwise she couldn't have gone on fighting when she was wounded and so on. I cannot quite believe that when I see ethereal Joans. I think that's another sort—that's Anouilh's *The Lark,* not Shaw's Joan.

It's not an easy role to play physically. It's very demanding, very exhausting, especially in hot countries. It's very difficult to get the sweat off your brow before you start on the next great thing, but Shaw gives you the time to do it, so that you don't have a whole lot of big terrible things to do all at once. Neither are you left languishing for too long. The Warwick scene is a welcome time to gather yourself together.

Judi Dench reflects:

I'm probably built quite like Joan. I'm amazingly strong, and small. I don't know whether she was small, but I just thought about that and I hope it informed the performance enough. I also trained as a designer, so I somehow have a very, very clear picture of what this person should look like. I was very relieved to hear Sir Laurence say that. I have to have that. I have to kind of design it in my mind first. I also had my hair chopped very, very roughly.

Joan is, in a way, like Juliet. When you're old enough to play it, you're too old. It is technically a very difficult play for an actress. If you're going to get someone nineteen or twenty to play it then they have to have the most incredible drive and energy. When you get to the trial, in a way you've done your physical work and then you've got the mental work. There is in a way that tremendous relief when they say "take her to the fire" and you think "oh, thank goodness," and that marvelous little, much gentler thing at the end of the Epilogue. The physical and mental resources called on for a woman are considerable. So it's not a part you can play at the beginning of your career and it's too late at the end, so I suppose for an actress if you can look very young at twenty-five to thirty, it's a kind of ideal time to play it. But one day of course someone will come along at nineteen and sweep the boards.

# Joan the Soldier

Physical strength and their own sturdy builds helped them capture Joan as soldier, the actresses agreed, and Barbara Jefford referred to the Maid's desire to be accepted like a man among her comrades-in-arms. Eileen Atkins felt that Joan did not think about herself as a soldier or as a sexual being:

That came out from a very interesting question I had from a publicity woman. She asked what were my favorite parts and I was listing them, and she said, "Don't you want to play the other roles in Shakespeare?" and I said no, I'd played the two—Rosalind and Viola—I'd wanted and that the breeches parts are his best. And she asked what else and I said Saint Joan, and she said, "Ew, you only seem to like it when you're dressed as a man."

I could see her getting at something and I thought, "Well, maybe she's right. Maybe I do like getting into drag." Then I went back and thought about it, and I saw her again the next day and said no, I had worked out what it is and had come across a really interesting thing about writers. All the parts that I've enjoyed playing are when the man writing it has not been bothered about writing a feminine woman. Sex hasn't come into it, and certainly Shakespeare is released as soon as his heroines get into male clothes. He stops worrying about they're being frightfully feminine and he writes as he'd write for a boy, and it's wonderful. And in Joan it's not worrying about her being sexual or not because I don't think sexuality comes into it. I think she's asexual. Whether it would have developed if she had lived one doesn't know, but certainly she had either stopped it or it didn't grow in her—the same is true, I think, of Elizabeth I, whom I also enjoyed playing. Again, the men wrote for a ruler, as for a saint who goes into battle. So there's something releasing about such works written for women.

I mean, I don't want to play Cleopatra. I think it's a nightmare to play. Some of the stuff between the two of them is wonderful, but there are very few parts of extremely feminine women—and Cleopatra is helped also by the fact that she's a ruler, so they give her a lot of balls, I suppose. Normally, with a role, there's the part that's obviously sexual where you fall in love or whatever and then you use your sexuality. In Joan it was something you didn't have to take into consideration. I don't think it's in her mind. I don't think she even flirts, and I think it's a wonderful bit when she says to Dunois about liking babies and wishing she could nurse him because that's what soldiers do.

# Joan as Intellectual

"The intellectual aspect doesn't exist at all from your point of view when you're playing Joan," comments Barbara Jefford. "You can't intellectualize it. You *are* a nineteen-year-old girl who has heard voices and who accepts absolutely that she is a child of God." Wendy Hiller reflects:

Joan was shrewd. But it is the kind of part, I swear, that doesn't want too much thought. Because she worked on entirely instinct, because she was one of the unique human beings who are put into the world at the right age at the right time. She never thought consciously what she was doing when she upped and said, "Look, do you know I'd rather do anything than live the life of a rat in a hole. My voices were right. They told me." That isn't a warrior who has thought and thought and intellectualized. That's a different wisdom, a wisdom of the blood. You act in a certain way with a wisdom of the blood when you're a certain age, and then you've got to take over with your worldly wisdom and your technique and do it in another way. And there's far too much conscious analyzing, which belittles so much. I really mean it when people ask, "Look, when you tackle a large Shaw role, what is the first thing you do?" and I say, "Take a small breath at the commas and a large one at the full stops and say his lines clearly." He's done it for you.

Most of what Shaw wrote was indisputably great. Everything that he wrote was enormously clear, and he never meant it to be overlaid. He always said to me that the best Morell he ever had in *Candida* was a man who didn't know what he was talking about, because he was a very personable and physically attractive man. G.B.S. didn't say without a thought in his head because he was far too charming, but I think that's what he meant.

Judi Dench and Eileen Atkins give somewhat different views of Joan's intellectual traits. Miss Dench

suspects that that is Shaw, because you know how he adored words. I remember my husband [actor Michael Williams] and I being at dinner with a great friend of ours, Joseph McCullough, who is director of St. Mary le Bow, the East London church famous for its Bow Bells. At this dinner were the Rev. Tom Carlinsky, who is a Jesuit, and Edward Carpenter, Dean of Westminster. They had a theological discussion, which Michael and I understood I suppose less than a third of.

Now sometimes very, very clever people or very sophisticated people speak in a language which somehow denies a direct straightforwardness. And Brother Martin, when he takes over at the trial and he actually is the person who speaks to Joan and makes her understand— just remember that in the trial it's sometimes like lateral thinking. Indeed she was intelligent; she couldn't not have been an intelligent girl. I think somebody of Joan's intelligence could go into, say, an Oxford college and sit down and be baffled by what people talk about. So I think there's a genuine portrayal of a person who comes from the country in the middle of a room with the princes of the Church and actually doesn't understand what they're saying and is just pursuing her own belief and assurance. And then the way she actually gets round some of those questions—I'd love to know how much was Shaw and how much the real Joan.

"I'm not a very intellectual actress," states Eileen Atkins. "I leave the intellectualizing really to people to discuss when I've done it. But I endlessly go back to scripts. I drive people potty by just going back all the time and saying, "Well, it's no use you all talking about it. What do we actually say?"

I don't know which are Shaw's words and which Joan's, but I was never bothered by that. I come from a working class family, very ordinary. In fact, my father was almost a simpleton in a way. He was very slow indeed, but he could say the most amazing things. And that was just my father, who was nothing in particular. I myself think there's an enormously wrong way of thinking that intellectuals are the only ones who can say things. How can I put this? It seems to me that intellectuals often frighten people into being quiet and not saying anything. But when quite ordinary people are left to it, there's amazing wisdom there. And Joan obviously had a lot more than most people do.

I suppose it's a philosophy of mine that I don't see how we can get rid of things that are taught, of layers of stuff that have gotten in there—that if you could endlessly pare away and just try—that's how I work on a part, certainly. I can't work on my life like it. I wish I could. But working on a part, I always imagine that the whole body inside me is covered in barnacles and somewhere in the middle is just the steel rod of the part. And one's got to chip away and chip away and chip away and chip away until you just get to the essence each time. Which is what Joan gets to in her life. She doesn't take in any of those outside things. She just says what she feels and knows to be true. Of course if we all behaved like that goodness knows what state the world would be in.

I do find it on the whole wonderful if you meet someone who can speak from a still center. It's pure and it's clear and it comes out what you really think and not what you think you should say. There is something wonderful when people just come out with it. Oddly enough I hadn't thought about that before, but I realize that I am very attracted to characters who are very direct and say what they think. I long to do a lot of Greek stuff, and people don't like it. I did a very successful Electra on television several years ago but no one would let us do it again. I don't know, they got nervous. But I don't agree with this thing of Peter Hall using men and masks and all as it was. For heaven's sake, we don't do Shakespeare as it was. Why the hell should we go that far back? Everybody's changed. Either the plays mean something today or they don't.

The interesting thing I discovered when I worked on Electra is that she says what she means in the same way that Joan is saying what she means. There's nothing underneath. She's not being crafty, and I have a tremendous feeling for those parts. I happen to be able to play the real devious ones rather well, and I think that's maybe more like I am really, but there is something wonderful about someone who just goes out there and says it with passion.

# Joan as Saint and Visionary

Stating an opinion shared by her colleagues, Barbara Jefford remarks of Joan, "She never thinks of herself as a saint." Says Judi Dench:

A lot that happens to Joan, I think, is luck. That may be a heinous thing to say, but in actual fact it is luck and drive. She was a catalyst, and that is as important as that maybe she was a saint. But it was a saint for somebody else to make up their minds about. Too many Joans make up their own minds that she's a saint from the moment she walks in. I don't think she is that. I think she's a rebel. Shaw himself was, you know, and I'm sure that Joan appealed to him because he saw something of himself in her—that immovability of somebody who thinks and knows they're right.

It is ignorance, I think, that makes part of Joan's mind so shut off—I mean not willing to see other people's points of view. And maybe that's also something to do with her youth, and the fact that she calls a spade a spade. I just remember that being the thread all the way through and certainly not playing in any way the saint. I mean, that very, very matter-of-fact bit about saying "I'll ask Saint Catherine and she'll send a west wind"—total assurance that she's on the level of the saints. That must have been intolerable for them.

I think I played Joan with a tremendous stubbornness and a dogged determination. I only pursued material, total belief, and under that canopy also came the saints and my belief that God had sent me and any belief I had about what was right and what was wrong. I hope it wasn't monotonous in that way, but I can't talk about that—I don't know.

But I did want to cut across—in a way it's the same as Juliet behaving so badly sometimes. She behaves terribly irrationally and hysterically. It's the intolerance of youth that I played in Juliet for Zeffirelli in 1961—that terrible intolerance of simply lying on the ground with

your hands over your ears and saying, "Don't speak to me about it."
That is the doggedness that can also go out and win battles.

# The Cathedral Scene

Musing that "I think I did make her, I should think G.B.S. would say,
sentimental instead of hard and tough," Wendy Hiller recalls Shaw
telling her that in the Cathedral scene:

> when I said, "I'll go out to the common people . . . and so God be with
> me," I probably said, "And so God be with me," in a wishy-washy way
> with my eyes to heaven. And G.B.S. said the man next to him threw
> up his arms and said "Good God," because I'd thrown it away by play-
> ing it as though I were in a church instead of saying it like "God is on
> my side. I've got Him, not you," and speaking of God as your best
> chum—in fact the only one you can trust.
>
> I don't think I made any decision about her voices. I think I played
> them entirely practically, as though somebody had been talking. I don't
> think I went off into hearing mad voices. I don't think I fell into that
> trap. That's a very easy one to fall into.

For Judi Dench, Joan's references to her saints and the bells were

> as matter-of-fact as saying "We have thirty head of cows." I didn't play
> against the music of the bells in "Dear child of God" because I had
> heard those bells in Domremy and that is what she would align it to,
> but I usen't to do it in a lyric way. In the aloneness speech, I just re-
> member taking off any soft corners. I don't know whether the produc-
> tion made people cry. I don't know. I've never talked to anybody for a
> long time about it.

Barbara Jefford thinks of the Cathedral scene as

> just lyrical, lyrical, lyrical. I remember being put in a very good place
> by my director and being absolutely still and just thinking literally of
> the voices. It's so wonderfully done in the play, you see, with the chimes
> coming in. I mean I can almost feel tears when I think of it now. She
> becomes ecstatic in the true sense of the word. I think she goes into
> the sort of ecstasy that Saint Bernadette was supposed to have—it's a

sort of trance. How do you play that? How do you play anything? It's very difficult to say.

A sort of parallel is the way that when you play Shakespeare you're not consciously playing in iambic pentameter. That's something that you've gathered during the experience of your life as an actress which becomes almost second nature, and the sense comes through of its own accord. You don't make line stops but they are there.

The loneliness speech is one of the best, even better than the speech in the trial, which is so well known as to be almost hackneyed. I don't as a rule cry real tears on the stage. I usually cry in rehearsals and then it's all over. Quite often I think actors who cry on the stage become less effective because the more you cry the less the audience does. But there's something about the music of the way the Cathedral scene was written and that loneliness speech particularly which does somehow bring tears. The emotion is there. It's very real.

I remember they were all ranged round the back of me—the Bishop and Dunois and Charlie—and they all sort of bore down on me and then gradually went away as they finished each rejection speech. And there she is on her own. It's just a sort of physical thing of direction and theatrical expertise which puts you in the right place and does help the emotion.

"I can remember at the beginning of the Cathedral scene when she talks about her bells. I found that the most difficult for a long time," recalls Eileen Atkins:

At the beginning she's very practical and we really see that side of her. But she's really got to start going because Dunois has got to say at the end of it all, "Now stop it. I'm with you when you're practical, but when you start going off I don't believe it." She has to do those bells, and I think it is the line at the end of them, "It's then that Saint Margaret etc.—then, oh then." If you're saying, "then, oh then," you know you're way beyond being practical. You know from the pure text that she's got to be gone by then.

Now, how does one do it? I don't know. The terrible thing about actresses is that you have enormous imaginations or you couldn't become one. It's not difficult for me to imagine a religious ecstasy. Maybe one calls on one's own earthly loves to help you through it, reminding yourself of when your body didn't matter, when the whole of you is enthused, is caught up, can only think, dream, talk of one thing, one person, one whatever it is. Certainly I've had plenty—well, not plenty, but two or three—examples of that in my own life. So if you attach that to this—but it isn't as clear as that. It's quite easy to sit and think and really imagine that you are someone who is utterly transported at the thought of an angel talking to you. I think if an angel talked to me I'd be utterly transported.

Now if you imagine that this girl thought even more that she could see something else—I can certainly imagine that I see things—so I can conjure maybe not Joan's ecstasy—we don't know what hers was—a kind of ecstasy that is the nearest I know about it. If that conveys itself to people, then that's fair enough.

But you do feel strange. I'd always remember that line "It's then that Saint Catherine"—you feel like lifting off. But there's another peculiar thing about acting altogether. I was discussing it with Albert Finney the other day. You know, somebody as prosaic as that and you think, "Oh, yes, we all feel the same way," and you feel so relieved. It sounds so camp, and actors I think are very nervous talking about it, but there are some parts when you're standing onstage and you feel that you are the vessel through which this person is talking. You have become somebody else as far as you can and there's a weird feeling as if the back of my head is opening up and there is like an energy, a god, whatever you want to call it—a great energy is coming through the back of my head and gives me that extra thing to go out there, to get it across to everybody, to absolutely make them see some raw, impossible thing. Albert gave me another version but it was the same thing. It happened with *Saint Joan* and it happened too with Celia Coplestone in Eliot's *The Cocktail Party*. It's like saying, "Yes, I'm the vessel, but it's coming from back there somewhere and I have to get it to you and I will be filled with it so you will get it." And it's on lines like "then, oh then" that it's wonderful if you can get it.

You could get it through the whole of the aloneness speech. Before when I heard of *Saint Joan* the only speech anybody ever talked about was the trial speech. I couldn't believe this speech when I read it. It is very like Celia's speech about aloneness. I'm afraid that, on this trip on earth, I'm probably as a person much more like Eliot's Lavinia. But if you are like Celia and like Joan—which I can imagine even though I'm not living it—then I think it is to know utter desolation and look it in the face and then to find this whatever you'd like to call it. We'll call it God because we're talking about Saint Joan. If she's thinking her way through the aloneness speech and reaches her god, it's just the most wonderful, wonderful speech.

# The Trial Scene

The transition between Joan's signing her confession and being taken to the stake, a process which took six days in real life, is accomplished in only a few pages in Shaw's play. Far from placing a burden on them, the actresses felt that the compression helped. "I think the scene is so well written and has such a very good rhythm that I never felt it as difficult to do," says Barbara Jefford. "In fact, it's highly dramatic and very satisfying to play those changes. And perfectly legitimate. I mean, what they say to her is appalling."

"It's so beautifully written, I can tell you, you just long to go out and do it," Eileen Atkins states:

> You're hanging on to the thing that you feel that everything you've said is right, and then they say they're going to burn you, and she is so frightened of being burnt. But being kept in a hole is worse, and once—I took the most tremendous pause at that point when she does the change to recant. As an actress you sit there thinking that being shut in a hole is so much more monstrous than burning that the burning becomes something she just has to go through. That's what I think is so wonderful about her. I think she starts to get it on "to condemn thee." She's not really been listening properly. She's done her work and she doesn't care. She's just thinking, "None of it's true. None of it's true. I am mad. I must have imagined all that, because to be burnt—I must have imagined all that." And then she hears "perpetual imprisonment," and being a very simple person it all clicks into place for her: Anyone who can put her in perpetual imprisonment is stupid and wrong; if they're stupid and wrong, then they are wrong about her angels and it is all true. And so it's a mixture of terrible anger at them for wanting to do such a thing and the elation that she's right that carries her out to the stake. I still think she's terrified. I think she makes that speech and then she's just utterly terrified from then on until she's burned. But that's the only answer.

Judi Dench thought the transition was "much quicker. In a way when you play it, it's like a door opening and an enormously bright light flooding in on her and her realizing exactly what she's done. When the Trial came, I was always immensely relieved. It was the work done before that I found difficult and more of a challenge to make her that much of a catalyst."

# The Epilogue

Proving that debate over Shaw's Epilogue is ongoing, Eileen Atkins recalls that her young director desperately wanted to cut the Epilogue. And Emrys James, who was playing Cauchon at the time, said "You cut it and I walk out. Don't you realize how brilliant that Epilogue is? You can't end a play with her being taken off to the stake. Everyone's too depressed for words. The Epilogue is wonderful for people."

Barbara Jefford remembers a conversation with Dame Sybil Thorndike on the importance of the Epilogue:

Now Sybil said to me, I remember very clearly, that *Saint Joan* without the Epilogue is like, I don't know—cutting *The Merchant of Venice* after the Trial scene. It's as bad as that, like Henry Irving cut everything after Shylock's exit. It's absolutely essential to the form of the play.

Miss Jefford believes that there are many different ways of playing Joan's final speech and recalls that in her many performances she

sort of played it differently every time. I think the simpler the better really. The main emotion around there is a terrible disappointment. I think it's the only time there's a hint of pessimism in her character, because she's the perennial optimist, isn't she? And suddenly she realizes it's not that simple, it's not a foregone conclusion as she always thought. And then they all run away from her.

"She is very depressed that they have all gone off then, and I think Joan's last line is a genuine question to Him. I don't think it's in the air," says Eileen Atkins, mimicking a breathy, goggle-eyed version of "How long?":

I think it's "How much longer have we got to bear people being such idiots and ruining what He's given us?" I think it's a direct question. Not totally direct—okay—it's comic if it's totally direct. Obviously the beginning of the play should be very funny, and I considered it a disaster if we didn't get a lot of laughs in the first scene. But you tread a very fine line when you try to make "How long" prosaic.

I think that if on "Oh God that madest this beautiful earth" you really get across how Joan thinks about the earth, which all comes into the Trial scene about the lambs and everything—which everybody in the audience can understand—they're all going to sit there and think "I'm on it. I'm here, now"—or that's what they should think. "He has made a beautiful earth." So that they're sitting there thinking about that, and then the actress says with real appeal and sadness "How long," I think they have a feeling of "Well, I can enjoy it tomorrow. I can make it all right tomorrow."

I think the audience should go out thinking, "You can do anything." They've seen somebody do anything. They've seen a young girl who has nothing do everything. And I think it's in the back of their minds that it has sprung from a true story. I love playing anything that says something so uplifting. It seems to me that whether you believe or not, you make people feel a sort of hope. Even non-believers come out of *Saint Joan* saying "Yes!"

"I believe that at the end of *Saint Joan* you should have tremendously mixed feelings about her," states Judi Dench.

The Epilogue is usually when the play gets holy and soft. I just remember doing the last line very angrily and very impatiently, and furious because they were so slow about it. I think that people should feel that history threw up this amazing person. I think they should probably feel ambiguous about her saintliness and her holiness, but they should feel that it was an extraordinary woman who was thrown up at this time and who achieved something very remarkable.

Because of the saints and the visions, people have felt she was always right. I don't believe the right is always on Joan's side. I think that sometimes she is just intolerant and doggedly determined. And because of the way she behaved they did achieve a victory. Not only the way she behaved. But it is an incident, and out of the incident it is up to you to make up your mind about her actual saintliness, whether she was totally chosen by God and the only one that was totally right.

Wendy Hiller recalls not how she played Joan's last line, but how she felt: "By that time I was jolly tired, I remember. I'd been rehearsing *Pygmalion* all day. I used to raise my arms to heaven and say 'How long, oh Lord, how long,' meaning 'How long can I stand here without passing out?'"

# The Most Difficult Scene

While the beginning of the Cathedral scene posed the most difficulty for Eileen Atkins, Barbara Jefford found the opening scene closest to her *bête noire:*

She rushes on as a sort of bright juvenile. The shepherd lass comes on. One critic in New York, I remember, said, "I had my doubts when Miss

Jefford pranced on, mutton dressed as lamb, in a red wool dress and a long wig." I think I'd probably play that a bit more cool, although Shaw says she's in a fever of excitement, so it's very difficult to do without being a bit winsome.

To Judi Dench, the Dunois scene

is fiendishly difficult to do. He makes Dunois such a charming hero and it's a thing of getting him to accept her, so it's not just a charming scene but it does work and precipitate the play forward. When she says, "You don't know how to use your guns"—then Dunois somehow sees more in her than a woman. She has that marvelous speech about not caring about the things women care for. But also she sees that they are compatible, but they shouldn't be when she comes on. It should be very prickly and difficult and then it should get to that and then to total belief in her. We discussed it a lot and worked on that.

# Comparison of Joan with Other Roles

The actresses readily agreed with Shaw's statement that actresses would want to play Joan as actors do Hamlet. Judi Dench mused:

I suspect that Joan is not so faceted for an actress as Hamlet is for an actor, because there are some bits of Hamlet that are so ambiguous and if you pursue too far along that line you lose the core. Joan is that on a small scale but not like Hamlet because it's in a much more accessible language, for one thing. We're still arguing about many things Hamlet says that we don't understand and that people interpret in different ways. We're still arguing about Joan, but what we have there is more accessible.

Eileen Atkins feels that for actresses,

Rosalind is the other great role, a comedy with great depth. But you can't get going with the emotion and the tragic side. I guess Hamlet is the part to end all parts and has everything, including even the sexuality. I suppose Hamlet is a complete man and Joan is not a complete woman, but I think it's the greatest challenge there is for an actress.

Wendy Hiller reflects:

> There are the Ibsen roles, there are the great Shakespearean roles, and there are the Shavian roles. We haven't really had many great writers writing for women. I would say coming up now I would have given a great deal to have been young enough to have played Priestley's *Time and the Conways*. I mean, it's not a great role but I think three or four of Priestley's plays are really magnificent for women, even men.

"Cleopatra is an obvious Shakespearean comparison," says Barbara Jefford,

> because particularly in the last part of the play she has the most wonderful things to do. Juliet is another. Yes, I would say Saint Joan is a woman's Hamlet. I don't think it's nearly as complex. I don't think there are so many different ways of playing Joan because Shaw is specific. Shakespeare is far more—how should I say—in our lifetime I've seen Hamlet played from a sort of scruffy student to the noblest of princes and everything in between. In a sense it's almost unplayable because there are so many aspects of him. I don't think that Saint Joan is nearly as difficult, but it is an amazing star role.

# Conclusions

"The actresses who have played Saint Joan since the war weren't in contact with Shaw," concludes Wendy Hiller:

> So much has changed it's light years away. My Joan, from your point of view, stands quite alone. Six rehearsals for no money. But the privilege of G.B.S. there, standing in front of me when I'm introduced and him saying, "My goodness, Wendy, what's the matter with your hair?" And me propped up with my armor at a dress parade absolutely terrified and saying, "Well, it's curly, G.B.S." And he says, "It's positively immoral." So I sleek it down with bay rum, but with the lights and the heat it began to curl up. And there was no time to get me a wig.
>
> There were things that he was quite absolutely adamant about, like his bringing out the watch and timing the Inquisitor speech of that wonderful actor Cecil Trouncer, and not a second above or beyond. It's like a piece of music. You must remember that Shaw was a music

critic and a fine musician with a great ear for music, and he's not going
to have anything legato if he didn't write it legato. He didn't want a lot
of false emotion between you and the audience.

"So there we are. Well, the old darling, in spite of ticking me off left,
right, and center, I remember something he'd given me." Dame
Wendy displays her copy of the Constable limited edition, with the
drawings of Charles Ricketts, the designer of the original British production, and opens it to the title page. Under *Saint Joan*, Shaw had
written "alias Wendy Hiller. G. Bernard Shaw. Malvern, August
1936." Dame Wendy comments: "So he did put that, so he really
didn't think that badly of me."[2]
Judi Dench reflects:

> I hope what I did was make Joan more accessible. We know she was a
> remarkable person, but somehow playing a unique, remarkable, saint-
> like person on the stage gives very little that people can identify with.
> If she starts off as a saint, then there's no way to go. Therefore, if you
> can make her more accessible—if people can understand more about
> her, even through anger or thinking "What an appalling way to be-
> have," then somehow the saintlike quality should be there anyway. You
> don't have to add it.

Eileen Atkins stresses:

> I think you never can have any self-pity. Any part with self-pity is a
> bore anyway—that's why I would hate to play Blanche DuBois. I'm
> not drawn to things like that, though they're good parts. There's no
> self-pity in Joan. She's like a clean arrow.
> I had to go talk to some kids in the East End when I was playing
> Joan, and it was very difficult because somehow it was a very political
> school. And of course Joan is a fanatic and I have very ambivalent
> feelings about fanatics. On the whole I think of them as dangerous
> people. It just happens that Joan is such an attractive fanatic. It be-
> came very tricky. The kids said: "You do admire Saint Joan, and if you
> admire her why not admire some of the more peculiar politicians on
> the left or right?" I never really worked out an answer.

"I remember going to Rouen long before I played her," says Barbara Jefford,

> and seeing the little market place and thinking of the ordinariness of
> it. That was the most impressive thing—somebody who is so extraor-
> dinary in such ordinary surroundings, being a shepherdess and being

so strong and doing the absolutely impossible. And for once—in spite of the wonderful discussions, particularly between Warwick and Cauchon, where you see the old Shaw that you know being discursive and a doler out of messages and an airer of opinions—but for the most part the play seems to be a deviation from his usual approach as a playwright. He's a man in love with his subject rather than standing away from it. How can one not respond?

# Notes

1. Brian Tyson, *The Story of Shaw's Saint Joan* (Kingston: McGill-Queen's University Press, 1982), p. 114.

2. Although not germane to this discussion of *Saint Joan*, these additional remarks by Wendy Hiller may be of interest to Shaw scholars. Speaking of the Malvern schedule after she was playing Joan and Eliza Doolittle in repertory with other plays in which she did not appear, Dame Wendy recalls that Shaw "invited me to the Restoration play—I forget what it was. Anyway, I sat in the dress circle with Mr. Shaw, who flirted outrageously, with Mrs. Shaw in a box.

"I always remember a London management asking me if I could play *Saint Joan* there, and my saying 'Oh, I say, I've just done that. Couldn't you do something else?' This is when you're twenty-two. The hair-raising stupidity! Later, when Shaw had promised the play to Sybil and Lewis's eldest daughter Ann Casson and she and her father were going on tour with it, I remember saying 'But G.B.S., the time is passing and I want to do the play again.' He said, 'It's all right, Wendy. It always was a good play.'

"We used to go to lunch with him and Mrs. Shaw. Mrs. Shaw was very sweet to me. Looking back now as one is older, one realizes that they were an elderly couple and they were delighted to meet somebody young. G.B.S. used to have me on and say 'All the actresses I know are dead, Wendy,' and look round for sympathy. And one realizes years later that they were being so charming, and we should have asked them round to our little maisonette in Bloomsbury.

"He was very, very friendly and kind and altogether holding out the hand of friendship. The war came, and I had a baby, but I could have—but I thought I mustn't take advantage. I mustn't intrude. I'd been brought up very strictly—you didn't intrude on elderly people, and all of that came into it. And yet I did go over when Mrs. Shaw was ill. Ronald and I cycled over into Hertsfordshire—no cars during the war—it was only about forty miles. We spent the night and came back the next day, and I remember G.B.S. and my husband had a long talk about Bevan's foreign policy. And we should have put all that down.

"What we did get down was when we went over to see him when he was alone and we took the movie camera and took a film of him and me. And Ronald spoiled half of it by letting some light in. G.B.S. was very old and a little bit deaf then. But when I was much younger before the war, I could have taken a good deal more that he obviously held out with both hands to offer me. He was a dear to me, a dear."

# Bernard Shaw

# TWO PIECES FROM *THE STAR*

## "Apostasy" Denied: An Unrecorded Shaw Letter to *The Star*

*A Shaw letter to the press, which if listed in the Laurence* Bibliography *would appear as C810a, denied that he had resigned from the Fabian Society and taken up "Individualism." The prankster who inserted the announcement is unknown, but Shaw's reply appears genuine: as a long-time contributor to* The Star *he would have been queried about the letter's authenticity, and denied it if somehow it appeared without authorization. The letter appeared on page 2 of the issue of 18 August 1891.*

To the Editor of *The Star.*

Sir, The *Agnostic Journal* has announced, somewhat too agnostically, that I have given up Socialism and become a convert to Individualism. After some handsome remarks about my "splendid mental abilities and logical acumen," with which I entirely agree, the writer goes on to chuckle over the dismay which my apostasy will create among "the cranks and frumps" known as the Fabian Society. He is careful to state that he has "good reasons for believing this to be true"; and I do not at all doubt him, though his assurance is only another illustration of the truth of Hegel's saying that "all mistakes are made for good reasons." It is quite true that I am a believer in Individualism, and have been trying this long time to convert the Individualists to it, without, unfortunately, succeeding in bringing them along any further than the recognition of the rights of at most one individual out of every five in the country. But the *Agnostic Journal* errs in supposing that I have been converted to Unsocialism, or that I have withdrawn from the Fabian Society. My splendid mental ability and logical acumen are not yet sufficiently impaired for that; and I am still on the best of terms with the cranks and frumps. If I feel any change coming on, I

shall hasten to publish a bulletin to that effect; but up to the present my Social-Democratic convictions remain as obstinate as ever. As I am beginning to receive letters of congratulations from deluded Unsocialists, and of dismay and remonstrance from startled Fabians, I venture to ask you to give a place in your columns to this contradiction.—
Yours, etc.

G. Bernard Shaw

29 Fitzroy–sq., W., 17th Aug.


# A.D. 3,000.
## The True Report of a County Council Candidate's Dream

## The People He Saw—What They Thought of Him and He of Them


*Shaw rarely took flights into prophecy. His most significant efforts in that line would come later, in the fantasies and prophecies of* Back to Methuselah, The Simpleton of the Unexpected Isles, The Apple Cart, *and* Farfetched Fables. *In some ways, all of his late plays were prophecies. In 1889, however, he was under the influence of William Morris's* Erewhon *and Edward Bellamy's* Looking Backward *when he drafted a political campaign appeal in the guise of a dream-vision. A few elements suggest the later plays— the long-lived people, the new means of locomotion, the telephone equipped with television screen (which causes an embarrassing moment in* Back to Methuselah).

*The experiment in fiction, not collected by Shaw later in* Short Stories, Scraps and Shavings *for the* Collected Edition, *appeared on page 6 of* The Star *for Thursday, 17 January 1889. It is not identified in the Laurence* Bibliography. *In the text below, several obvious typographical errors typical of newspaper publication are silently corrected. The original publication was anonymous. "I was nearly 17," Shaw wrote in his diary for 14 January 1889, "when I got to work on an article, 'A County Councillor's Dream,' for the double number of* The Star *on Thursday."*

I felt sure of being returned when I got to bed at last after addressing four meetings in the course of the day. My chief opponent is only a workman, and as the division for which I am standing is inhabited chiefly by men of his own class, he has not the slightest chance against me; for I am a member of the Board of Works, and an old Vestryman.

No sooner had I blown out the candle and committed my head to the pillow than I began to imagine myself delivering speeches about what the new County Council would do for the people. The darkness swam with faces, but instead of listening they shifted in all directions like bubbles, in soda water. I was still hard at work trying to make myself heard when I suddenly found myself in full sunshine on a handsome bridge in the middle of a splendid city. Something about the general hang of the place and the course of the broad river seemed familiar to me; and yet I could not quite make up my mind about it. At first it seemed that nobody was about, but presently a colored man, with a tattooed face—

QUITE THE GENTLEMAN THOUGH—

turned away from the balustrade and asked me politely whether I could point out which was St. Paul's. Taken aback by the question, I instinctively turned to the northeast shore, and there, sure enough, the first thing I saw was unmistakably the Monument; but I recognized nothing else except the slope of Fish-street-hill. As for St. Paul's, there was not a sign of it. I looked rather foolish, and told him that it must have been pulled down. "But the ruins, sir," says he; "where are the ruins?" I looked again, but could only say as pleasantly as possible, "They don't keep ruins here, I am afraid." He seemed annoyed, and slipped the elastic band abruptly on a sketch book he had taken out. "I thank you," says he; "these Whig historians are not to be depended on," and he turned away. But just as he was half-way round, his heels went as if he had trod upon a piece of ice, and down he came smash on the back of his head. I was hurrying to give him a lift up when, to my astonishment, his body was drawn along the ground, as if invisible horses were harnessed to it, and had vanished into Gracechurch-street (so to speak) before I recovered my presence of mind—for you may be sure my hair was standing on end at this piece of

SPIRITUALISM IN BROAD DAYLIGHT.

I would have taken to my heels, but I could not get the County Council out of my head even then, and the fear of being seen running through the streets by some of my constituents helped me to keep up my dignity.

As I walked away, I noticed that there was a magnificent embank-

ment all along the north and south sides. The water in the river was
so clear that I could see the bottom covered with grey-blue pebbles.
There were heaps of goldfish and things. But what surprised me most
was to see several people in jerseys in the water, swimming. I soon
saw that they were not bathing, like boys do at Millbank, but just
going from one side to the other, for all the world as if they were
crossing a street. When they got out, they ran up the steps and
### SHOOK THEMSELVES LIKE A DOG,
and went off without thinking of a towel or as much as a handker-
chief. Some of them walked along the embankment like any ordinary
person out walking; but others stooped until I could only see their
heads over the wall, and shot off like mad at about 30 miles an hour.
At last one of them came up on the bridge at the south end, and I
put my dignity in my pocket and was about to make a bolt for the
north, when four appeared there. I was fairly in it this time, so I
strolled along towards the four as if nothing was the matter. First I
thought they were men. Two of them wore plain grey jerseys and
pants; the other two wore cinnamon color tunics about as long as a
cut-away morning coat, and their pants had a sort of fringe along
where the stripe would be down a pair of trousers. They had no col-
lars nor cuffs, and they all wore wide-awake hats. The colors and materials were fine, but I couldn't make out exactly what they were. But
what was my horror and blushes when we came closer, to see that the
two in the tunics were young women,
### AS UNCONCERNED AS YOU PLEASE.
They none of them looked fat, healthy and strong—not to my no-
tions of health at least; but they were very fine drawn and cultivated
looking, as it were; and in spite of the brazen get-up of the women, I
felt sheepish before them. They all carried something like a camp-
stool in their hands. Suddenly they went over to the pathway, opened
their campstools, sat down with a little hop and a twist, and—I
thought I should have dropped—streamed off along the bridge just
as the tattooed man had done when he fell; only, when they were
passing me, they all stared and then rose, caught up their stools, and
came to a stand with a little jump to one side, like as it were getting
off a tramcar without stopping it. Then I saw the whole secret. The
footpath was in motion, like a belt over two wheels, and it was a mercy
I had not stepped on it without knowing and perhaps broken my
neck. But with these four people coming at me I had no time to think
of patent street improvements. I grabbed my umbrella fast; but somehow they were not the sort of people you could offer to fight exactly.
They had low, quiet, impressive, and high-class sort of voices, though

not a word could I understand. I didn't half like their manners; they made too free considering they were strangers; and all the same they were uppish, as if they thought themselves as good as me. By this time the person I had seen at the other end of the bridge had slid up to us. He was in a brown jersey, and I took him for a man of 50. He was reading as the pavement carried him along; but when he looked up he got off, and seemed twice as curious as the others.

"Well, ladies and gentlemen," says I, "I'm sure I hope you'll know me again."

"Sir," says the old fellow, in a finicking way, "you speak like a phonograph. You are evidently a perfect master of old English vernacular. I am a professor of our obsolete national dialects. Your costume is historically accurate, and even your person reproduces with singular fidelity the
BLOATED AND SOMEWHAT UNPLEASANT TYPE
common to the 19th century."

"You might be aware, perhaps," I said stiffly, "that I am a candidate for the London County Council."

"That is curious," he says, as cool as you please; "for anyone can perceive without the trouble of exact anthropometric measurement, that you are neither intelligent nor trustworthy."

I didn't say anything, but I just gave him a look to teach him his place. Then I made a jump and got on to the pavement, which carried me off at a fearful pace. He was after me like a shot, and I was glad to catch hold of him to keep from falling.

"At my age I generally go on the slow tack," he said, steadying me politely enough. "Only our very young people care to go so fast; I have not done so myself since I turned 70."

"Why, you don't look more than 50," I says.

"I am 98," he replied. "Nineteenth century ghosts always mistake our age."

"Do you call me a ghost?" I said indignantly.

"Come," says he quietly: "do you call yourself a contemporary?"

That shut me up. "Whatever I am," I says, "I may as well make myself at home. Is there any place about here where we could have a snack of fish and a glass of—Halloe! Stop thief! Stop thief!"

It was a young fellow that had just reached his hand into a shop window full of magnificent fruit, and taken a bunch of grapes like hen's eggs. There was no one in the shop; and he took them and walked away as coolly as if the whole place belonged to him.

"My good sir," says old Ninety-eight, stopping me, "I think I know what you mean. In your time a citizen was not allowed to take what he wanted without depositing a metal token, which was received by an official, who weighed out a certain portion of the desired commodity in return for it. We cannot afford to waste our time on such cumbrous forms. We do our day's work and take what we want. As a guest of the City you are also welcome.

PRAY TAKE WHAT YOU PLEASE."

"Me steal!" I says. "No!" I says. "Thieving is thieving, whatever your time may be worth. I'll die honest. I'll have a bunch, but I'll pay for it like a man." And I planked down half-a-crown, and took up about half-a-dozen big grapes.

"Do you not require this any more?" he says, looking covetously at the half-crown.

"Of course not," I said, "It belongs to the shop now—not to me."

"Very good of you, I'm sure," he says, pocketing it with a face of brass. "If it is genuine it will form a valuable addition to our museum."

This was too much. "*If it's genuine!*" I says. "Damn your impudence, do you know who I am? I might have known by your uniform that I was among the criminal classes. Where are the respectable people?"

"Well, there are only three ghosts at present in London—or four, counting you. Two of them claim, I believe, to be respectable. The other, a female, allows her hair to grow down to the small of her back, dresses in a ridiculous and indecent fashion, and is curiously useless and helpless. She lays great stress on her respectability. Had you not better step into this store and steal—since you prefer that expression—something less noticeable to wear. The people we pass are too considerate to stare now that you are under my wing, but we are attracting a great deal of attention."

"I wish I could find a policeman," I said, gruffly.

"We have four at the British Museum," he said; "but one of them has been half eaten by rats."

"Eaten by rats!" I explained, getting a dreadful turn.

"Yes; they stuffed him with some tasty substance, I suppose. If you wish to see them we can do so by photophone at the Ludgate-hill panopticon; or we can get to the Museum in

FOUR SECONDS BY PNEUMATIC TUBE."

"May I ask you whether those four policemen are under the control of the County Council?"

"No; they are under the control of the trustees of the British Museum. Before we go into the laboratory you had better have a brush down. That singular garment of yours—made of wool adulterated with cotton, if I judge rightly—is full of dust. May I ask why the stiff black cylinder on your head has a flange? The white-tubes on your wrists and neck have no such appliance."

"They are

## A MARK OF CASTE,

sir," I said haughtily, as I followed through the hall of a splendid club-house into a room where there was a treadmill—as I thought—turning very fast. On a second look it turned out to be a huge brush. My companion went up and held himself against it as coolly as if he was a cat, and it the cook's skirt. I tried it rather gingerly, and found there was a draught to take the dust down; but it was too penetrating for the stuff I wore, and I soon had enough.

"How do you work it?" I asked, wishing to show an intelligent curiosity after his late remarks. "Steam or electricity?"

"We don't call it anything particular," he said. "We store it in accumulators, which we fill from windmills, tidemills, watermills, and

## SUPERFLUOUS ENERGY CRANKS,

in our gymnasia. In the old days a good deal of it was produced by a noisy arrangement worked by audiences at theatres, public meetings, and so on when they wished to applaud; but we are not so demonstrative now. We still find that five out of every six men use more force in pushing open a swing door than is necessary to let them through, and this we store. We export millions of foot-pounds of it. It works everything—the drums on which the *trottoirs* revolve, the flying machines—everything. You see very little of its effects here; for, of course, London, lying so low, is a mere village. All our big cities are on the tops of the hills and ridges. The flying machine led inevitably to that."

"If you call this only a village, you must have pretty high ideas of good living," I said, staring at him to see whether he was in earnest.

"The less developed of us find time hanging heavy on hand. They keep pulling down the buildings for the mere sake of putting them up again, so that you do not recognise a town if you have been away for a week. One man—he was quite an idiot, hardly three grades higher than you—actually tried to revive one of the antique handicrafts. He made an obsolete instrument called a saw. But he cut his finger off and, of course, died."

"Died of losing a finger!"

"Certainly. We are not lizards or lobsters; you cannot dismember so highly organised a creature as man without killing him. This is the laboratory."

It was a splendid place; but such an examination I never underwent in all my born days. He said they were

## WEIGHING AND MEASURING ME,

but though I went into places where I was shut in and let out again, I saw no scales and no standards. They nearly made me ill, putting things on my tongue that had no more taste than sawdust. They showed me dozens of stuffs, all of the same silly grey color, and asked me which was which. One joker wanted to question me in mental arithmetic, but I wouldn't stand that. I don't remember half their dodges; but at last Ninety-eight says:

"I have noticed that you do not like to be spoken to about your own powers. You will be able to understand—at least we think you can with a little effort—that how we determine a man's capacity is no more a matter of opinion than his weight or stature. Personalities, as you would call them, are therefore never resented among us. However, as we are therefore still apt to be pleased when our points are exceptional, you will be glad to learn that in order to estimate you we have had to fall back on the instruments used with the anthropoid apes. Your color blindness, your obtuseness of palate, your insensibility to stimuli, and your sloth in responding to those coarse enough to be felt by you, your incapacity for dealing with abstract conceptions, your egotism, your love of notoriety, your greediness, your dulness, your complacent imbecility, your superstition, and, in short, your stupidity, are

## PRODIGIOUS AND UNIQUE."

"Do you mean to say that I am not a fit person to act on the County Council?" I said, getting very red—as I felt—in the face.

"Beyond a doubt you are not a fit person to sit even on a coroner's jury," he replied.

My conviction of the truth of what he said was that deep that I walked out, made straight for the bridge, and chucked myself right over. Instead of finding myself in the water, I found myself on the floor of my room, where I had fallen slap out of bed. The relief of finding that it wasn't true was beyond all description. Not to revive the Metropolitan Board of Works, would I dream it again, though my seat there was worth two thousand a year to me one way or another.

I hope I shall get in at the top of the poll to-day; but I don't feel so sure as I did. The dream has taken the pluck out of me.

# Reviews

## Archer on Ibsen

Thomas Postlewait, editor. *William Archer on Ibsen: The Major Essays,* 1889–1919. Westport, Ct.: Greenwood Press, 1984.

The editor has performed a distinct service to scholarship in providing students of the drama with a representative though admittedly incomplete collection of William Archer's writing on Henrik Ibsen. The first part of the book consists of a dozen essays presented with Archer's and the editor's notes. Most of these pieces have been long out of print—available only in moldy late-nineteenth/early-twentieth-century library volumes of such periodicals as *The Fortnightly Review, The International Monthly, The New Review, The Pall Mall Gazette, Edda,* etc. The second part offers Archer's introductions to 14 of Ibsen's plays translated by William Archer and collected in the 1906–8 Heinemann edition.

The major argument of Postlewait's introduction, and presumably also of his forthcoming book, *Archer: Prophet of the New Drama,* is that Archer has been misunderstood and "for various reasons" misrepresented by generations of critics (among whom this reviewer, though misidentified as "William" Quinn, is cited as a leading example). Such misrepresentation apparently comes in two forms: (1) failing to give Archer his due as leader of the Ibsen campaign, and (2) underestimating Archer's involvement in behind-the-scenes stagecraft. As one thus hauled to the dock I plead innocent to the first charge and a qualified nolo contendere to the second.

Postlewait attests to have found evidence in the form of prompt books among Archer's papers in the British Theatre Association which indicates that his role in Ibsen productions was greater than hitherto supposed. Thus, even his great friend and contemporary, G. B. Shaw, may have misled subsequent commentators by writing in his memorial tribute, "How William Archer Impressed Bernard Shaw" that "the theatre was not to him a workshop but part of his fairyland. He never really got behind the scenes and never wanted to." At any rate we shall wait for proof of Postlewait's pudding.

Similarly, Archer's capacity to be misunderstood was also recognized by Shaw, who describes Archer in the same essay as "in person and manner the most deceptive man of his time . . . he took in all his contemporaries, even those who were fairly intimate with him." So insidious was the inclination to portray Archer as a "dour Scot" that Shaw predicts that "Not until the last London journalist who has met him has perished will William Archer be judged by his writings. . . ."

It is therefore possible that Postlewait may be the first to judge William Archer by his writing and without being unduly influenced by the views of those who knew him in the flesh. If the result is a fresh and more accurate appraisal of this forgotten man, more power to him.

Martin Quinn

# Another Introduction to Shaw

Arthur Ganz. *George Bernard Shaw.* New York: Grove Press, 1983. 227 pp. Illustrated. $17.50.

Professor Ganz's small and helpful book on Shaw is part of the Grove Press Modern Dramatists' Series. On balance, this is a worthwhile addition to Shaw criticism, with only a few minor problems that are worth mentioning. First, the author has a strange propensity to overwork dashes and parentheses, to the point where they become an annoyance and an intrusion in his text. Second, the book has an unsatisfactory conclusion. From a discussion of the late plays, Mr. Ganz moves abruptly into a one-paragraph, rushed ending, contrasting sharply with his long, leisurely beginning. It is almost as though he suddenly lost interest in his topic, or else his publisher told him he had exceeded the planned length for a Grove book. Having treated us to a pleasant repast, Mr. Ganz has jumped up from his chair without the grace to offer even a modest dessert or cup of coffee.

Third, and most important, I kept wondering about this book's niche. If it is an introduction to Shaw, as the series editors indicate in their preface, it certainly demands a great deal of its readers; the discussions of a number of plays presume a fairly sophisticated and thorough prior knowledge of Shaw's work. If, on the other hand, Professor Ganz intends this book for the advanced Shaw scholar, it is not sufficiently new or insightful. Any general book on a major author faces this problem of audience, and if Professor Ganz does not always succeed in overcoming it, there are enough rewarding moments to permit his readers to overlook the problem most of the time.

Mr. Ganz manages nicely to summarize key elements of Shaw's early life, with psychological insights into family relationships which go far in explaining Shaw's later writing. Shaw's life in Dublin is treated sufficiently to allow the full later development of biographical relationships to characters, scenes, and ideas in his plays. His problems in school and his early attempts to support himself in various ways are also treated well. Best of all are the discussions of his life with his mother, his problems with sexuality, his frequently-chronicled flirtations, his strange marriage and stranger, mainly intellectual, love affairs. Ganz also discusses the Fabian days in London with clarity and economy.

After covering Shaw's music criticism and theatre criticism, Ganz moves to the plays themselves. In discussing this major body of Shaw's work, Professor Ganz properly emphasizes Shaw's theatrical connections, stressing at the same time a Shavian consistency in both style and thought. Ganz's enthusiasm and love of Shaw's work shine through every chapter; early on he calls Shaw's plays "the most notable body of drama to be written in English, perhaps in any language, since Shakespeare," and he never wavers from this judgment.

Mr. Ganz uses *Man and Superman* effectively as the touchstone play, bringing up variations and interrelationships constantly through reference to this central work. He devotes full and careful analysis to *Pygmalion* (dwelling particularly on the problem ending), less to *Heartbreak House* and *Saint Joan,* and gives unreasonably short shrift—one paragraph—to *Back to Methuselah.* Shaw would certainly not have been cheered by that kind of ratio. Nonetheless, if this is not a balanced treatment of all of Shaw's works, it is a frequently stimulating one. Professor Ganz sees and develops numerous fresh relationships among the plays, and he manages as well as any critic of Shaw that I have read to handle the seeming inconsistencies, the serious humor, the maddening paradoxes of GBS.

Michael J. Mendelsohn

# John R. Pfeiffer*

# A CONTINUING CHECKLIST OF
# SHAVIANA

## I. Works by Shaw

Shaw, Bernard. "Barker's Wild Oats" (1947) in *An American Retrospective. Writing from Harper's Magazine, 1850–1984*. Edited by Ann Marie Cunningham. Harper's Magazine Foundation. 1984. This volume was offered as a "Free Book" ("you can't buy it") to accompany a new subscription to *Harper's*. *Harper's* made an exception and sent a copy for $3.95.

————. *Bernard Shaw. The Diaries, 1885–1897.* Edited by Stanley Weintraub. University Park: The Pennsylvania State University Press, 1986.

————. *Bernard Shaw's Letters to Siegfried Trebitsch.* Edited by Samuel A. Weiss. Stanford: Stanford University Press, 1986.

————. "Crossing Switzerland: Thun to Zürich. The Truth about the Brünig Pass and the Speed Limits." *Shaw Abroad: The Annual of Bernard Shaw Studies,* Volume Five. University Park: Pennsylvania State University Press, 1985. GBS's Royal Automobile Club piece on automobiling in Switzerland.

————. "G.B.S. in the Holy Land: Two 1931 Interviews." *Shaw Abroad: The Annual of Bernard Shaw Studies,* Volume Five. University Park: Pennsylvania State University Press, 1985. Newspaper pieces on Shaw in what was then Palestine, which quote him.

————. Excerpts from the music criticism. In Donald V. Mehus's "A Musical Critic: George Bernard Shaw on the London Scene." *Opera News,* XLIX (February 2, 1985), 15–16. Includes G.B.S. on Gluck's *Orfeo ed Euridice,* Verdi's *Falstaff, Siegfried* at Covent Garden, Amending Mozart, Critics and Musicians, *Aida* at Covent Garden, *Don Giovanni, Cavalleria Rusticana, La Damnation de Faust, Tristan und Isolde* at Bayreuth, *Il Trovatore,* Verdi, and "Shaw's Critical Credo." See Mehus, Donald V., under "Periodicals," below.

————. *Heartbreak House.* Produced by Howard K. Grossman and John H. Williams. Long Island City: Silvercup Studios, 1984. Stars Rex Harrison as Shotover, Rose-

*Professor Pfeiffer, *SHAW* Bibliographer, welcomes information about new or forthcoming Shaviana: books, articles, pamphlets, monographs, dissertations, reprints, etc. His address is Department of English, Central Michigan University, Mount Pleasant, Michigan 48859.

mary Harris as Hesione Hushabye, Amy Irving as Ellie Dunn, and Anthony Page as director. This taped and cut production is said to run two hours to the nearly four hours required for performance of the uncut play. Scheduled for airing on Showtime in April 1985; later on Public Broadcasting Service's "Great Perform-ances." This information taken from Schneider, Steve, in "Periodicals," below.

―――. *John Bull's Other Island*. London: Penguin Books, 1984. Not seen.

―――. *Last Plays*. London: Penguin Books, 1985. Includes *King Charles, Billions, Fables, Shakes vs Shav*, and *Why She Would Not*.

―――. Letters. In *Granville Barker and His Correspondents*. A Selection of Letters by Him and to Him. Edited by Eric Salmon. Detroit: Wayne State University Press, 1986. Not seen. Information from advertisement. "Intriguing comments about Barker's work and the British theatre from George Bernard Shaw, John Galsworthy, T.E. Lawrence, and others."

―――. *Letters III (1911–1925)*. Edited by Dan H. Laurence. London: Bodley Head, 1985; New York: Viking, 1985.

―――. Quotations. In Victor Bonham-Carter's *Authors by Profession*. Los Altos, Califor-nia: William Kaufmann, Inc., 1984. Quotations of some length from GBS's For-ward to G. H. Thring's *The Marketing of Literary Property* (Constable 1933), on "lei-sure," "authors," "publishers" and ownership of copyright. See also Bonham-Carter under "Books and Pamphlets," below.

―――. "The Sanity of Art" (1908). Reprinted in *Impressionists in England, The Critical Reception*. Edited by Kate Flint. London: Routledge and Kegan Paul, 1984, pp. 141–43.

## II. Books and Pamphlets

Adams, Elsie B. "In Pursuit of Art: Shaw's Italian Tours of 1891 and 1894." *Shaw Abroad: Annual of Bernard Shaw Studies*, Volume Five. University Park: Pennsylvania State University Press, 1985.

Adrian, Arthur A. "'Why was I ever a father!': Charles Dickens as Father" in *Victorian Literature and Society*. Essays Presented to Richard D. Altick. Edited by James R. Kincaid and Albert J. Kuhn. Columbus: Ohio State University Press, 1984, pp. 276–99. Several insights on Dickens' fatherhood are shared with GBS in letters from Dickens' daughter, Katey: "That Katey came closer than any of the other children to assessing her father's genius is borne out by her correspondence with George Bernard Shaw while the disposition of Dickens's letters to his wife was under consideration. 'You wrong me,' she told Shaw, 'when you think for one sec-ond that I would suggest any comparison between my father and any other artist in the world—. I believe my father to have been a man apart—as high above his fellow men—as the children of such great and exceptional men, are generally . . . below them.'" Other extracts from Katey's letters express similar testimony.

Albert, Sidney P., and Matoba, Junko. "Shaking the Earth: Shaw in Japan." *Shaw Abroad: Annual of Bernard Shaw Studies*, Volume Five. University Park: Pennsylvania State University Press, 1985.

Amalric, Jean-Claude "A Playwright's Supertrips: Shaw's Visits to France." *Shaw Abroad. Annual of Bernard Shaw Studies*, Volume Five. University Park: Pennsylvania State University Press, 1985.

Barker, Granville. *Granville Barker and His Correspondents*. A Selection of Letters by Him and to Him. Edited by Eric Salmon. Detroit: Wayne State University Press, 1986. Not seen. See Letters under "Works by Shaw," above.

Berst, Charles A. "Passion at Lake Maggiore: Shaw, Molly Tompkins and Italy, 1921–1950." *Shaw Abroad: Annual of Bernard Shaw Studies*, Volume Five. University Park: Pennsylvania State University Press, 1985.

Bloch, Robert. *Night of the Ripper*. Garden City: Doubleday, 1984. Not seen. From an advertisement: A "splatter novel" set in Victorian London of 1888, with a cast of characters that includes Wilde, Doyle, and GBS.

Bonham-Carter, Victor. *Authors by Profession*, Volume Two (from the Copyright Act of 1911 until the end of 1981). Los Altos, California: William Kaufmann, Inc., 1984. One of the several references to GBS puts into perspective the great importance to the financial solvency of the Society of Authors of Shaw's invitation in 1945 to the Society to assume management (at commercial fees) of all of his theatre and literary business. Shaw's lifelong distrust of the ordinary literary agent is noted in this connection.

Beichmann, Arnold. *Herman Wouk, The Novelist as Social Historian*. New Brunswick, New Jersey: Transaction Books, 1984. "In his notebooks, Wouk describes how the *Caine Mutiny Court-Martial* came into being. In January 1952, Wouk saw . . . *Don Juan in Hell* which, he said, 'was the most electrifying theatrical event to my mind in recent years.' It occurred to him that a dramatic reading of a similar kind could be made of the *Caine's* court-martial scene."

Bradby, David. *Modern French Drama, 1940–1980*. Cambridge: Cambridge University Press, 1984. Georges Pitöeff and his wife Ludmila shared with Dullin and Jouret a belief that theatre is not best suited to a naturalist mode of representing reality. "They held that the production of any given play had to give scenic form to the invisible forces contained in that play. A famous example of this was their setting for Shaw's *Saint Joan* (1925) which stressed the idea of saintliness by using a permanent scenic structure reminiscent of an altarpiece: a central gothic arch with two half arches on either side, and stage groupings that concentrated the audience's attention on the upward thrust, suggesting a constant movement heavenward."

Brady, L. W. *T. P. O'Connor and the Liverpool Irish*. London: Royal Historical Society; New Jersey: Humanities Press, 1983. A number of references here to Shaw's involvement as a writer with O'Connor's newly founded *The Star* in the 1880s. The note on p. 115 is wrong, however, as Shaw *was* first employed by *The Star* to write political pieces (unsigned, of course).

Brown, Gene, ed. *The New York Times Encyclopedia of Film*. New York: Times Books, 1984. Thirteen volumes. Volume thirteen is an index which lists sixty-seven newspaper story references to GBS from 1896 to 1979.

Bullock, Alan and Woodings, R. B. *Twentieth-Century Culture, A Biographical Companion*. New York: Harper and Row, 1983. Lists about 2000 persons, including GBS. Entry is three-quarters of a page in space—above average. The latest secondary source is from 1979.

Carlson, Marvin. *Theories of the Theatre. A Historical and Critical Survey, from the Greeks to the Present*. Ithaca and London: Cornell University Press, 1984. Samples of the treatment of Shaw's theory of theatre dwell upon his didactic and utilitarian propositions. "What work does it do in the world? That question is the ultimate touchstone in all of Shaw's criticism of both playwriting and performance."

Dukore, Bernard F. "GBS, MGM, RKO: Shaw in Hollywood." *Shaw Abroad: Annual of Bernard Shaw Studies*, Volume Five. University Park: Pennsylvania State University Press, 1985.

Edel, Leon. *Writing Lives, Principia Biographia*. New York and London: W. W. Norton &

Co., 1959; 1984. Edel, in a single reference reports he met GBS, as well as Edith Wharton, Granville-Barker, Yeats and others.

Edwards, Anne. *Matriarch. Queen Mary and the House of Windsor.* New York: William Morrow and Company, 1984. "In a very rude manner" GBS refused to contribute a handwritten miniature book for Queen Mary's doll house library. Kipling, Milne, Maugham, Doyle, Beerbohm and others did contribute. See also Rose, Kenneth, below.

Evans, T. F. "Myopia or Utopia? Shaw in Russia." *Shaw Abroad: Annual of Bernard Shaw Studies,* Volume Five. University Park: Pennsylvania State University Press, 1985.

Falk, Candace. *Love, Anarchy and Emma Goldman.* New York: Holt, Rinehart and Winston, 1984. Goldman, free love advocate, birth control pioneer, and anarchist, respected GBS.

Gifford, Barry. See Lee, Lawrence, below.

Gray, Piers. "Hong Kong, Shanghai, The Great Wall: Shaw in China." *Shaw Abroad: Annual of Bernard Shaw Studies,* Volume Five. University Park: Pennsylvania State University Press, 1985.

Grene, Nicholas. "Visitor or Returning Exile? Shaw in Ireland." *Shaw Abroad: Annual of Bernard Shaw Studies,* Volume Five. University Park: Pennsylvania State University Press, 1985.

Hall, Peter. *Peter Hall's Diaries, The Story of a Dramatic Battle.* Edited by John Goodwin. New York: Harper & Row, 1984. There are half a dozen interesting pages. However, apparently Hall likes only one GBS play—*Heartbreak House:* "It's the only Shaw play I really enjoy. I think I persuaded John [Schlesinger] to do some more cuts. I hope I also persuaded him that the madness and emotion should be greater in the second act—particularly after the burglary. Once something odd has happened, people's adrenalin remains high. They want to talk, to drink, to dispute. One thing is certain from this afternoon, Kate Nelligan is a star. Absolutely no doubt about it."

Hession, Charles H. *John Maynard Keynes. A Personal Biography of the Man Who Revolutionized Capitalism and the Way We Live.* New York and London: Macmillan, 1984. Includes a number of references to Shaw whom Keynes respected greatly. There is a substantial account of the lively published and unpublished exchange between the two over the merits of the Soviet system, Prints a photo of GBS and Keynes on the steps of the Fitzwilliam Museum, Cambridge, 1935.

Hugo, Leon. "Upset in a 'Suntrap': Shaw in South Africa." *Shaw Abroad: Annual of Bernard Shaw Studies,* Volume Five. University Park: Pennsylvania State University Press, 1985.

Jacobs, Arthur. *Arthur Sullivan. A Victorian Musician.* Oxford and New York: Oxford University Press, 1984. Shaw's criticism of the "Operas" is mined for some of this account of the most widely known, perhaps, of all English composers.

Kalogjera, Damir. "A Political Game: Shaw in Yugoslavia." *Shaw Abroad: Annual of Bernard Shaw Studies,* Volume Five. University Park: Pennsylvania State University Press, 1985.

Kazantzakis, Helen. *Nikos Kazantzakis, A Biography Based on His Letters.* Translated by Amy Mims. Berkeley: Creative Arts Book Co., 1983. Based on the original French Language copyright edition of 1968. In London in 1946 Kazantzakis got a chance to give three broadcasts on the radio. The first was an S.O.S. to intellectuals. The second and third were dedicated to Angelos Sikelianos and Bernard Shaw. There is no elaboration.

Lagercrantz, Olof. *August Strindberg.* Translated by Anselm Hollo. New York: Farrar,

Straus, Giroux, 1984. First published in Stockholm in 1979. In summer of 1908 Strindberg was visited by GBS in Stockholm. He proudly took Shaw to see *Miss Julie*. In 1926 Shaw did not remember this performance of *Miss Julie*. It was given, of course, in Swedish. Shaw also visited Strindberg at home and conversed with him in French and his (Shaw's) rather poor German.

Laurence, Dan H. "'That Awful Country': Shaw in America." *Shaw Abroad: Annual of Bernard Shaw Studies*, Volume Five. University Park: Pennsylvania State University Press, 1985.

Lawrence, Lee, and Gifford, Barry. *Saroyan, A Biography*. New York: Harper & Row, 1984. In London in 1944 as a Pfc. Saroyan's most memorable encounter was with GBS at Ayot St. Lawrence. "An Australian newspaperwoman arranged the meeting, and the invitation came . . . from Shaw himself. . . . Shaw was in a deliberately provocative mood when the younger man arrived: "Armenian? But didn't the Turks *kill* all of the Armenians?" Saroyan was impressed by his piping voice, his knickers, and his evident worry that the American guest would consider him some sort of saint, a notion he was at pains to correct. "But he couldn't fool me, and he remained the gentlest, kindest, the most decent fellow in England, and possibly in the world." Shaw said he felt that he was dying, and Saroyan reassured him— correctly, as it turned out—that he had productive years remaining.

Lewis, Robert. *Slings and Arrows, Theater in My Life*. New York: Stein and Day, 1984. Lewis considers GBS a first-class critic, possessing the hallmarks of the great critic, "exemplary taste" and the acumen to "point the way," among other qualities.

Lindblad, Ishrat. "A Good Holiday: Shaw Visits Sweden." *Shaw Abroad: Annual of Bernard Shaw Studies*, Volume Five. University Park: Pennsylvania State University Press, 1985.

Malina, Judith. *The Diaries of Judith Malina, 1947–1957*. First edited by James Spicer. New York: Grove Press, Inc., 1984. Malina's liking for GBS is evident in a number of entries. Samples: "Finished *Back to Methuselah*. . . . In his preface he writes a critical appraisal of Darwinism, a refutation of atheism, a detailed defense of Lamarckian evolutionary theory, a Fabian analysis of Marxism, materialism, vitalism *et al*. When I take issue with him, he invariably downs my arguments in the next paragraph. He is the perfect sophist." "At the Theater Guild: In this monumental mansion I am resentful, like an ambitious servant girl. (paragraph) The bronze bust of Shaw enshrined like a Roman household god between the two grand stairways tempts me to idolatry and perhaps brought about the solemn thoughts that I attributed to the hospital."

Martin, Murray. "'If I Showed My True Feelings': Shaw in New Zealand." *Shaw Abroad: Annual of Bernard Shaw Studies*, Volume Five. University Park: Pennsylvania State University Press, 1985.

Matoba, Junko. See Albert, Sidney P., above.

Maxwell, D. E. S. *A Critical History of Modern Irish Drama 1891–1980*. Cambridge: Cambridge University Press, 1985. The references to Shaw are only passing ones. To Maxwell, GBS is not really an Irish playwright beyond the accident of birth and GBS's enjoyment of 19th-century Irish plays.

McKay, Nellie. *Jean Toomer, Artist*. A Study of His Literary Life and Work, 1894–1936. Chapel Hill and London: University of North Carolina Press, 1984. The influence of GBS on Toomer, an Afro-American novelist, is noted here more than once, suggesting it might be studied in depth.

Molin, Donald H. *Actor's Encyclopedia of Dialects*. New York: Sterling Publishing Co., 1984. The chapter on "Cockney" notices Shaw's use of this dialect in *Pygmalion*, and provides an explanation of why this lower-class dialect could represent the great leap in social status that takes place in the play.

Orgel, Joseph R. *Undying Passion. A Book of Anecdotes about Men, Women, Love, Sex and the Literary Life*. New York: William Morrow and Company, 1985. Three about GBS are for Jenny Patterson, Alice Lockett, and Mrs. Pat. There is another for Charlotte.

Peters, Margot. *Mrs. Pat, The Life of Mrs. Patrick Campbell*. New York: Alfred A. Knopf, 1984. The life and works of Shaw are, of course, a huge content here. See reviews by Findlater, Richard, and Jackson, Russell, under "Periodicals," below.

Pryce-Jones, David, ed. *Cyril Connolly, Journal and Memoir*. New York: Ticknor & Fields, 1984. A few references to Shaw, who rated very low with Connolly.

Rao, Valli. "Seeking the Unknowable: Shaw in India." *Shaw Abroad: Annual of Bernard Shaw Studies*, Volume Five. University Park: Pennsylvania State University Press, 1985.

Rose, Kenneth. *King George V.* New York: Knopf, 1984. Notes a rare subject upon which GBS and the King would be allies. The King told his prime minister that the country was unlikely to accept a pension of just 5s for widows of soldiers killed in action. "Mr. Bernard Shaw," he continued, "is 'out for' £1 a week and 35s a week pay for every soldier." Also describes the contributions of handwritten miniature books for the library of the Princess's dollhouse at Windsor by famous authors—except for GBS who "in a very rude manner" refused the invitation. See Edwards, Anne, above.

Rota, Anthony. "The Life as Bibliography" (Review of *Bernard Shaw: A Bibliography* by Dan H. Laurence). *Shaw Abroad: The Annual of Bernard Shaw Studies*, Volume Five. University Park: Pennsylvania State University Press, 1985.

Salmon, Eric. *Granville Barker, A Secret Life*. Fairleigh Dickenson University Press, 1984. A British edition came from Heinemann Educational Books in 1983. See Salmon under "Books and Pamphlets" in Checklist for *SHAW* 4.

Shainess, Natalie. *Sweet Suffering: Woman as Victim*. Indianapolis and New York: Bobbs-Merrill, 1984. Female masochism is the problem she wants to solve. GBS's women never reflect it, illustrated especially in *Mrs. Warren, Candida,* and *Saint Joan*. "All of . . . Shaw's women reflect different facets of the feminine personality; they have shortcomings, but they are far from masochistic. On the contrary, Shaw's women are flesh-and-blood creations endeavoring to maintain authenticity in the midst of struggle. Shaw, despite misogynist tendencies of his own, wrote heroines much more often than he did heroes, intelligent active women capable of taking a hand in their own destinies, even though those destinies were necessarily circumscribed by the restrictions of the society in which they lived."

Watt, George. *The Fallen Woman in the Nineteenth-Century English Novel*. Totowa, New Jersey: Barnes & Noble, 1984. Shaw did not admire George Moore. In a chapter on *Esther Waters*, Moore's best known novel, Watt uses GBS's disapproval as a challenge. He finds Esther Waters "one of the most finely drawn of the late Victorian fallen women."

Weintraub, Stanley. "A High Wind to Jamaica." *Shaw Abroad: The Annual of Bernard Shaw Studies*, Volume Five. University Park: Pennsylvania State University Press, 1985.

Weisert, John J. "A Wagner Pilgrim: GBS in Germany." *Shaw Abroad: The Annual of Bernard Shaw Studies*, Volume Five. University Park: Pennsylvania State University Press, 1985.

Welch, Denton. *The Journals of Denton Welch*. Edited by Michael De-La-Noy. London: Allison & Busby, 1984. Includes a recollection of Edith Sitwell's opinion of censorship: Sitwell: "The law, I think, is absolutely right. As Bernard Shaw said to me when we were all called to give evidence over the *Well of Loneliness* [by Radclyffe Hall about lesbianism] fuss, 'Here I am, asked to say something about this pathetic book, and I don't know what to do, because I know it's serious, unpornographic, but it's so bad as literature.'" Sitwell continued, "Let those poor people think or behave like that, if they cannot help it, but don't let them write bad books about it. It is dangerous. In the hands of young people they might do great damage—not because of stimulation, but because of the terrible revulsion they might cause."

Wells, H. G. *Experiment in Autobiography, Discoveries and Conclusions of a Very Ordinary Brain (since 1866),* with Drawings by the Author. Boston and Toronto: Little, Brown and Company, 1984. First copyrighted in 1934. A number of references to GBS, of course. One recalling 3 January 1895 is a tribute to Shaw. "On that eventful evening I scraped acquaintance with another interesting contemporary, Bernard Shaw. I had known him by sight since the Hammersmith days but I had never spoken to him before. Fires and civil commotions loosen tongues. I accosted him as a *Saturday Review* colleague and we walked back to our respective lodgings northward while he talked very interestingly about the uproar we had left behind us and the place of the fashionable three-act play amidst eternal verities. . . . He talked like an elder brother to me in that agreeable Dublin English of his. I liked him with a liking that has lasted a lifetime."

Wells, H. G. *H. G. Wells in Love. Postscript to an Experiment in Autobiography.* Edited by G. P. Wells. Boston and Toronto: Little, Brown and Company, 1984. Two references report that GBS helped get Wells through his wife Catherine's funeral, and the following: "A furtive sexual system grows up detached from the general activities. It does not approve the normal demands of vanity. Release may come too late. This, I think, is what explains much that is perplexing in the life of G. B. Shaw; and it goes far to explain Odette Keun. Essentially they are masturbators. With me she led a normal sexual life; but . . . when we got separated. . . ."

Wood, Barbara. *E. F. Schumacher, His Life and Thought.* New York: Harper and Row, 1984. The brilliant and visionary German economist, especially after WW II, loved Shaw as one among people who "combine high morality with constructive and progressive ideas." Shakespeare and Shaw were the only playwrights he thought worthwhile.

Wright, Anne. *Literature of Crisis, 1910–22. Howards End, Heartbreak House, Women in Love* and *The Waste Land.* London: Macmillan, 1984. Chapter three is on *Heartbreak.* "In *Heartbreak House* the chronic Condition of England becomes acute, and quite possibly terminal. In this extremity the play asks: who can save the country?" "Salvation—'Life with a blessing' . . . in Ellie Dunn's terms—is the urgent and persistent concern of *Heartbreak House.* This is the end and solution, expressed in religious language, towards which the action is directed. The play seeks salvation for the individual as well as society." "The maintained tension of *Heartbreak House* is impatient for finality, but with the emphasis on waiting, on '*intense expectation,*' and the continuing poise of 'hope.'" For *Heartbreak* the "Zeppelin is forever approaching, the sun forever about to set. Apocalypse is imminent but withheld, and Judgement suspended."

# III. Periodicals

Adams, Patricia. Review of Haymarket Production, June 4, 1983, of *Heartbreak House. Theatre Journal,* XXXVI, no. 2 (May 1984), 270–72.

Barr, Alan P. Review of *The Unexpected Shaw: Biographical Approaches to G.B.S. and His Work* by Stanley Weintraub; *The Playwright and the Pirate, Bernard Shaw and Frank Harris: A Correspondence*, edited by Stanley Weintraub; and *Bernard Shaw and Alfred Douglas: A Correspondence*, edited by Mary Hyde. *Victorian Studies*, XXVII, no. 2 (Winter 1984), 279–81.

Burgess, Anthony. "When to lend an ear." *TLS* (December 28, 1984), p. 1491. The famous novelist and author of *A Clockwork Orange* with its special linguistic concerns, in a review of Raymond Chapman's *The Treatment of Sounds in Language and Literature*, addresses himself briefly to Shaw's mostly frustrated attempts to render dialect with conventional orthography, particularly in *Captain Brassbound*.

Carpenter, Andrew. "Despairingly Optimistic" (review of Arthur Ganz's *George Bernard Shaw* and *Shaw's Plays in Performance: The Annual of Bernard Shaw Studies*, volume 3, edited by Daniel Leary). *TLS* (June 15, 1984), p. 663.

Carpenter, Charles A. "Shaw" in "Modern Drama Studies: An Annual Bibliography." *Modern Drama*, XXVII, no. 2 (June 1984), 198–99. Thirty-two entries, several of which have not been listed in this Checklist, by the former Bibliographer of *The Shaw Review*. Carpenter's yearly section on GBS in *Modern Drama's* bibliography is indispensible.

DeVine, Lawrence. "Ontarians have fun with Shaw's 'Devil's Disciple.'" *Detroit Free Press* (May 24, 1984), p. 6B. "The Shaw Festival, once small but mighty, now simply looks mighty. Evidence its 1984 season premiere, 'The Devil's Disciple,' that sometimes troublesome George Bernard Shaw melodrama with which a grand Canadian cast here had no trouble at all." Provides a photo of Jim Mezon as Dick Dudgeon.

———. "Shaw Festival goes for Broke." *Detroit Free Press* (May 18, 1984), pp. 1; 9C. "Without undue modesty, Shaw Festival chief Christopher Newton said this summer is the year the theater near the Falls goes for broke, for world-class stature. Shaw, he said, already is the best in Canada. 'There's nobody to compare with us.'" The rival is the Stratford Festival, mentioned later in the article.

Everding, Robert G. "Staging Shaw: Insights for Directors." *Theatre Southwest.* Journal of the Southwest Theatre Conference (1984), 19–23. Simplified considerably, Everding's insights are that 1) Shaw's plays are bristling with action; 2) the sound effects of the plays are very important; 3) the speeches are strongly contrapuntal; and 4) Shaw makes fine use of lights, costumes, settings and properties. "When directing Shaw, careful analysis is imperative because of the way he uses every detail of the script to structure the dramatic experience, and because of the extensive notes he provides the director."

Findlater, Richard. "The Anarch on Stage" (review of Margot Peter's *Mrs. Pat: The Life of Mrs. Patrick Campbell*). *TLS* (August 31, 1984), p. 961. "George Bernard Shaw" in 1983–1984 Annual Review number of *Journal of Modern Literature*, XI, nos 3/4 (November 1984), 503–4. The five immediately listed items have been noted in this Checklist. Several cross-referenced ones have not.

Gibbs, A. M. "Pygmalion." *TLS* (July 13, 1984), p. 783. A letter taking issue with Harold Hobson's review (see Hobson, Harold, below) praising the Shaftsbury Theatre production for using "the original text." Gibbs notes it was not the *original* text.

Harrison, David B. "A New Source for Shaw's *Major Barbara.*" *English Literature in Transition*, XXVIII, no. 2 (1985), 56–57. "An examination of Engels' 'The Attitude of the Bourgeoisie Towards the Proletariat' reveals the extent of Engels' influence on *Major Barbara*. Act Two, which provides the theoretical foundation for the play, is, in fact, not only a dramatization of Engels' treatise, but also a mirror image of Engels' analysis of charity."

Hobson, Harold. "The Anti-Cockney Hero" (review of Shaftsbury Theatre production of *Pygmalion*). *TLS* (June 8, 1984), p. 639. See "Pygmalion" letter under Gibbs, A. M., above.

Jackson, Russell. Review of *Mrs. Pat: The Life of Mrs. Patrick Campbell* by Margot Peters. *Theatre Research International*, X, no. 1 (Spring 1985), 80–82.

Levin, Milton. Review of *The Story of Shaw's Saint Joan* by Brian Tyson. *Eire-Ireland*, XIX, no. 2 (Summer 1984), 154–56.

Mehus, Donald V. "A Musical Critic: George Bernard Shaw on the London Scene." *Opera News*, XLIX (February 2, 1985), 14–19. Mehus surrounds a group of excerpts from Shaw's music criticism with an account of his achievement as a music critic before he made it big as a playwright, noting that today many believe GBS's music criticism is the best ever by an English critic.

Myer, Michael Grosvenor. "Dickensian Echoes in Shaw: *Our Mutual Friend* and *Pygmalion*." *Notes and Queries*, New Series, XXXI, no. 4 (December 1984), 508. "Doolittle's conversation on his first visit to Higgins and Pickering in Act II of *Pygmalion* contains several distinct echoes of Riderhood's first visit to Lightwood and Wrayburn in Book 1, Chapter 12 of *Our Mutual Friend*."

Needham, Bob. "Just Loverly: Players Stage 'My Fair Lady.'" *Morning Sun* (Mount Pleasant, Michigan) (April 12, 1985), Entertainment, pp. 1–2. This story on the Gratiot County, Michigan, Playhouse Production is puffed by a front-page headline, "'My Fair Lady' Opens on Gratiot Stage." The newspaper serves an area population of about 40,000.

Nickson, Richard. "The Lure of Stalinism: Bernard Shaw and Company." *The Midwest Quarterly*, XXV, no. 4 (Summer 1984), 416–33. "Shaw should not be judged exclusively by such a passage as this, from the Preface to *Farfetched Fables*, written in his nineties: 'The soviet system . . . includes all the conventional democratic checks and safeguards against despotism now so illusory, and gives them as much effectiveness as their airy nature is capable of. Incidentally it gives Stalin the best right of any living statesman to the vacant Nobel peace prize, and our diplomatists the worst. This will shock our ignoramuses as a stupendous heresy and a mad paradox. Let us see.' The ignoramus in these matters was, alas, Bernard Shaw—tragically duped as have been so many other staunch world betterers. The shock is a great one indeed."

———. "Using Words on the Stage: Shaw and Granville-Barker." *Modern Drama*, XXVII, no. 3 (September 1984), 409–19. "A reflection on that time early in the century when Shaw and Granville-Barker were in their primes as writers and created the finest drama of the late Victorian and Edwardian periods may stimulate in some of us, besides nostalgia, certain evaluative comparisons among some of the differing theories about language in drama—as well as a few of the notable practices—of these two masters of dialogue." GBS and Granville-Barker were "essentially observing Ibsen's practice of 'writing in the straightforward honest language of reality.'" Their plays show that speech "looms large" in the interpretation of life in action.

O'Reilly, Jane. "'Lemme Tell Ya'—and Did She Ever." *Time* (January 7, 1985), p. 60. Has Robert Kennedy quoting GBS: "You see things, and you say, 'Why?' But I dream things that never were; and I say, 'Why not?'"

Saddlemyer, Ann. Review of Brian Tyson's *The Story of Shaw's Saint Joan*. *English Studies in Canada*, X, no. 3 (September 1984), 377–8.

Schneider, Steve. "Shrinking 'Heartbreak House' for TV." *Sunday New York Times* (December 23, 1984), p. 26H. Describes the production of and the story of a videotaped version of the play. See *Heartbreak House* under "Works by Shaw" above. See Simon, John, below.

Simon, John. "George Bernard Shaw. Did He Really Think He was Better Than Shakespeare?" *TV Guide*, XXXIII (April 13, 1985), pp. 38–40. The title of this background piece to accompany the week's Showtime debut of a cut-down made-for-TV version of *Heartbreak House* is somewhat misleading. Simon gives GBS a glitzy biographical sketch, and some paragraphs on *Heartbreak*. This number of *TV Guide* also contains a blurb on *Heartbreak* by Stanley Marcus—a "warning" to viewers, "the urbane talk may be of marriage and money and the battle of the sexes, but Shaw has other things on his voluminous mind, and he's not going to let you in on them without a fight." See Schneider, Steve, above.

Warner, Nicholas A. "Shaw, Tolstoy and Blake's Russian Reputation." *Blake, An Illustrated Quarterly*, XVII, no. 3 (Winter 1983–84), 102–4. The article begins by referring to Shaw's 1910 letter to Tolstoy, wherein GBS mentions Blake. This may have been the first that Tolstoy had ever heard of Blake.

Weintraub, Stanley. "Evidence of Success" (review of Dan H. Laurence's *Bernard Shaw: A Bibliography*. TLS (May 18, 1984), p. 563.

*The Independent Shavian*, 22, no. 1 (1984). Journal of the Bernard Shaw Society. Includes "Conversations with Shaw: Stella Mervyn Beech and Patrick Beech" by Margot Peters, "Some Animadversions on Shaw as Music Critic" by George Levinson, a review of *Bernard Shaw and Alfred Douglas: A Correspondence* by Richard Nickson, a review of *A Stroll With Henry James* by Daniel Leary, a review of *The Kleist Variations* by Daniel Leary, "Society Activities," "News About our Members," "Shaw the Communist," and "Our Cover."

*The Independent Shavian*, 22, nos. 2/3 (1984). Journal of the Bernard Shaw Society. Includes "A Conversation with Shaw" by Patrick Beech, "Another Look at Shaw as Music Critic" by Jacques Barzun, "Shaw on Nuclear War" by Richard Nickson, "GBS in New Zealand: The Interested Visitor" by Katrine Keuneman, "A Word about our Society" by Richard Nickson, "Vera Scriabine" by Douglas Laurie, "Our Founder" by Daniel Leary, "My Aunt, Vera Scriabine" by Andrew Littauer, "Announcement," "Shavian Idolator," "Loathing Mr. Shaw," "Free, Adult, Uncensored," "Our Man in Minsk," "News about our Members," "Society Activities," and "Our Cover."

*The Independent Shavian*, 23, no. 1 (1985). Journal of the Bernard Shaw Society. Includes "Shaw on Conductors" by Benjamin Grosbayne, "Shaw and Shakespeare: Why Not!" by Daniel Leary, "*My Fair Lady* Serenaded by Cats," "Letter from London" by T. F. Evans, "Again, Shaw's Musical Invective" by George Levinson, review of *Bernard Shaw: A Bibliography* by Daniel Leary, "The Discreet Lunch," review of *Mrs. Pat: The Life of Mrs. Patrick Campbell* by Lillian Wachtel, "Housebreaking," "Androcles and the Tunesmiths," "A Knot Never Tied," "Shaw in the Lead," "Society Activities," "Notice," "Literary Gifts," "News about our Members," and "Our Cover."

# IV. Dissertations

Al-Douri, Madi Weis. "Bernard Shaw's Cosmopolitan Perspective: An Approach to Selected Plays in International Settings." University of Birmingham, 1980. "Examines the nature and the background of Shaw's cosmopolitanism, comparing him to some of his major contemporaries: Yeats, Joyce, Conrad, James, Hardy, and Lawrence. The other seven chapters deal with the ramifications of Shavian cosmopolitanism as revealed in . . ." plays with settings outside Britain and Ireland: *Arms, Man of Destiny, Caesar, Joan, Disciple, Brassbound,* and *Methuselah.* From a synopsis supplied by the author.

Williams, Arthur Ernest. "Comparative Dramaturgical Structure in Selected Plays of Bernard Shaw and Bertolt Brecht." Ohio State University, 1984. *DAI,* 45 (December 1984), 1574–5A. "Examines the structural relationships between plays from each playwright's early, middle, and later periods, seeking to prove a correspondence between the construction and purposes of the works rather than a causal or influential relationship between the men themselves. The plays considered in this study are . . ." *Mrs Warren, Pygmalion,* and *Joan* by GBS, and *Baal, Saint Joan of the Stockyards* and *Caucasian Chalk Circle* by Brecht.

# V. Recordings

Shaw, Bernard. *Heartbreak House.* Produced by Howard K. Grossman and John H. Williams. Long Island City: Silvercup Studios, 1984. See *Heartbreak House* under "Works by Shaw," above.

"Shaw, Bernard" and "Shaw, George Bernard Shaw Festival." *The Magazine Index.* Belmont, California: Information Access Company. Microfilm reel: 1979 to January 1985. Seven new entries since March 1984—mostly not listed in this Checklist.

"Shaw, Bernard" and "Shaw, George Bernard." *The National Newspaper Index.* Los Altos, California: Information Access Company. Microfilm reel: May 1981 to December 1984. Two new items since March 1984—neither listed in this Checklist.

# CONTRIBUTORS

Susan Albertine is on the faculty of the Department of Language & Literature, University of North Florida, Jacksonville.

Alan G. Brunger is Associate Professor of Geography at Trent University, Peterborough, Ontario.

Bert Cardullo is Assistant Professor of Dramatic Literature at Louisiana State University.

Fred D. Crawford is on the English faculty at the University of Oregon, Eugene.

Holly Hill is an Assistant Professor of Speech and Theatre at the John Jay College of the City University of New York.

J. Scott Lee has taught criticism and drama for the University of Chicago, Office of Continuing Education. His Ph.D. dissertation traces the development of Shaw's comic artistry.

Katherine Lyon Mix is the author of *A Study in Yellow,* the definitive study of *The Yellow Book,* and of *Max in America,* on Max Beerbohm. She was formerly on the faculty of Baker University in Kansas.

Sean Morrow is a lecturer in History at the University of Malawi, Zomba, Malawi.

Desmond J. McRory is a Senior Technical Writer for the Burroughs Corporation, Flemington, N.J.

Martin Quinn, collaborator with Dan H. Laurence on a recent book on Shaw and Dickens, is an officer with the United States Information Service overseas.

Michael J. Mendelsohn is Professor of Humanities at the University of Tampa and a member of the Editorial Board of *SHAW.*

John R. Pfeiffer, *SHAW* Bibliographer, is Professor of English at Central Michigan University.

Paul Sawyer is Professor of English at Bradley University, Peoria, Illinois.

Stanley Weintraub is Editor of *SHAW* and a Research Professor at The Pennsylvania State University.